CAP AND BELL

© This collection: Susan and Asa Briggs 1972

First published in 1972 by
Macdonald and Company (Publishers) Ltd
St Giles House, 49/50 Poland Street
London W1

Printed in Great Britain by
Waterlow & Sons Limited
London and Dunstable

SBN 356 03521 2

CAP AND BELL

Punch's Chronicle of English History in the Making, 1841-61

Collected and edited by Susan and Asa Briggs

MACDONALD · LONDON

CONTENTS

PREFACE XI
SUGGESTIONS FOR FURTHER READING XXXV
KEY TO ARTISTS' SIGNATURES XXXVI

I THE WATCHER

Peel takes Office (1841)   3
The Letter of Introduction (Vol. I, 1841, p.91)

Electioneering: The Practitioners . . .   4
Candidates under different phases (Vol. I, 1841, p.6)

and the Practice   5
'On the Science of Electioneering' (Vol. I, 1841)
Newcastle's Freedom of Election (Vol. X, 1846, p.91)

Whig and Tory   6
Punch's Monument to Peel (Vol. XIX, 1850, p.157)
Lord John in a Fog (Vol. XIII, 1847, p.195)
Dombey and Son (Vol. XIII, 1847, p.75)
Whig Progress (Vol. XIII, 1847, p.25)

Education: State or voluntary?   7
The Educational Question (Vol. XII, 1847, p.159)

Dealing with Ireland (1846) . . .   8
Where Ignorance is bliss (Vol. XI, 1846, p.203)

but Ireland has her own Methods   9
Young Ireland in Business for himself (Vol. XI, 1846, p.79)

At Home the Radicals want to move faster (1848) . . .   10
The Hour and the Man (Vol. XIV, 1848, p.211)

but the British note an Object Lesson across the Channel   11
'The Kings in their Cock-Boats' (Vol. XIV, 1848, p.146)

British Revolutionaries   12
A Physical Force Chartist arming for the Fight (Vol. XV, 1848, p.101)

Across the Atlantic: a true Picture of the Land of Liberty   13
The Land of Liberty (Vol. XIII, 1847, p.215)

At Home there are Avenues of Escape   14
The Currency Question (Vol. XII, 1847, p.211)

There are, of course, Family Outings, and the Children have their own Social Occasions   15
A Pic-nic (Vol. XVIII, 1850, p.216)
A Juvenyle Partye (Vol. XVIII, 1850, p.174)

Adults go to the Theatre or to Concerts . . .   16
'The Theatres' (Vol. VII, 1844, p.152)
A Monster Concert (Vol. XVII, 1849, p.136)

and, above all, to the Opera   17
'Italian Opera Fashions' (Vol. XII, 1847, p.194)
Melancholy Scene at the Opera (Vol. XIII, 1847, p.60)

Whilst Every One goes to the Seaside 18
North-East Wind – Thermometer several Inches below Freezing (Vol. XXI, 1851, p.220)
'How to calculate the Height of the Season at the Seaside' (Vol. XXXIII, 1857, p.97)
Sea-side Literature for Young Ladies (Vol. XVII, 1849, p.96)

A Cambridge Diversion 20
A Row of Heads (Vol. XII, 1847, p.114)
H.R.H. Field Marshal Chancellor Prince Albert taking the Pons Asinorum (Vol. XV, 1848, p.225)

London Landmarks 21
'The Ups and Downs of King's Road, Eaton Square' (Vol. XIX, 1850, p.38)
'The Ten Towns' (Vol. XXXII, 1857, p.51)

In 1850 the Exhibition raises Hopes, and also Fears 22
London in 1851 (Vol. XIX, 1850, p.132)
'The Industrious Boy' (Vol. XVIII, 1850, p.227)
'Albert! Spare those Trees' (Vol. XIX, 1850, p.10)

Rich and Poor meet at the Crystal Palace 23
The Pound and the Shilling (Vol. XX, 1851, p.247)

Foreigners are everywhere 24
Perfidious Albion lets his Drawing-Room Floor to a distinguished Foreigner (Vol. XX, 1851, p.174)
Rather Alarming: or Hotels in 1851 (Vol. XX, 1851, p.28)

What were the Lessons? 25
'The Morals of the Great Exhibition' (Vol. XX, 1851, p.233)
'A Whisper to Prince Albert' (Vol. XX, 1851, p.198)

The Crimean War 26
Consultation about the State of Turkey (Vol. XXV, 1853, p.119)
A Bear with a sore Head (Vol. XXV, 1853, p.219)
Aberdeen on Duty (Vol. XXV, 1853, p.259)
England's War Vigil (Vol. XXVI, 1854, p.184)

Russia has other Enemies 27
General Février turned Traitor (Vol. XXVIII, 1855, p.95)

At Home Victory is extolled, but Punch grows impatient of Mismanagement 28
Enthusiasm of Paterfamilias (Vol. XXVII, 1854, p.213)
The Queen visiting the Imbeciles of the Crimea (Vol. XXVIII, 1855, p.145)

Britain gains a new Friend 29
La Belle Alliance (Vol. XXIX, 1855, p.87)

There are mixed Feelings about the Peace 30
A distressed Agriculturist (Vol. XXX, 1856, p.44)
'Rejoicings for Peace' (Vol. XXX, 1856, p.177)

Punch already recognises the new Powers of the Time, and their possible Applications 31
'The two Giants of the Time' (Vol. XXXIII, 1857, p.132)
'Chit-Chat by Telegraph' (Vol. XVIII, 1850, p.13)

Already (1856) Englishmen are looking West, and there is a strong Feeling against Slavery . . . 32
The Dis-united States – A black Business (Vol. XXXI, 1856, p.185)
'The Split in the States' (Vol. XXXI, 1856, p.124)

although, by 1861, Punch sympathises with the President 33
The American Difficulty (Vol. XL, 1861, p.193)

Australia is now the Land of Opportunity . . . 34
'Know'st thou the Land?' (Vol. XV, 1848, p.261)
A Gold Field in the Diggins (Vol. XXIII, 1852, p.59)
Not a bad Customer (Vol. XXIV, 1853, p.107)

though Punch appreciates the social Drawbacks of Emigration; Home is best after all 35
Distressing Result of Emigration (Vol. XXIV, 1853, p.24)
An English Gold Field (Vol. XXIII, 1852, p.59)

In 1852 Punch honours a dead Hero 36
'Wellington' (Vol. XXIII, 1852, p.135)

A few Years later (1855–7) Palmerston becomes Punch's Hero 37
Seeing the Old Year out and the New Year in (Vol. XXVIII, 1855, p.5)
Pam – Winner of the great National Steeple-Chase (Vol. XXXII, 1857, p.125)

Patriotism proclaimed (1857) 38
The British Lion's Vengeance on the Bengal Tiger (Vol. XXXIII, 1857, pp.76–7)

Another Imperial Proclamation (1858) 40
The Accession of the Queen of India (Vol. XXXV, 1858, p.107)

La Belle Alliance loses its Charm 41
French Fashion (Vol. XXXV, 1858, p.237)
MR BULL (Vol. XXXVII, 1859, p.197)
The Volunteer Movement (Vol. XXXIX, 1860, p.24)

Punch recognises his Friends (1860) . . . 42
Garibaldi the Liberator (Vol. XXXVIII, 1860, p.243)

and his Enemies (1861) 43
Papal Allocution – Snuffing out modern Civilisation (Vol. XL, 1861, p.151)

At Home the Radicals are more interested in Reform; but Punch knows that Reform means different Things to different People 44
It will soon boil! (Vol. XXXV, 1858, p.187)
The Reform Janus (Vol. XXXVIII, 1860, p.183)

Meanwhile Punch predicts social Disaster if Darwin's Theories are true 45
'Monkeyana' (Vol. XL, 1861, p.206)
The Lion of the Season (Vol. XL, 1861, p.214)

And on all Questions Punch never fails to give Advice 46
'Wonderful Things' (Vol. XXIV, 1853, p.120)

II CURATOR, PROTECTOR, CHASTISER

The Sense of Contrast 49
Substance and Shadow (Vol. V, 1843, p.23)

Priorities (1844) 50
The Game Laws (Vol. VII, 1844, p.197)

One Law for the Rich: Another for the Poor 51
'The Case of Mary Furley' (Vol. VI, 1844, p.223)
Fine or Imprisonment (Vol. VII, 1844, p.243)

Punch takes a Stand 52
'Man *versus* Machine' (Vol. II, 1842, p.26)

A second Stand 53
'A Royal Wife of – £3,000!' (Vol. IV, 1843, p.256)

A social Metaphor (1844) 54
Prince Albert's Bee-Hives (Vol. VII, 1844, pp.90–1)

The Image of Death 55
The Poor Man's Friend (Vol. VIII, 1845, p.93)

Social Commentary 56
The Home of the Rick-Burner (Vol. VII, 1844, p.17)
The Mayoralty – The Coming In, The Going Out (Vol. VII, 1844, pp.208–9)
'Distress of the Country' (Vol. I, 1841, p.215)

The Railway Class System 58
'Railway Politeness' (Vol. VIII, 1845, p.101)
'The Railway Monitor' (Vol. VII, 1844, p.258)

Railway-mania 59
'Railway Charges' (Vol. XIV, 1848, p.218)
The Railway Juggernaut of 1845 (Vol. IX, 1845, p.47)

The genteel Oppressed 60
'Wanted a Governess by a "Small Family"' (Vol. XX, 1851, p.52)
'The March of Morality' (Vol. XV, 1848, p.153)
Splendid Opening for a young Medical Man (Vol. XIV, 1848, p.59)

The continuing Struggle for Education 61
Battle of the Alphabet (Vol. V, 1843, pp.22–3)
Who shall educate? Or, our Babes in the Wood (Vol. XXIV, 1853, p.165)

Punch loathes Cant . . . 62
'A Dose of Cant' (Vol. XXX, 1856, p.129)

'Religion for the Higher Circles' (Vol. XXIII, 1852, p.10)

and Canters 63
'Consequences for Canters' (Vol. XXIV, 1853, p.77)
'"Brummagem" Piety' (Vol. XXXII, 1857, p.40)
A great Sunday Example, by the Archbishop of Cant (Vol. XXX, 1856, p.85)

Anti-Semitism 64
'Cartoon for the Merchant Tailors' (Vol. VI, 1844, p.261)
'The Triumph of Moses' (Vol. XXXV, 1858, p.12)
'A Jew to Canterbury' (Vol. XXX, 1856, p.221)
Christmas in the Minories (Vol. XX, 1851, p.10)
MR NEBUCHADNEZZAR (Vol. X, 1846, p.239)

Anti-Advertising 65
'A Nation of Advertisers' (Vol. XII, 1847, p.14)
'A Little Elysium' (Vol. XI, 1846, p.156)

Religious Capers 66
'Puseyite "Histrionics"' (Vol. XIX, 1850, p.215)
'The Bishop's Wish' (Vol. XXXI, 1856, p.59)
The New Oxford Costume (Vol. XXIV, 1853, p.80)

The Church in Danger? 67
The Guy Fawkes of 1850 (Vol. XIX, 1850, p.197)
The Thin End of the Wedge (Vol. XIX, 1850, p.207)
Religion à la Mode (Vol. XXXIV, 1858, p.257)

Going to Church 68
'The Two Churches' (Vol. XXXIII, 1857, p.136)
'Genteel Christianity' (Vol. VIII, 1845, p.153)

Punch champions the Agricultural Labourer . . . 70
'Agricultural Revels' (Vol. XXVII, 1854, p.134)
The Cottage (Vol. XL, 1861, p.19)

but he warns Strikers that they will hurt only themselves, and criticises their Leaders 71
Effects of a Strike (Vol. XXII, 1852, p.27)
The Strike, a Subject for the Consideration of the Real Working Man (Vol. XXXVII, 1859, p.187)

Punch does not forget the Great Unemployed 72
'Pity the great Unemployed' (Vol. XXXII, 1857, p.74)
The Homeless Poor (Vol. XXXVI, 1859, p.35)

III THE SCALPEL OF REFORM

The Poor Law questioned   75
The 'Milk' of Poor-Law Kindness (Vol. IV, 1843, p.47)

A Poor Law Case History   76
'The "British Labourer" at Andover' (Vol. XV, 1848, p.241)

The Income Tax: a necessary Evil   77
'Sevenpence in the Pound' (Vol. II, 1842, p.118)
'An Income-Tax Apologist (Wanted)' (Vol. VIII, 1848, p.101)

A famous Page by Thomas Hood (1843)   78
'The Song of the Shirt' (Vol. V, 1843, p.260)

Unholy Poverty   79
'A "Warm, Woollen Prison Dress"' (Vol. VIII, 1845, p.32)
'A Trifle from Brighton' (Vol. XV, 1848, p.259)

Punch calls himself the Commissioner for Everywhere . . .   80
'Punch's Commission to Inquire into the General Distress' (Vol. I, 1841, p.169)

and dispenses useful Advice   81
'Fustian Jackets!' (Vol. III, 1842, p.74)
'A Front for a Workhouse' (Vol. VIII, 1845, p.131)
'Hints to Visiting and Relief Societies' (Vol. VII, 1844, p.108)

The Social System   82
Capital and Labour (Vol. V, 1843, pp.48–9)
'Elbow-room' (Vol. XV, 1848, p.42)

Crime and Punishment   84
'Crime and Ignorance' (Vol. XI, 1846, p.77)
'Hints for calling a Spade a Spade' (Vol. XIII, 1847, p.89)
'A Cry from the Condemned Cell' (Vol. XIII, 1847, p.158)

A Plea for Mercy   85
'Old Bailey Holidays' (Vol. II, 1842, p.240)

Pollution: On Land and Water   86
'A Colloquy between the Invalids' (Vol. XIII, 1847, p.33)
A Court for King Cholera (Vol. XXIII, 1852, p.139)
'Dirty Father Thames' (Vol. XV, 1848, p.151)
'To the Thames' (Vol. XXXV, 1858, p.7)
The 'Silent Highway'-Man (Vol. XXXV, 1858, p.15)

Cemeteries, and Homes . . .   88
'An Elegy, written in a London Churchyard' (Vol. XVII, 1849, p.111)
'The Model Court' (Vol. XXVII, 1854, p.204)

a more salubrious London   89
'Our Mean Metropolis' (Vol. XXVII, 1854, p.158)

More Campaigns: Adulteration   90
The Use of Adulteration (Vol. XXIX, 1855, p.47)
The Great Lozenge-Maker (Vol. XXXV, 1858, p.207)
'The Adulterator's Alphabet' (Vol. XXIX, 1855, p.105)

The Licensing Laws: Some Contrasts   91
The Roadside Inn (Vol. XXIX, 1855, p.5)
The Club (Vol. XXIX, 1855, p.6)
'A Drop of Gin!' (Vol. V, 1843, p.223)

Episcopal Reform   92
Sauce for the Gander (Vol. XXXV, 1858, p.147)
A Proper Charge (Vol. XXXV, 1858, p.217)
'Christmas in the Church' (Vol. XIII, 1847, p.247)

The Repeal of the Window Tax, and a Call for Saturday Half-Holidays   93
A Vision of the Repeal of the Window-Tax (Vol. XVIII, 1850, p.165)
'The Saturday Early Closing Movement' (Vol. XXVI, 1854, p.266)

The Scalpel laid down – by all Classes   94
'The Sorrows of the "Star"' (Vol. XXXVIII, 1860, p.221)
'Too Full of Beer' (Vol. XXXVI, 1859, p.70)

IV LANCET OF SATIRE

At the Hustings   97
'Catechisms for the Hustings' (Vol. XV, 1848, p.254)
Bribery is Detestable; but Politeness costs Nothing (Vol. XIII, 1847, p.64)

The Electorate   98
'Intelligence of the People' (Vol. XVII, 1849, p.21)
'Emigration for the Upper Classes' (Vol. XV, 1848, p.73)

Political Theory and Practice   99
'The Political Euclid' (Vol. I, 1841, p.149)
'Hints to New Members' (Vol. I, 1841, p.82)

Political Romance   100
'Young England's "Old Nobility"' (Vol. VI, 1844, p.241)

The Body Politic   101
'Young England's Lament' (Vol. VIII, 1845, p.127)

'A Nice Young Man for a Small Party' (Vol. VIII, 1845, p.267)
'Poisons' (Vol. XXXI, 1856, p.197)

Peel's Progress   102
'The Political Pecksniff' (Vol. VII, 1844, p.25)
'Political Railway Accident' (Vol. IX, 1845, p.111)
'Peel's Mechanical Members' (Vol. VIII, 1845, p.212)

The Machinery of Government   103
'The Government Offices' (Vol. II, 1842, p.178)
'A New Cabinet Library' (Vol. VIII, 1845, p.202)

The Fabric of Society   104
'How to live on nine Shillings a Week' (Vol. VII, 1844, p.125)
Advice gratis to the Poor (Vol. XI, 1846, p.97)

Doctors and Medicine   105
'Doctors' Bills' (Vol. VI, 1844, p.66)
Bubbles of the Year (Vol. VIII, 1845, Almanack)

Romance and Reality of the Railways   106
'Views on Railroads' (Vol. IX, 1845, p.14)
'Panorama of the Blackwall Railway' (Vol. IX, 1845, p.124)
'Railway Pastorals' (Vol. IX, 1845, p.26)
'A Railway Map of England' (Vol. IX, 1845, p.163)
'Railway Maxims' (Vol. XXIV, 1853, p.92)

The Romance (and Reality?) of Royalty   108
'The Royal Rhythmical Alphabet' (Vol. I, 1841, p.62)
'Preparations at Brighton' (Vol. VIII, 1845, p.63)
'Royal Sport' (Vol. VII, 1844, p.157)
'Juvenile Court Circular' (Vol. VI, 1844, p.85)
'Costumes of the Royal Children' (Vol. XIII, 1847, p.70)

National Attitudes to Manners and Morals across the Channel . . .   110
'Small Change for Persons going on the Continent' (Vol. IX, 1845, p.71)

and across the Atlantic   111
'A Yankee Notion' (Vol. VII, 1844, p.56)
The Californian Outfit (Vol. XVI, 1849, p.137)
'Yankee Doodle in 1851' (Vol. XX, 1851, p.161)

National Likes and Dislikes   112
'National Characteristics' (Vol. XXIII, 1852, p.147)
OLD GENT (Vol. XXII, 1852, p.13)
Too Civil by Half! (Vol. XXIII, 1852, p.226)
'Christmas in Ireland' (Vol. XIV, 1848, p.3)
'Irish Game Laws' (Vol. XIV, 1848, p.29)

French Demonstrations of Democracy   113
'La Presse est Morte; Vive la Presse' (Vol. XV, 1848, p.178)
'The French Constitution' (Vol. XXII, 1852, p.41)

Women's Rights and Duties   114
'Club des Femmes' (Vol. XIV, 1848, p.218)
'The Women's Charter' (Vol. XIV, 1848, p.249)

Punch's Female Charter   115
'How to treat the Female Chartists' (Vol. XIV, 1848, p.3)
A Poser for a Bloomer (Vol. XXI, 1851, p.208)

The Shape of Things to Come   116
Bloomeriana. A Dream (Vol. XXI, 1851, pp. 204–5)

Maxims on Art Criticism   118
'Articles and Art' (Vol. VIII, 1845. p.247)

A Confrontation with the Architectural Experts   119
'The Duke that Trench Built' (Vol. XI, 1846, p.107)

Writing made easy, and difficult   120
'Writing made easy' (Vol. VI, 1844, p.79)
'Catalogue of the British Museum' (Vol. XIX, 1850, p.190)
'The New Patent Novel Writer' (Vol. VII, 1844, p.268)

War and Peace – some Rules and Definitions   121
'Patriotism by the Yard' (Vol. XXII, 1854, p.199)
'Extracts from a Peace Dictionary' (Vol. XXX, 1856, p.3)

Statistics, applied and misapplied   122
'A Female Library' (Vol. XII, 1847, p.121)
'Steam-Boat Statistics' (Vol. III, 1842, p.75)
'Ministerial Measures' (Vol. XX, 1851, p.127)
'Analysis of our Collective Wisdom' (Vol. XXXII, 1857, p.97)

Census and (female) Sensibility   123
'The Perpetual Youth of the Women of England' (Vol. XXVII, 1854, p.69)
Filling up the Census Paper (Vol. XX, 1851, p.152)
The Census (Vol. XL, 1861, p.162)

Life goes on: Follies at Home and Abroad   124
A Wholesome Conclusion (Vol. XXXIV, 1858, p.54)
GENTLE SUBSCRIBER! (Vol. XXV, 1853, p.108)

V LIGHTNESS OF HEART

Punmanship   127
'Lessons in Punmanship' (Vol. III, 1842, p.221)

Social Entertaining   128
The Evening Party (Vol. I, 1841, p.31)

Courters' Etiquette 129
'The Natural History of Courtship' (Vol. III, 1842, p.103)

The Niceties of Love 130
'A Dictionary for the Ladies' (Vol. I, 1841, p.263)
'The Chemist to his Love' (Vol. V, 1843, p.236)
The Fox and the Grapes (Vol. XI, 1846, p.138)

Love in Motion 131
'The Poetry of the Rail' (Vol. IX, 1845, p.20)
'Love on the Ocean' (Vol. IX, 1845, p.135)

Love at Home 132
Youth at the Prow (Vol. XXVII, 1854, p.132)
Domestic Bliss (Vol. XIII, 1847, p.74)
Domestic Bliss (Vol. XIII, 1847, p.84)
A Perfect Wretch (Vol. XXX, 1856, p.58)

Love and Duty 133
'More Hints to make Home happy – to Wives'
(Vol. VI, 1844, p.208)
'Matrimonial Weather Report' (Vol. XXXVI, 1859, p.70)

With the Servants: Above the
Stairs . . . 134
Flunkeyiana – A Fact (Vol. XXVI, 1854, p.44)
Flunkeiana (Vol. XXXVI, 1859, p.194)

and below 135
'The Knee-Plush Ultra' (Vol. XXXII, 1857, p.207)
BUTLER (Vol. XXXVI, 1859, p.78)
SERVANT MAID (Vol. XIII, 1847, p.94)

The Delights of the Table:
Anticipation . . . Experiment . . . 136
ANGELINA (Vol. XII, 1847, p.64)
Very Proper Diet for this Hot Weather (Vol. XXIII, 1852, p.40)
Quite a Novelty (Vol. XXVII, 1854, p.40)

Arrival . . . Departure 137
OLD PARTY (Vol. XXXVIII, 1860, p.192)
Bachelor Housekeeping (Vol. XXIII, 1852, p.78)
A Rise in Bread-stuffs (Vol. XXXIX, 1860, p.200)

The Rising Generation 138
HOSTESS (Vol. XII, 1847, p.30)
Sound Advice (Vol. XXII, 1852, p.23)
OLD GENTLEMAN (Vol. XIV, 1848, p.204)
Nothing like Prudence (Vol. XVI, 1849, p.214)
Comparative Love (Vol. XX, 1851, p.165)
A Word to the Wise (Vol. XXXVIII, 1860, p.88)
Bon-bons for Juvenile Parties (Vol. XX, 1851, p.72)

Wives and Daughters 140
'The Best Sewing-Machine' (Vol. XXXVI, 1859, p.91)
'How to "Finish" a Daughter' (Vol. XXIII, 1852, p.161)
YOUNG LADY (Vol. XXVIII, 1855, p.74)

The Value and Values of a
Gentleman 141

Consolation (Vol. XXX, 1856, p.30)
A Delicate Creature (Vol. XXVIII, 1855, p.210)
A Gent at Cost Price (Vol. XXXI, 1856, p.228)
'The Value of a Gentleman' (Vol. V, 1843, p.258)

The Art of Conversation 142
'Polite Conversations' (Vol. V, 1843, p.223)
PARDON ME (Vol. XL, 1861, p.246)
Very Interesting, if one did but know a little more
(Vol. XXX, 1856, p.41)

The Laws of Etiquette 143
'Punch's Guide to Parties' (Vol. VII, 1844, p.206)
'Etiquette of Burglary' (Vol. XXXI, 1856, p.219)

The wrong Size: More Incongruities 144
YOUR BATH (Vol. XI, 1846, p.212)
Comfortable Lodgings (Vol. IX, 1845, p.145)
A Puzzling Order (Vol. XI, 1846, p.4)
Fancy Dress Ball (Vol. X, 1846, p.106)

Shopping 145
'Directions to Ladies for Shopping' (Vol. VII, 1844, p.142)
Taste (Vol. XXIX, 1855, p.10)

The lighter side of Politics 146
'The Merry Commoners' (Vol. XIX, 1850, p.27)
'The New Periodical' (Vol. XL, 1861, p.35)
COLONEL SIBTHORP (Vol. XIV, 1848, p.165)

The lighter side of Science 147
'Domestic Hydropathy' (Vol. XVII, 1849, p.34)
'Fun in a Fossil' (Vol. XXVI, 1854, p.24)
'Progress of Science' (Vol. XXXVII, 1859, p.135)
The Hat-Moving Experiment (Vol. XXIV, 1853, p.214)

The lighter side of Art 148
Ignorance was *bliss* (Vol. XXXVII, 1859, p.160)
Young Dawdlemore (Vol. XXXVII, 1859, p.233)
ENTHUSIASTIC ARTIST (Vol. XL, 1861, p.246)

The lighter side of Religion 149
HOUSEMAID (Vol. XIX, 1850, p.160)
All is Vanity (Vol. XXV, 1853, p.185)
GRANDMAMA (Vol. XX, 1851, p.144)
A Moral Lesson from the Nursery (Vol. XXXII, 1857, p.130)

The lighter side of Learning 150
'Liberal Education' (Vol. XXXI, 1856, p.23)
'The Things to teach at Cambridge' (Vol. XV, 1848, p.228)
'Something for the next Cambridge
Examination Paper' (Vol. XIII, 1847, p.14)

The lighter side of Language 151
Too Fastidious (Vol. XXV, 1853, p.203)
'Fashionable Translations' (Vol. XV, 1848, p.264)
A Horrid Boy (Vol. XXXI, 1856, p.74)

The Stuff of Dreams 152
'Dreams for the Million' (Vol. IV, 1843, p.229)

Problems of Travel by Rail: Luggage
and Timetables 153
RAILWAY PORTER (Vol. XXVII, 1854, p.102)
Wednesbury Station (Vol. XXXIX, 1860, p.242)
The Beard and Moustache Movement (Vol. XXV, 1853, p.188)

Holidays at Home and Abroad 154
Life in London (Vol. XXVIII, 1855, p.134)
2AM (Vol. XXIII, 1852, p.87)
Mr 'Arry Belville (Vol. XXV, 1853, p.134)
SNOB (Vol. XXXVIII, 1860, p.186)

Always the Englishman 155
'Why Englishmen are so beloved upon the
Continent' (Vol. XXXIV, 1858, p.8)
'What an Englishman likes' (Vol. XXX, 1856, p.217)

The Seaside, or the Art of making
pleasant Discoveries 156
A Sketch at Ramsgate (Vol. XXIII, 1852, p.140)
Common Objects at the Sea-side (Vol. XXXV, 1859, p.76)

The Perils of Photography 157

A Photographic Positive (Vol. XXV, 1853, p.48)
A Photographic Picture (Vol. XXV, 1853, p.69)
Art-Progress (Vol. XXXII, 1857, p.174)

Advertisements banned!
(except in Punch) 158
'Catching People's Eyes' (Vol. XXV, 1853, p.267)

Sporting Variations 159
Fishing off Brighton (Vol. XI, 1846, p.188)
THE DEER (Vol. XL, 1861, Almanack)
New Cricketing Dresses (Vol. XXVII, 1854, p.60)

All at Sea 160
BOATING (Vol. XV, 1848, p.114)
Notice to Correspondents (Vol. XXV, 1853, p.30)

Country Life 161
'The Music of Nature' (Vol. XXXIV, 1858, p.21)
*Astounding Announcement from the Small
Country Butcher* (Vol. XXXII, 1857, p.232)

The World sweeps past 162
Utility combined with Elegance (Vol. XXXV, 1858, p.193)

VI PUNCH'S IMAGES

The First Image Projected 165
'The Moral of Punch' (Vol. I, 1841, p.1)

Punch the Regent: Crowned King
(and Queen) 166
King Punch, Queen Judy (Vol. VI, 1844, pp. 18–19)
'Punch's Regency' (Vol. IX, 1845, p.94)

Punch's Images in Stone and at the
Wax-works 167
'Punch's Statue' (Vol. VIII, 1845, p.141)
'A Vacancy in the Public Amusements' (Vol. XV, 1848, p.108)

Punch expelled from France (1843) . . . 168
Punch turned out of France! (Vol. IV, 1843, p.77)

but welcomed in the Provinces 169
'Punch's Tour in the Manufacturing Districts' (Vol. X, 1846, p.123)

Punch the Pope (1847) 170
Roman Punch (Vol. XIII, 1847, p.135)

Punch with Weapons 171
'Punch Tonans' (Vol. XIII, 1847, p.198)
First of September (Vol. XIII, 1847, p.85)

Punch and his Rivals 172
'To Senior Wranglers' (Vol. V, 1843, p.268)
Mrs Gamp (Vol. XI, 1846, p.170)

Punch admonishes the New Boys,
advises a Patient, and addresses the
House of Commons 173
The New Boy (Vol. XIII, 1847, p.255)
Ministerial 'Advice Gratis' (Vol. XXII, 1852, p.159)
*Punch telling the Members to go about their
Business* (Vol. XV, 1848, p.100)

Punch the Instructor in 'Subjects
grave and gay' 174
*Specimens from Mr Punch's Industrial
Exhibition of 1850* (Vol. XVIII, 1850, p.145)
A Pleasant Holiday Task (Almanack, 1859, p.174)

Punch 'the Protector of the High and
the Low' 175
PRINCE ALBERT (Vol. XXV, 1853, p.208)
A Picture for the Intemperate (Vol. XXXVIII, 1860, p.259)
'To All Whom it may concern' (Vol. XXXVI, 1859, p.172)

Punch's Dream of Peace, despite which
he is the best Shot in England 176
Punch's Dream of Peace (Vol. XVI, 1849, p.253)
The Volunteer Movement (Vol. XXXVIII, 1860, Almanack)

Punch, V.C. 177
'Mr Punch and the Victoria Cross' (Vol. XXXIII, 1857, p.4)
Mr Punch receiving the Victoria Cross (Vol. XXXIII, 1857, p.4)

Punch praises himself as an immortal
Institution in a Year of Revolution . . .   178
'Punch's Birthday Ode to Himself' (Vol. XV,
1848, p.1)

and immortalises his Almanack   179
A Page of an Almanack (Vol. X, 1846)

Punch the Priest-baiter   180
' "His Eminence" fighting with Punch' (Vol.
XX, 1851, p.22)

Punch the Critic, the Schoolmaster,
and Member for Everywhere   181
Behind the Scenes (Vol. XXXII, 1857, p.135)

Young 1860 (Vol. XXXVIII, 1860, p.17)
Triumphant Re-election of Mr Punch (Vol.
XXXVI, 1859, p.191)

Punch the Wizard and the Scientist   182
Punch the Wizard (Vol. XXXII, 1857, p.1)
Punch the Scientist (Vol. XL, 1861, p.1)

Punch the Capitalist (1861)   183
'Strike, but hear me!' (Vol. XL, 1861, pp.140–1)

A Footnote: Punch examines his own
Image   184
'Fifty thousand Cures' (Vol. XXV, 1853, p.267)
Cause and Effect (Vol. XIII, 1847, p.158)

VII RETROSPECT AND PROSPECT

A Prophecy   187
'The Reconciliation' (Vol. VIII, 1845, p.122)

1066 and All That   188
'First Causes of the Liberty of the English
Nation' (Vol. XV, 1848, p.137)

Punch's Guide to the Mediaeval
Court of the Crystal Palace   189
'Punch's Handbooks to the Crystal Palace'
(Vol. XXVII, 1854, p.37)

An historical Contrast, and an
historical Parallel   190
'A Contrast' (Vol. XIII, 1847, p.44)
An Historical Parallel; Or, a Court Pastime
(Vol. IX, 1845, pp.130–1)

Five Georges   191
'The Georges' (Vol. IX, 1845, p.159)
'Beau Brummell's Statue, Trafalgar Square'
(Vol. VI, 1844, p.218)

The Course of Modern French History   193
'The Seven Ages of the Republic' (Vol. XV,
1848, p.226)
'Three Epochs of Half-a-Century' (Vol. XXVII,
1854, pp.106–9)

Changing Times: the Course of
Modern British History   194
'America versus England' (Vol. XXI, 1851,
p.128)
'The Good Old Days of Joseph Hume' (Vol. XL,
1861, p.103)

The Present as History   195
'Persecution and Punch in 1851' (Vol. XX, 1851,
p.81)

The Taste for Antiquity: Punch
identifies some cultural Fads –
Archaeological, Antediluvian and
Architectural   196
'More Archaeology' (Vol. XV, 1848, p.72)

The Effects of a Hearty Dinner (Vol. XXVIII,
1855, p.50)
'A Good Goth Wanted' (Vol. XXXVIII, 1860, p.137)

A Glimpse into the Future:
a hundred Years hence (A.D. 1947)   198
'The Middle-Age Mania' (Vol. XII, 1847, p.126)

Five hundred Years hence:
London in 2346   199
'London in A.D. 2346' (Vol. XI, 1846, p.186)

Three Dreams of the nearer Future   200
'What may be done in fifty Years' (Vol. XXXVI,
1859, p.128)
'Palmerston at the Antipodes' (Vol. XXIX, 1855,
p.125)
A Dream of the Future (Vol. XXXVII, 1859, p.10)

Punch's Aerial Courier   201
'Grand Invention!' (Vol. IV, 1843, p.152)

The Electric Telegraph: Punch views
the Implications – social,
technological . . .   202
'Electric Telegraph for Families' (Vol. XI, 1846,
p.253)
'Music by Electric Telegraph' (Vol. XV, 1848,
p.275)
'Letter-writing by Telegraph' (Vol. XI, 1846,
p.238)

aesthetic, moral   203
'The House Telegraph' (Vol. XXXV, 1858, p.244)
'The London District Telegraph Company'
(Vol. XXXVI, 1859, p.29)
'The Electric Story-teller' (Vol. XXVII, 1854,
p.143)
'The Universality of Electricity' (Vol. XXXV,
1858, p.165)

More Travel Prophecies:
Subterranean, astronautical   204
'The Last New Railway Scheme' (Vol. XI, 1846,
p.133)
'Mars', 'The Moon' (Vol. XL, 1861, Almanack)

Two more Predictions with social Consequences 205
'Photography for Criminals' (Vol. XXVII, 1855, p.19)
'Advertising Ingenuity' (Vol. XII, 1847, p.62)

Feminine Fantasies: Comment or Prophecy? 206
Sporting for Ladies (Vol. XI, 1846, p.206)
The Parliamentary Female (Vol. XXIV, 1853, Almanack)
'Woman's Emancipation' (Vol. XXI, 1851, p.3)

Some Metropolitan Prophecies 208
'Enlarged and (not) beautified' (Vol. XIII, 1847, p.140)

'Completion of the Nelson Column' (Vol. XXXII, 1857, p.100)

Royal Prospects (1844) 209
A Royal Nursery Rhyme for 1860 (Vol. VII, 1844, p.79)

Social Transformations 210
'Servantgalism *versus* Schooling' (Vol. XL, 1861, p.3)
'Crinoline's Raging Fury' (Vol. XXXII, 1857, p.41)
The Modern Governess (Vol. XL, 1861, p.52)

Tout change, tout passe 212
'The Future of the Fashions' (Vol. XXXVIII, 1860, p.248)

VIII PLUS ÇA CHANGE

Economic Grumbles 215
Capital and Labour (Vol. XXVIII, 1855, p.48)
'Activity in the Dockyards' (Vol. XXIV, 1853, p.182)
'The Markets' (Vol. X, 1843, p.84)

Taxation and Bureaucracy 216
'A Cool Question and a Courteous Answer' (Vol. XXXVIII, 1860, p.71)
'The Uncivil Civil Service' (Vol. XXIX, 1855, p.208)
Touching Simplicity (Vol. XXX, 1856, p.170)

Students 217
'Code of Instructions' (Vol. I, 1841, p.225)
PROCTOR (Vol. XIX, 1850, p.70)
'The University Boys' (Vol. XIV, 1848, p.26)

Demagogues, and Drugs 218
'The Model Agitator' (Vol. XIV, 1848, p.130)
'Fashionable Laboratories' (Vol. XIV, 1848, p.88)

Baby Worship 219
Domestic Bliss (Vol. XIII, 1847, p.113)

Civil Rights 220
'American Liberty – American Eggs' (Vol. XIII, 1847, p.154)

The Rights of the Customer 221
'Customers' Protection Circular' (Vol. XX, 1851, p.81)
'Advertisements' (Vol. X, 1846, p.269)

Novelties 222
'Old and New Toys' (Vol. XIV, 1848, p.76)
'Fine Ladies and their Tailors' (Vol. XXXII, 1857, p.184)
A Startling Novelty in Shirts (Vol. XXV, 1853, p.31)

Poultry Prophecies 223
'Steam Chickens' (Vol. XIV, 1848, p.127)
'Chicken for the Million' (Vol. XIV, 1848, p.82)

The English Climate 224
Portrait of 1855 (Vol. XXVIII, 1855, p.224)
Oh! The Merry Merry Month of May (Vol. VIII, 1845, p.238)

Decimals, and Smoking 225
'The Decimal Coinage' (Vol. XXV, 1853, p.101)
'A Few Simple Rules against Smoking' (Vol. XL, 1861, p.73)
'Songs of the Hearth-rug' (Vol. VI, 1844, p.175)

Smoke in the Streets 226
'The Battle of the Streets' (Vol. IX, 1845, p.64)
'King Smoke' (Vol. XXVII, 1854, p.84)

Disturbance in the City 227
'Our Anglo-Italian Climate' (Vol. XVII, 1849, p.54)
'The Anti-Street Noise League' (Vol. XXXIV, 1858, p.103)

Advice to those about to Travel 228
'Hints How to Enjoy an Omnibus' (Vol. I, 1841, p.250)
The Threepenny Fare Mystery (Vol. XVI, 1849, p.197)

Don't! 229
LONDON CABS (Vol. XXIV, 1853, p.84)
The Thaw and the Streets (Vol. XL, 1861, p.48)

The Royal Family criticised . . . 230
'Dreadful Destruction in Buckingham Palace' (Vol. XI, 1846, p.84)
A Case for Real Distress (Vol. XI, 1846, p.89)

and (over-)chronicled. Punch issues a Warning 231
'A Prince in a Yankee Print' (Vol. XXXIX, 1860, p.71)
'A Prince at High Pressure' (Vol. XXXVII, 1859, p.126)

The Christmas Spirit 232
'It is lucky that Christmas does come but once a Year' (Vol. XXIV, 1853, p.17)
'The Christmas-Box Nuisance' (Vol. XV, 1848, p.271)

Holiday Mood 233
'Tripping Time' (Vol. XXXVII, 1859, p.92)

Finis 234

This anthology of the first twenty years of *Punch* covers a period of striking changes both in the structure and in the mood of English society. In 1841, when the first number appeared, the country was in the midst of the worst industrial depression since the introduction of steam power nearly sixty years before. There were bitter social conflicts in which different classes were arrayed against each other, and the politics of the governments of the day seemed to the many social and political critics of the time to be impeding rather than assisting any effort to answer 'the condition of England' question. The Whigs gave way to Sir Robert Peel's Tories within weeks of *Punch*'s first appearance, but it was certainly not clear then that large-scale practical reforms would be introduced by the new prime minister.

By 1861, when *Punch* celebrated its twentieth birthday, the mood of the country was so mellow that it was difficult to arouse any sustained interest in further political reform. There were few outspoken radical critics, and most commentators on society dwelt not on its tensions but on its harmonies, not on its conflicts but on its conformities. Above all, they concerned themselves with the implications of its unprecedented rate of material progress. The dark years at the end of the Napoleonic Wars had receded into the distance and when most people thought of Napoleon they had Napoleon III in mind, not Napoleon I.

It is easy to see in retrospect that the England of 1861 had not disposed of its

problems. As G. M. Young has written, the extremes of wealth and poverty, civilization and savagery, literally jostled each other in the streets. This was the year, indeed, when Henry Mayhew, one of the founders of *Punch*, published in book form the first part of his *London Labour and the London Poor* which had first appeared in the form of articles in 1849–50 when revolution and cholera had jolted social complacency. Yet Mayhew had long ceased to be connected with *Punch*, and the magazine, which had started off 'squeaking in the streets', had become 'respectable'. This was, indeed, the favourite social attribute of 1861 when the great dividing line in society was between the 'respectable' and the rest. Already by 1850 *Punch* was hailing himself as 'a householder with fine plate-glass windows' and the dedication in the volume of that year was not to the Nine Pins but to the Nine Muses. During the 1850's there was no longer any need to be self-conscious about the transformation. Mark Lemon, *Punch*'s editor throughout the whole period covered in this volume, was told frankly by his friend Sir Joseph Paxton, ex-gardener, railway magnate, designer of the Crystal Palace, Liberal member of parliament and hero of self-help in the eyes of both Queen and People, 'The circulation keeps up – so keep up the tone.'

The tone of 1841 had certainly been very different. Douglas Jerrold, Lemon's right-hand man and Mayhew's father-in-law, prided himself, with full justification, on being a 'champion of the poor', and the new magazine was completely lacking in what the mid-

Victorians were to call 'deference'. Whether or not politicians were ignoring 'the condition of England' question, journalists were not. Nor were some of the most lively novelists. The founders of *Punch* were mainly young men. Jerrold, who had started an earlier magazine called *Punch in London* in 1832, was 38 years old. Yet Lemon was only 31 and Henry Mayhew was only 29.

There was nothing new either about the philosophy (if such a term can be applied to it) or the format of *Punch*. It had many predecessors, most of them short-lived, and Lemon, Mayhew and Gilbert à Beckett, another of its first writers (aged 30), had all been involved, like Jerrold, in earlier publishing ventures with periodicals which included both text and pictures. So, too, had its first printer, Joseph Last, whose *Figaro in London* (1831–9) was one of the sources of inspiration of *Punch*; *Figaro* is said to have reached a peak circulation of 70,000.

The name *Punch* was a last-minute choice. *The Funny Dog; or the London Charivari* was the title first proposed (with a glance across the Channel at Charles Philipon's Paris *Charivari*), and a woodcut of dogs in male and female costume with the caption 'Funny Dogs with Comic Tales' figured in the first prospectus. The periodical was announced as a 'new work of wit and whim', although in the first number Jerrold promised also in an article called significantly 'The Moral of Punch' that there were to be judgements as well as jokes. Jerrold liked to address his readers directly, to appeal to their consciences as well as to seek to entertain. He continued to do so until his death in 1857. Already in his earlier *Punch in London* he had offered the same ingredients as were offered in 1841:

'*Mr Punch* is a man of few words; but those words, like the syllables of the girl in the fairy tale, come with pearls and diamonds; they are also often mixed with snakes and scorpions . . . He hath a long time been the oracle of highways and byways – the "Wisdom that crieth out in the street" – the delight and councillor of all men from their cradles to their coffins . . . Is it not evident that *Punch* possesses, above all personages, the amplest means of becoming "the best public instructor"?'

In 1841 the new *Punch* did not immediately prosper, and it was on the basis of its annual almanack, first published in 1842, rather than on its regular weekly issues, that it established its fortunes.

Funny Dogs with Comic Tales

It very soon lost both its first printer (Bradbury and Evans became printers and proprietors in 1842) and Henry Mayhew. In the meantime, Lemon consolidated his own position and began to build up a remarkable team, the secret of *Punch*'s success. It was a team of people with different views, some of them conflicting. Jerrold's presence guaranteed that the periodical would both support the underdog and probe social inequalities, yet the novelist W. M. Thackeray, who began writing for *Punch* in 1842 and continued doing so regularly until 1851, had quite different sympathies. He told his mother in 1842 that *Punch* was 'a very low paper' and that he would write for it only because of 'its good pay and a great opportunity for unrestrained laughing, sneering, kicking and gambadoing', and although he could be just as irreverent as any other contributor to *Punch* he thought of Jerrold as 'a savage little Robespierre'. Whereas Jerrold set out to expose the contradictions of society Thackeray sought to depict it ironically, critically, but basically not unsympathetically. Jerrold pointed to exploitation, Thackeray to snobbery. Both men were in their different ways moralists, but 'the moral of *Punch*' for Thackeray was very different from that originally enunciated by Jerrold.

If the difference in outlook between the two men was the most important of the differences behind the scenes, it is true also that the other members of the team were diverse in their attitudes and characters. Horace Mayhew,

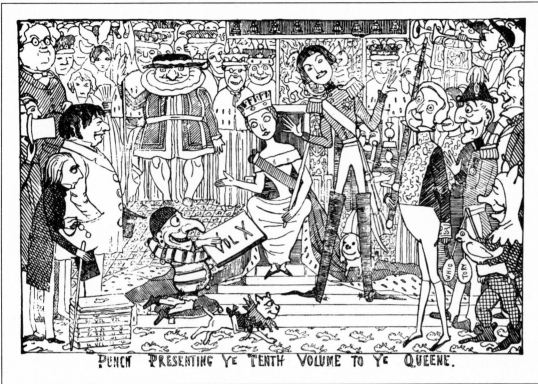

PUNCH PRESENTING Yᵉ TENTH VOLUME TO Yᵉ QUEENE.

Punch personalities as seen by Richard Doyle, 1846. Thackeray is in the top left hand corner: below him are Lemon and Jerrold

Henry's younger brother, who joined *Punch* in 1843 and continued to serve it until 1872, two years after Lemon's retirement as editor, shared his brother's curiosity and willingness to penetrate hidden, even forbidden, areas of mid-Victorian society. But 'Professor' Percival Leigh, who had written a highly successful *Comic Latin Grammar*, remained more interested in the classics and in Shakespeare than in London labour and the London poor: he is said to have written his articles for *Punch* on 'the assumption of scholarship in its readers'. Tom Taylor, who was to be editor of *Punch* for six years after 1874, was for a time a real professor at University College, London. Learned and eloquent, he became a barrister in 1846 and later on secretary of the Board of Health. À-Beckett was a Poor Law Commissioner and a Metropolitan magistrate.

Of the first artists – and the very first artists were hired as cheaply as possible on a commission basis – John Leech had been a friend of Thackeray at Charterhouse. He was only 24 when he joined *Punch*, and was quite uninterested in 'the condition of England' question. Richard ('Dickie') Doyle, who was only 19 when he was first employed by *Punch* in 1843, was a Roman Catholic who resigned in 1850 when *Punch* became brutally and obsessively anti-papal. Older artists were

quickly got rid of as the paper established its own personality. Among them were the wood engraver Ebenezer Landells, born in 1808, an early example of whose work appears on the title-page of this book, and Archibald Henning, who produced the first cover, and whose work was in line with an older tradition of comic journalism from which *Punch* very quickly and successfully broke free.

Some of the tensions within the *Punch* team may be thought of, to use a cliché, as creative. Whatever readers might think of the whole publication, parts at least they would find excellent. In addition there was an edge to some of the individual contributions which resulted from interplay and argument behind the scenes. The fact that in the early days members of the *Punch* set were attacked *en masse* in conservative circles undoubtedly pulled them together. In 1848, for example, Thackeray wryly recorded in 'Author's Misery' the illustrated conversation (reproduced overleaf right) which he and Jerrold overheard in a railway carriage.

Even during the mid-1850's, when Lemon and many of his *Punch* colleagues travelled as a group to Boston to support the election campaign of Herbert Ingram, the founder of the *Illustrated London News*, several newspapers, doubtless echoing established sections of public opinion, accused the *Punch* men of making a cheap and vulgar bid for publicity. Such comment cannot have been stilled by the *Boston Guardian's* rejoinder that 'we have inaugurated a new era in political life'.

XIII

The Punch Team, 1854

Yet the creativity of the *Punch* team was not simply a matter of group dynamics. Lemon, a perfect editor for his times, recognised that there had to be diversity in unity. He was frank enough to realise that some members of the team were more clever than he was, and skilful enough to draw the best out of each of them. He entreated, persuaded and cajoled, but in the last resort he could give orders. He was willing also to take a gamble at critical moments. It was at his instigation, for example, that Thomas Hood's 'The Song of the Shirt' was published in the Christmas number in 1843 even though most members of his team advised him not to do so. The poem was a winner and totally eclipsed his own 'Pauper's Christmas Carol' which appeared in the same number. Year in, year out, Lemon took an intense personal interest in what was going on, visiting the homes of his artists to make sure that they were working on the right lines and would produce their cartoons in time. He also argued freely with his writers about art and politics, always from an instinctive rather than systematic liberal standpoint. While Henry Mayhew gave the impression to his intimates

that there was a committed sociologist seeking to break out from inside him, it was clear that in the case of Lemon there was no such demon. He was adaptable to changing moods and circumstances, and unlike editors of a later generation he was vigilantly aware of the dangers of proceeding by formula.

There were two other significant features of his approach to the editing of *Punch*. First, he insisted that there should be a basic nucleus of 'regulars'. Writers, in particular, should be paid well. Piece work and payment by the column might be adequate for writers, young or old, who had not established themselves, but for those who had survived the necessary period of probation there had to be a definite attachment and obligation to *Punch*. He allowed, even encouraged, his contributors to write for other periodicals also – he himself organised the Christmas supplements of the *Illustrated London News* and collected items from *Punch* writers and artists – yet every column contributed by 'regulars' to *Punch* was recorded in a Day Diary which was kept in the *Punch* office. Some writers, like à Beckett, contributed hundreds of jokes and verses each year, yet they never became jaded hacks. Second, he encouraged *Punch* to become the

Old Gentleman   *Miss Wiggets*   *Two Authors*

OLD GENTLEMAN. 'I am sorry to see you occupied, my dear Miss Wiggets, with that trivial paper PUNCH. A railway is not a place, in my opinion, for jokes. I never joke – never.'

MISS W. 'So I should think, Sir.'

OLD GENTLEMAN. 'And besides, are you aware who are the conductors of that paper, and that they are Chartists, Deists, Atheists, Anarchists, and Socialists, to a man? I have it from the best authority, that they meet together once a week in a tavern in Saint Giles's, where they concoct their infamous Print. The chief part of their income is derived from Threatening Letters which they send to the Nobility and Gentry. The principal writer is a returned Convict. Two have been tried at the Old Bailey; and their Artist – as for their Artist . . .

GUARD. 'Swin-don! Sta-tion!'   *Exeunt two authors*

centre of a social circle – this was perhaps the best way of avoiding the feeling of hackwork – and not simply a periodical produced at a distance by scattered writers and artists. Every Wednesday evening editors, proprietors and staff met for dinner at the *Punch* table not only to discuss business – the subject of the principal cartoon for the next week's issue (called at first 'Mr Punch's Pencillings' and later 'The Big Cut') – but any matter, topical or otherwise, which appealed to them. 'The Punch Brotherhood,' Lemon himself wrote later, 'has been one of the most extraordinary literary brotherhoods the world has ever seen.' 'Sociality,' claimed Evans, the printer and proprietor, 'is the secret of the success of *Punch*.'

The *Punch* circle was difficult to enter, but it was never completely closed. Shirley Brooks, who was to become one of Lemon's closest friends and his successor as editor, was deliberately drawn in from a rival journal *The Man in the Moon* in 1851. *The Man in the Moon* had been founded by one of *Punch*'s first contributors, Albert Smith, who had been sacked by Lemon: Smith, who remained active in Fleet Street and beyond until 1860, had his own circle which included G. A. Sala. He was

described later in the century as the 'smartest and wittiest phrase-maker of the later Cockney school'.

Brooks was an experienced and sophisticated writer who very quickly made his mark with *Punch*; unimpressed by noisy radical causes, he was fascinated by the in-fighting of parliamentary politics: his 'Essence of Parliament', which was very much the essence of Brooks, first appeared in 1855. It was the ubiquitous Brooks who made ambitious politicians feel that they could not afford to be neglected by *Punch* or, for that matter, to miss *Punch*'s jokes.

After Doyle's sudden withdrawal from *Punch* in 1851, John Tenniel (to be made Sir John in 1881 – the one *Punch* artist to be knighted) began contributing the cartoons which established not only his own reputation but that of *Punch* as a national institution. Tenniel's remarkable capacity to handle 'great affairs' in terms of symbols (and stereotypes) as well as of running commentary guaranteed his success. His 'courteous highmindedness', as Spielmann, the first historian of *Punch*, called it, was in keeping with the changing image of *Punch* in the mid-Victorian years, and he lived long enough to become the Grand Old Man of *Punch*,

XV

enjoying what Spielmann also called an apotheosis. 'Many complain,' Spielmann went on, 'that *Punch* no longer hits out straight from the shoulder. This peaceable tendency obviously arises from neither fear nor sycophancy, but from an anxious desire to be entirely just and good-natured and to avoid coarseness or breach of taste. Much of the change of *Punch* has simply been the inevitable accompaniment of change in the times – in the tastes, manners, social polish and sensitive feelings of the courteous and urbane.'

Certainly new recruits, amongst whom Brooks and Tenniel were outstanding, were strong and distinctive enough both in talent and temperament to guide *Punch* through the changing social and political conditions of the 1850's. Tenniel was neither radical nor liberal: Brooks had Tory sympathies. So, too, had Charles Keene, who even when *Punch* had become thoroughly respectable said after a new member of staff had been engaged, 'I hope he's a Tory. We want some leaven to the set of sorry Rads that lead poor old *Punch* astray at present.' George du Maurier, for whom social pictorial satire meant satire of Society with a large rather than with a small s, contributed his first drawing in 1860 and his first signed sketch a year later, but he did not become a 'regular' until after this anthology closes: he was to be known as 'the Thackeray of the pencil', and his social 'types' and 'series' were to be thought of as supremely English in all parts of the world, not least in the United States.

It is interesting to trace, as R. G. G. Price has done in his admirably compact and perceptive *History of Punch* (1957), the stages by which *Punch* became respectable between 1841 and 1861, turning from a 'guffawgraph' with a social message into a national institution. For all the importance of the contributions made by Brooks and Tenniel and later by du Maurier, Lemon was the main agent of the great transformation. As England prospered, *Punch* prospered and Lemon prospered. He started at a stipend of 30 shillings a week and was soon earning £1,500 a year. With both eyes on his readership, he was careful even during its early 'unrespectable' years to superintend the weekly contents page, keeping out of *Punch* anything which might be thought to be either brutal or improper. '*Punch*,' he once said, 'keeps up by keeping to the gentlemanly view of things and its being known that Bohemians don't write for it.' One of the sources of inspiration of *Punch*, as we have seen, was the Paris *Charivari*, yet in the 1850's there was little in common between *Punch* and its French contemporaries. There was little in common, either, with its satirical predecessors in London, like *The Town*, which made the most of 'fun after dark' and included in its titillating pages sketches of 'metropolitan gaming houses, free and easies, the swell mob, cigar shops and pretty women, Bow-street Officers and the doings of courtesans, demireps of quality etc., etc.'

Moreover, attacks on individuals, prominent in the early numbers of *Punch*, were soon muted. Lord Brougham, in particular, had been an early target of scathing criticism, as had been Peel's Home Secretary, Graham, and Colonel Sibthorp, ultra-Tory M.P. for Lincoln, had been an unquenchable source of fun.

OUR COLONEL'S CORNER

THE hearing in the new House of Commons is, as every one knows who wishes to make a fine speech, extremely indistinct. SIBTHORP being asked what was the loudest tone generally heard in it, replied on the spot, 'A Barry-tone.'

A person who was reading in the streets, ran violently against him. The Colonel took hold of him and held him by the button-hole, till he delivered himself of the following *jeu d'esprit*: – 'Sir, it is perfectly true that "those who run may read;" but that is no reason why those who read should run;' having said which, he good-naturedly released him, with a poke in the ribs.

It is needless to state that the Colonel is strongly imbued with all the JOHN BULL prejudices of the fine 'Old School,' of which he has always been one of the proudest ornaments. He was asked what he would do in case the Crystal Palace were attacked by these French Socialists. 'Do, Sir!' he answered quite angrily, 'why, Sir, I would simply call into operation the Cold Water Cure. I would have a small fire-engine stationed in the Exhibition; and if they attempted any of their foreigneering tricks here, I would begin playing upon them, like a house on fire. Depend upon it, Sir, they would all begin running, to a man; for if there is one thing a Frenchman has a greater horror of than another, it is Cold Water. I never met with a foreigner yet who could face it.'

He was asked what was his opinion about Communism. He was very angry at first, and wouldn't answer. At last his brow gradually relaxed, and he said, in the calmest manner, 'Communism, my dear Sir, is the equal division of goods. That is to say, if I have a dickey, and you have no shirt, I must share my dickey with you. Now I should like to know how we should all look with only half a dickey a piece?'

Despite a continuing distaste for Disraeli, *Punch* found no new Sibthorp. Yet it was even more prepared to take on all foreigners than Palmerston was, and took advantage of every tricky situation to beat the national drum. The thirteenth volume stated eloquently that 'Mr Punch has a lively belief that the world will feel the benignant influence of his teaching. . . . In the meantime, the Briton will be pleased to feel duly proud with the conviction of the fact that Mr Punch as the Schoolmaster is Abroad [ironically the phrase came from Brougham], and that even crowned heads are made to listen to him. Every crowned head, too, like every medal, has its reverse. If Mr Punch can twine the bay, can he not also bind the birch?'

On many occasions *Punch*, never inhibited about itself, claimed proudly that it was speaking for all England. As it burst out in one of its many self-congratulatory odes:

But of our Constitution
    There's one peculiar boast,
Its finest Institution –
    That is to say, almost –
With warmest exultation,
And self-congratulation,
With admiration utterly unbounded
    Should every mother's son
Regard THAT Institution, founded
    In Eighteen Forty-one . . .

Thy celebrated Journal
    The proudest feelings must awaken
In every patriotic breast
That throbs beneath a British vest.

The same message could be stated more economically in pictures (see below):

The National Claim (*1847*)

There is a temptation for the historian of the nineteenth century simply to use old numbers of *Punch* through these changing years in the same way as he uses novels or poems – as illustration or decoration of his narrative. Thus, he may reproduce one of the famous Crimean War cartoons to lend extra colour to the tale told many times over of militant nationalism and military mismanagement, or re-cast *Punch*'s attitudes to slavery and to the American Civil War. The verse and prose in *Punch* have tended to be neglected even in terms of this strictly limited ransacking use.

This anthology, however, has a different purpose. It is designed to offer something more than a series of bright illustrated glosses to the appropriate paragraphs of a historical monograph or textbook. It seeks by assembling chosen samples of items from *Punch* to 'place' the periodical in the history of communication. In other words, it puts *Punch* into the picture rather than extracts pictures out of *Punch*. It treats the periodical as a medium rather than as a source.

It is only during the last two decades that we have come to consider carefully, in the light of our own unfinished 'communications revolution' (radio, television and so on), earlier patterns of communication. Our understanding of the role or rather the roles of *Punch* in its nineteenth-century context will be broadened and deepened if we compare it with other media of communication then and since, including not only newspapers but novels and television. The pictorial element in its composition is particularly interesting since it was not until 1886 that F. C. Gould took up the first regular post as cartoonist with a political journal, *The Pall Mall Gazette*, and it was not until the twentieth century that photography (a subject of great interest to *Punch*) made its way into newspapers.

Very little has been written about *Punch* within this context. For all its attractiveness to historians as a source of illustrations, it has been given little attention by students of reading habits in the nineteenth century or by critics concerned with the changing relationship between academic writers, men of letters and journalists. It falls outside the scope both of Louis James's *Fiction for the Working Man* (1963), which in the course of examining different strata of readers turns to a number of forgotten popular periodicals read by larger numbers of people than *Punch*, and of John Gross's *The Rise and Fall of the Man of Letters* (1969), which leaves out all the members of the *Punch* circle, with the exception of Thackeray who is not considered as a contributor to *Punch*. It is not mentioned in the chapter on reviews and magazines in the Pelican Guide to English Literature *From Dickens to Hardy* (1958), although as R. G. Price has pointed out in his *History of Punch*, as early as 1842 the sober

Westminster Review in a survey of periodicals stated that *Punch* was considerably better written than many papers with higher pretensions.

As a weekly, *Punch* was always concerned with deadlines. The effort to get it out in time always involved writing and drawing for the clock. Last-minute changes were sometimes made in the interests of topicality, above all in cartoons. 'Journalism,' wrote Henry James, 'is the criticism of the moment *at* the moment, and caricature is that criticism at once simplified and intensified by a plastic form.' In *Punch* the influence of caricature affected prose and verse as well as drawing, and there was always a link, through Lemon even before Brooks, with the daily and weekly press. Douglas Jerrold edited *Lloyd's Weekly Newspaper*, for example, from 1852 to 1857: according to a contemporary, he discovered the newspaper in the gutter and annexed it to literature. There was no regular *Punch* feature, as there has been in other places since, concerned with what the papers say, although for a time there was an item called 'curiosities of advertising literature' and there were frequent references to other newspapers and periodicals. Brooks 'devoured' material from the press and was proud of the fact that *Punch* 'set its watch by the clock of *The Times*'.

If *Punch* had the advantage over the newspapers that it had time to sum up the events of the week that was, it also had the advantage over the prestigious quarterlies that it could comment on ideas and events before they became stale. It was the *Illustrated London News*, not *Punch*, which pointed to the change of rhythm and pace during the railway age. 'In the palmy days of the *Edinburgh* and *Quarterly*,' it argued in 1849, 'the conversation in every man's mouth was the tone, temper and ability of the last review. . . . Now, who asks, except on rare occasions, which is the grand article in the last *Quarterly*? Railways and revolutions have put the finishing stroke to this sort of excitement which has been gradually declining for many years past.' Not that novelists, some of whom wrote for *Punch*, did not have some advantages over journalists or social commentators, particularly during the 1840's when, in the words of a reviewer in *Fraser's*, 'whoever has anything to say . . . puts it forthwith into the shape of a novel or tale'. In comparing the handling of themes common to novels and to *Punch* it is usually the novel, 'multiform and multitudinous', which wins. In dealing with railways, for example, *Punch* had much of importance to say both in words and in pictures, but it did not reach the interpretative depth of Dickens. Though Humphry House considered Dickens to be 'tainted with the prevailing facetiousness about refreshment-rooms and luggage and wrappers, the stand-bys of *Punch*', he added that Dickens used such material 'infinitely better than *Punch*'.

XVIII

The same point cannot be made so easily about the comparative merits of illustrations in books and in *Punch*, even when the work of George Cruikshank, who never drew for *Punch*, except for one announcement on its advertisements page in 1844, is taken into account. Cruikshank thought that the idea of *Punch* had been stolen from his *Omnibus* and that the *Punch* pocket-books were directly copied from his *Comic Annuals*. Yet this was an unfair charge. *Punch* was not alone among periodicals in dealing in images as well as in quips, for, leaving on one side its rivals, the Sunday newspapers and many other cheaper periodicals carrying copious illustrations, there had been no shortage of illustrated political broadsheets in England, particularly from the eighteenth century onwards. There was an even more ambitious idea behind the *Illustrated London News* – that of providing a regular pictorial pageant or 'panorama' encompassing references to 'arts' and 'fashions' as well as to the main public events of the week, 'a living and moving panorama' before 'the eye of the world'. The term 'panorama' thus spans the communications revolution, linking the 1840's with the 1950's and 1960's. Indeed, the first number of the *Illustrated London News* already spoke of a revolution. 'We have watched with admiration and enthusiasm,' its editor exclaimed, 'the progress of illustrative art and the vast revolution which it has wrought in the world of publication. It has converted blocks into wisdom, and given wings and spirit to ponderous and senseless wood. It has adorned, gilded, reflected and interpreted nearly every form of thought.'

Wordsworth, among others, like many conservatives since, had no sympathy with this new development, and his comments about it anticipate twentieth-century comments about television:

Discourse was deemed Man's noblest attribute,
And written words the glory of his hand;
Then followed Printing with enlarged command
For thought – dominion vast and absolute
For spreading truth, and making love expand.

Now prose and verse sunk into disrepute
Must lackey a dumb art that best can suit
The taste of this once-intellectual Land.
A backward movement surely have we here,
From manhood, back to childhood; for the age –
Back towards caverned life's first rude career.
Avaunt this vile abuse of pictured page!
Must eyes be all in all, the tongue and ear
Nothing? Heaven keep us from a lower stage.

This was certainly not the language of *Punch*, and it is fascinating to trace the way in which its artists developed new pictorial styles between 1841 and 1861 without their art undergoing a real technical revolution. Throughout the period, in the absence of photographic methods, boxwood blocks were used for line engraving. Designs were drawn by artists on the face of the blocks and cutting was then laboriously carried out by wood engravers: the task took up to twenty-four hours. Given the limitations of the technology and the initial shortage of skilled wood engravers (in 1827 there had been only twenty wood-cutters in London who claimed artists' wages), it is remarkable how skilful the *Punch* engravers proved themselves to be in coping with the artists' attempts to introduce tone by what was called 'cross-hatching', the use of shaded lines at angles to each other.

From the start the styles of the different artists varied at least as much as their abilities. Some followed the example of the broadsheet: their drawings (for example of Mr Punch himself in the early numbers) were crude and lacking in subtlety. Some enjoyed great fame in their own time, and have been little appreciated since: among them was Kenny Meadows, 51 years old when he joined *Punch*. His designs, wrote his nephew, 'were intended to portray something more than a burlesque view of a current event or a popular abuse', yet Henry Vizetelly, journalist and artist, argued more accurately that 'he was a singularly incorrect and feeble draughtsman' who 'abounded with clever and often highly poetic ideas'.

A Kenny Meadows Fantasy (*1843*)

ST DAVID'S DAY, OR THE PRINCE AND HIS PATRON

Back to the Middle Ages (Doyle, *1846*) YE TOURNAMENT

A Broad Caricature

Dickie Doyle, son of a famous father, and as inexperienced as Meadows was over-ripe, had been given no regular teaching and was never permitted to draw direct from the model. There was a charm and sweetness about his work which marks an immense break with the parody, burlesque and brutality of James Gillray. The 'dicky bird' sitting on a branch was his signature, and his most lasting achievement was an 1849 design for the cover of *Punch* which was still being used more than a hundred years later. He was at his best in purely decorative work, with fairies and elves appealing irresistibly to his Irish imagination. They skip and gambol around the borders of the pages, settling provocatively in elaborate initial letters. The Irishness did not prevent him making the most of the lost days of 'Merrie England', and the Pre-Raphaelites are said to have bought issues of *Punch* to study Doyle's groupings.

John Leech, drawing straight on the wood block with a lead pencil, established the full-page cartoon (the word was invented in its modern sense within the *Punch* circle in 1843), working very closely at that time with Jerrold, as in his influential drawing 'The Poor Man's Friend' of 1845 (see below, p. 55). He was to employ a very similar treatment ten years later in one of his most famous cartoons, 'General Février turned Traitor' (see below, p.27) during a period when domestic themes were being eclipsed in the public mind by foreign affairs. Leech, indeed, as has often been pointed out, climbed the social ladder with *Punch*. He had made his mark with drawings from 'low life'. Yet ten years later, after he had created a *Punch* world of urchins, 'stout parties', policemen, scraggy maiden ladies and over-fed elderly gentlemen, Thackeray was right to say of him

that he was surveying society 'from the gentleman's point of view'. There was, indeed, a new Leechian angle on the world. When du Maurier wrote of him, he dwelt on his 'love of home, his love of sport, his love of the horse and the hound – especially his love of the pretty

A Leech 'Social' (*1853*)

PREPARATIONS FOR WAR

Officer (who is going to the East). 'Of course it's rather a Bore just at the beginning of the Season – and I shall miss the Derby! Wish they could have had the Russians over here, because then we could have Thrashed 'em in Hyde Park, and dined at Greenwich afterwards, you know.'

woman – the pretty woman of the normal, wholesome English type'. (Sir John Millais produced an admirable skit on Leech's 'Pretty Girl'.)

Du Maurier made much also of Leech's 'Englishness', the 'Englishness' that foreigners associated with *Punch*. 'He conformed quite spontaneously and without effort to upper-class British ideals of his time, and had its likes and dislikes.' Yet du Maurier claimed finally that Leech was 'a king of impressionists, and his impressionism becomes ours on the spot – never to be forgotten! It is all so quick and fresh and strong, so simple, pat and complete, so direct from mother Nature herself!'

It is strange to read of the term 'impressionism' being applied to Leech's work, even though it may be applied with more meaning to another *Punch* artist of the period, Charles Keene, whose work was greatly admired in Paris. Sickert called him 'the first of the moderns', and Whistler was a close friend. Keene had no respect for the medievalism of the Pre-Raphaelites nor did he approve of Victorian official or even unofficial narrative art. Once, after a visit to the Royal Academy, he commented on 'how bad' a great number of the pictures were, 'especially among the R.A.s and the great guns'. Keene left behind for posterity only three or four oil paintings, a few water colours and a number of etchings and original drawings. The great bulk of his work is to be found in the pages of the *Illustrated London News* and *Punch*. He lacked the native humour of Leech, who was always adept at integrating 'legend' and picture, but occasionally, particularly when depicting the art world, he

Keene's First Contribution to *Punch* (1851)

SKETCH OF THE PATENT STREET-SWEEPING MACHINES LATELY INTRODUCED AT PARIS

Taken on the Spot (A, the Spot) by our own Artist (Who being naturally rather a nervous man, confesses that the peculiarity of his position certainly *did* make him feel a little shaky; and, looking at his sketch, we think our readers will not be disinclined to believe him.)

COTTON LORD (*'coming' the Noble Patron*). 'Haw – I was indooced to buy a little Picture of yours, the other day, Stodge, haw –'
ARTIST (*who does not seem to see it*). 'Lucky Fellow!!'

(Keene, *1861*)

could get to the point with remarkable incisiveness.

When Leech retired in 1864 Keene was to take his place. He always drew from the model and devoted infinite pains even to 'cuts' on the most trivial themes, displaying wonderful powers of composition and, most remarkable of all, great ability to suggest light and shade.

The subtlety of Keene's effects makes much of the highly praised work of the next outstanding *Punch* artist, John Tenniel, seem coldly academic and over-correct by comparison. Yet it was Tenniel who, as Spielmann has written, 'dignified the cartoon into a classic composition'. His humorous captioned drawings possess little visual wit and he had no gift for 'fooling'. Moreover, he never drew from life, and as he got older and more and more of a national institution he was criticised for not having moved sufficiently with the times. The interest of his work does not lie in his grasp of social material, but rather in his ability to present at particular moments of history a sense of the meaning of great events in terms of association and symbol. If Leech has claims to be considered one of the best social historians of the nineteenth century, no political historian of

Mr Punch at St Paul's, Covent Garden

that century can leave Tenniel out of the reckoning.

In her detailed study of opinion and propaganda, *English Political Caricature, 1793–1832* (1959), M. Dorothy George has pointed out that the historian of cartoons must concern himself not only with chronological sequences or running commentaries on the news but with 'the framework of allegory and metaphor which both reflects and colours opinion, which is deeply traditional and yet responds to the fashion of a moment'. John Bull first appeared in a cartoon of 1756, when caricature drew deeply on symbolism. *Punch* himself was an even more ancient symbol (Pepys recorded a Punch and Judy show in 1662 and a tablet recording the event can be found in St Paul's, Covent Garden).

Below: A Tenniel lion (*1856*). It is very interesting to compare this lion with Leech's (*1846*) *above right*, and with Doyle's (*1847*) *below right*

THE BRITISH LION SMELLS A RAT

XXII

THE BRITISH LION IN 1850;
or, the effects of free trade

Tenniel created powerful new nineteenth-century symbols. 'The British Lion's Vengeance on the Bengal Tiger' (see below, pp.38–9) still impresses by its vigour and forcefulness. He was equally confident – masterful would perhaps be a better word – in his portrayal of French eagles and Russian bears. But the symbol that meant most to him was the British lion. Along with Landseer's stags, it immediately transports us back to the high-Victorian period. Du Maurier called Leech 'John Bull himself, but John Bull refined and civilised – John Bull polite, modest, gentle – full of self-respect and self-restraint, and with all the bully softened out of him; manly first and gentlemanly after, but very soon after'. This is an inadequate verdict on Leech: it could never have been made at all on Tenniel. There seems to be something peculiarly appropriate in the fact that Tenniel drew with a specially-manufactured 6H pencil on the wooden block and in the fact that the very first cartoon which he drew for *Punch* had the title 'Lord Jack, the Giant Killer'. For the deeper sources of inspiration of Tenniel's art – and the fantasy – it is necessary, perhaps, to turn away from politics to the superb

THE BRITISH LION UNDER DIFFICULTIES

WHEN a General Election is coming on, that unhappy beast, the British Lion, gets into a most distressing predicament, for his growl is invariably invoked for all sorts of purposes. 'No Popery' is now the cry that is being poured into the ear of the harassed brute, and while he is being taken in the rear by the Nonconformists, who are raising the shout, with which he is expected to growl in unison, an attempt is being made to stir him up in the front with the long pole of popular opinion, and excite his fury by brandishing before his eyes the flaming banner of Protection. We really think it is high time to pension the unhappy British Lion; for, with all his teeth knocked out by the blows he has received in the course of his career, and with a mane grey from old age, he is becoming miserable to himself and useless to others. The British Lion ought to be placed on the Superannuation Fund at once; or, at all events, the British Unicorn ought to be made to take his turn in the public service, after the enjoyment of his long sinecure.

illustrations in Lewis Carroll's *Alice's Adventures in Wonderland* and *Alice Through the Looking Glass*. The Jabberwocky must be introduced into the Tenniel menagerie. And there is a great gulf between Tenniel's Alice and Leech's 'pretty girl', not to speak of Mrs Leech who so often made her way into the pages of *Punch*.

There was a gulf, too, between Tenniel and du Maurier, who contributed his first drawing to *Punch* in 1860 with little suspicion that, as Spielmann puts it, he would eventually be counted with Leech, Tenniel and Keene as 'one of the four great pillars on which would rest the artistic reputation of the paper'. Du Maurier considered himself to be 'the tenor or rather the tenorino of that little company for which Mr Punch beats time with his immortal baton'. He believed that he was expected to 'warble in black and white such melodies as I could evolve from my contemplations of the gentler aspect of English life'. In 1861 his great days were still ahead of him. He was eventually, among other things, to create his own ideal of willowy, gracious, ageless feminine beauty for more than one generation – but already in 1861 he was set in his styles (see cartoon below).

In looking at all the pictorial material in the *Punch* of the first twenty years it is worth noting that none of the artists were successful in capturing movement in their drawings. The day of the strip cartoon was still in the future

(although Dr Syntax, not to speak of Goya, had already pointed the way ahead). Even Leech's stags and horses portrayed in motion or his children playing games in the streets do not really move. They are caught in single 'stills', like some of the first and most famous mid-Victorian photographs. We are very far away from the McLuhan world of instant circuitry and continuous flow, even though Professor Plateau of Brussels had tried to reconstitute motion in his 'phenakistocope' of 1833, the 'zoetrope' or 'wheel of life' had made its appearance about 1860, when this anthology is closing, and the first patents for devices to take photographs in rapid series were issued to du Mont in France in 1861. The *Punch* world is still 'the fragmented visual world', McLuhan's 'old world of the wheel and nuts and bolts'.

Punch always lagged behind the *Illustrated London News* in its use of processed blocks and in its application of photographic techniques. Nor did it emulate the lithographs of Paris. It is interesting in examining the work of its team of artists to compare what was being produced across the Channel by Daumier, an artist of genius, who depicted the contemporary scene with scarcely a break between 1832 and 1872. Daumier seldom sketched his designs on stone until he had prepared initial jottings of lines, forms and shapes. He used four types of crayon and was able to produce greys and blacks outside the technical range of any *Punch* artist.

CONSIDERATE!

Young Pugge (*mysteriously*). 'Ahem! Captain – it strikes me there's something on between you and the fairhaired party with the coronet? If so, between friends, you know. Eh? As *I* had some thoughts, – eh? don't you know?'

Captain (*facetiously*). 'Oh! ah! I see – *very* delicate of you – quite takes a load off my mind, 'sure you!'

He was able 'to suggest the silkiness and brilliance of fine materials'. His range included not only 'social types' and political caricature but also detailed individual character studies. It is worth speculating what would have happened to Keene had he been working in France within a French tradition. As it is, we must recall him as a man in breeches and glengarry sketching on a camp stool, a clubbable bachelor who would have been easily absorbed into one of his own backgrounds. When Felix Bracquemond asked his permission to publish examples of his prints in *Graveurs du XIXe Siècle*, Keene replied modestly that they were 'the merest experiments', and he replied to a request for an autobiographical note with the words, 'as to my writing my life-story, God bless you, Sir, I've none to tell.'

Historians of art have suggested that the work of both Daumier and Gustave Doré reveals a 'strong sense of sculpture'. The *Punch* artists by comparison were very close to the stage. Mark Lemon wrote plays and had his first farce produced in 1836 at the Strand Theatre: he also tried his hand at burletta and even opera. Jerrold, à Beckett and Henry Mayhew had similar propensities, and Tom Taylor wrote many plays. Leech joined in the entertainments which the *Punch* team arranged even if he showed little enthusiasm for the acting roles assigned him. From Christmas 1842, when *Punch's Pantomime or Harlequin King John* was

presented at Covent Garden, the home of Punch and Judy, down to the end of the period covered in this volume, *Punch* had a direct link with the theatre which explains something of the style of the publication and the balance between the different constituent elements which Lemon fused so successfully into one whole. 'Our weekly show-box is anxiously sought by all who are unwilling to let their minds moulder' was the way *Punch* itself thought of the connection.

This approach contrasts sharply with that of the French caricaturists who in an age first of political uncertainty and then of authoritarianism tried, whenever they could, to identify 'the objectionable characteristics of individuals' with a view to securing basic political change. *Punch*, however critical it might be both of individuals and of movements, never played a straight party political game. Nor was it seeking to undermine a whole regime. This is not to say, of course, that the political impact of its 'big cuts' was negligible. *The Man in the Moon* said of Leech's 'No Popery' in 1851 that *Punch* with his cut had 'wakened up those whom his letterpress had sent to sleep', while hostile critics (Doyle was among them) spoke of *Punch* stoking up the coals of popular prejudice in a way which *The Times*, bereft of pictures, could not imitate. (Its editor, Delane, said in private that he thought the whole anti-papal scare 'gross humbug and a pack of nonsense'.) In an

THE HAYCOCKS IN 1851

THE PRIVATE THEATRICALS

age of national politics at a distance, when few electors ever saw national politicians and when there were no photographs of them (at best, cheap prints or Staffordshire pottery had to do), *Punch* provided 'images' of politicians for the electorate. When a Welsh postman once recognised Palmerston and Palmerston asked him how he had done so, he replied simply, 'seen your picture in *Punch*, my Lord'.

There were probably very few postmen who ever read *Punch*. This was an age not of mass but of minority communication, and even within this context *Punch* had a small circulation (40,000 in the mid-1850's against 50,000 to 60,000 for *The Times* and over 100,000 for the *Illustrated London News*). It appealed, moreover, not to a cross-section of the whole community but to a series of segments within it. It was not exceptional in its early radicalism: it was estimated in 1840 that radical Sunday newspapers were outselling conservative ones at a ratio of ten to one. Yet its radicalism had a 'middle-class' flavour even in the golden years of Jerrold. There had already been a crucial social and cultural cleavage in the history of the radical press during the 1830's, particularly after the Reform Act of 1832, a cleavage neatly revealed in the biographies of the Mayhew brothers who had been associated in their early youth both with *Figaro in London*, one of *Punch*'s predecessors, and with *The Poor Man's Guardian*, an avowedly and self-consciously working-class paper. As Edward Thompson has put it succinctly, 'after 1832 the ways were clearly dividing. One way led to political Owenism and to Chartism and the other to *Punch*.' Henry Mayhew, unorthodox and limitlessly inquisitive, might find it possible during the late 1840's to 'pierce the protective shell of Podsnappery' in his *Morning Chronicle* articles on London labour and the London poor, but already ten years earlier Thackeray in an article in *Fraser's Magazine* had noted just how great the social distances were beginning to be. After reading a number of 'lower-class periodicals' circulating in larger numbers than *Punch* ever was to circulate in the crowded cities, he said that it was possible only at second hand to discover the secrets of 'a tremendous society moving around us and unknown to us – a vast mass of active, stirring life, in which the upper classes form an insignificant speck'. 'An English gentleman,' he went on, 'knows as much about the people of Lapland or California as he does of the aborigines of the Seven Dials or the natives of Wapping.'

The distances certainly did not narrow as the country became more comfortable during the 1850's, and as *Punch*, with Leech as a chief agent (he was a Special Constable during the Chartist disturbances of 1848), turned increasingly from articles and cartoons about the contrasts between rich and poor to articles and cartoons about holidays and servants (*Punch* staples) and hunting and dancing. It was recognising quite frankly the character of its readership and the limits to the possible extension of its circulation. It might still expose 'scandals', flay 'abuses' or exploit 'panics' – these three key words were all important in the psychology of what W. L. Burn has called 'the age of equipoise' during the 1850's and 1860's – but its concerns and its angles were very much middle-class concerns and angles. It was in favour (after initial opposition) of the Great Exhibition of 1851, and it was Jerrold who invented the name 'Crystal Palace' and Thackeray who wrote an ode on it; it was passionately involved in support of Britain entering the Crimean War, and bitterly opposed, in consequence, to Cobden and Bright; it disliked strikes, though it sometimes tried to see both sides, and it despised demagogues; it was vigilantly pro-Volunteer, though it saw the fun of middle-class citizens pretending to be soldiers; and it fumbled inconclusively on the issue of parliamentary reform (see below).

Above all, it became 'happy'. 'All our ideas connected with *Punch* are happy ones,' Lemon said. (Compare the irony of his article 'Substance and Shadow' in 1843, when he had observed that 'there are silly dissatisfied people in this country, who are continually urging upon ministers the propriety of considering the wants of the pauper population under the impression that it is as laudable to feed men as

AN UP-HILL JOB

MR POLICEMAN PUNCH (*Compassionately*). 'Now, little'un, do you *think* you'll be able to shove that perambulator up them steps?'

(*1860*)

A BRITON IN THE TIME OF PEACE

From a Sketch taken at Notting Hill

to shelter horses'.) Du Maurier made exactly the same point about life as described by Leech: it was 'an optimistic life in which joyousness prevails, and the very woes and discomfitures are broadly comical to us who look on – like someone who has sea-sickness or a headache after a Greenwich banquet.' (Compare his remarks about the way both he and Leech had thought of things in their youth: 'we hated and despised the bloated aristocracy, just as we hated and despised foreigners without knowing much about them.')

Punch forgot much as he grew respectable. Take two examples of early comment. 'A company,' we read in 1844, 'has just been formed in Paris for the purpose of destroying rats. If such a company were to be formed in England, Lord Brougham, Lord Stanley and Sir James Graham would be entitled to ask for protection on the plea of their lives being in danger.' 'Sir James Graham,' *Punch* wrote a few weeks later, 'begs to announce that it is his intention during the Easter vacation to give instruction in *Vulgar Abuse.* Lord Brougham is already engaged as his principal assistant.' Compare a comment made by John Ruskin in 1883: Leech's cartoons, he claimed, had served as 'the finest definition and natural history of the classes of our society, the tenderest flattery of its pretty and well-bred ways with which the modesty of

subservient genius ever amused or immortalised careless masters.' While Ruskin became increasingly disturbed about English society, *Punch* became increasingly content. For the most part, he was more interested in 'law and order' than in experiment, with the need being stressed for the honest Briton to protect himself against any kind of rogue and malefactor (see the cartoon of 1856 above).

Only very rarely did he penetrate beneath the respectable surface of society, as in Leech's famous drawing which was published in 1857 in Lemon's temporary absence, and which is reproduced overleaf.

During the 1850's there was certainly little that was comparable to drawings like the one of 1845 which appears at the foot of the following page, with the message made all the sharper in that the drawing was surrounded by agreeable pictures of more fortunate people dancing the polka.

Likewise, there was a change in tone even when familiar themes which had been handled in the early years were taken up again. During the 1840's, for instance, the abuses of the London fashion market had been frequently exposed, particularly the long hours and low wages of seamstresses and milliners, but during the 1850's 'the bonnet-maker's dream' was simply to be at the ball herself (see p. XXIX).

THE GREAT SOCIAL EVIL

*Time: – Midnight. A sketch not a Hundred Miles
from the Haymarket.*
BELLA. 'Ah! Fanny! How long have you been
Gay?'

As for the banquets, which had been savagely
satirised during the 1840's (see below, page 57),
they were now – by 1853 – handled far more
gently:

A SENSIBLE CIVIC DINNER

THE object of education is not accomplished by the mere
cultivation of the intellect. To teach that which is
simply true is insufficient: it is also necessary to inculcate
the knowledge of what is good. We thus moralise in
reference to a rich intellectual treat, thus described in
the *Times*: –

ENTERTAINMENT AT THE MANSION HOUSE. – THE LORD
MAYOR gave a dinner last evening to about 80 Mayors and
Provosts of the principal cities and towns of Great Britain and
Ireland. This, we understand, is the first of several entertain-
ments, the special object of which is to aid the efforts of HER
MAJESTY'S Government by promoting a uniform organisation
throughout the country for the Diffusion of a more General and
Practical Knowledge of Science and Art among all Classes.

What could be a better beginning for such an end? In
dining eighty Mayors for the Diffusion of Useful Knowledge, the City contributes to promote public enlightenment by a proceeding no less judicious than appropriate.
Teaching those eighty municipal magistrates how to
live, it affords them a lesson which they will be not slow
to communicate to their respective Corporations, whose
members, in their turn, will impart to others the benefit
of the instruction they have thus received. To commence
with an entertainment at the Mansion House, is to lay a
good solid foundation for subsequent acquirements. The
digestive function, for example, so important in physi-
ology, is studied on a sound basis of turtle in addition to
capon and sirloin, besides a great many other of the
choicest substances of the vegetable as well as of the
animal kingdoms. To the information capable of being
communicated by plates, that which may be derived
from dishes is wisely adjoined; and it is obvious that a
taste for Art may be expected to be developed through
the gratification inspired by good cuts. We hope the
eighty Mayors who were regaled the other day at the
Mansion House, for the extension of learning, will

Bubbles of the Year – Cheap Clothing

XXVIII

THE BONNET-MAKER'S DREAM

earnestly endeavour to fill their minds as largely as they filled their stomachs on that occasion. The next Civic Educational Dinner, perhaps, will be given to eighty Masters in lieu of Mayors, in order to cram them for their respective tasks. In conclusion, we may observe, that if the LORD MAYOR's banquets should make no bookworms, they will constitute very considerable grubs.

*

Before turning to the arrangement of this anthology and some of the problems involved in the selection of text and pictures, three other points should be emphasised about *Punch* as a medium of communication – first, it was very much a metropolitan paper; second, it was always 'masculine' in its management and in its approach; third, it had family appeal.

These were the golden years of the provincial press, yet *Punch* visited the provinces only on holiday or for the sake of a laugh. Manchester or Birmingham always figured less than Brighton. The problems which preoccupied it even during its most radical phases were London problems – the corruption and gluttony of the London aldermen; the foul state of the River Thames; the fate of the Crystal Palace buildings after they had moved from Hyde Park to Sydenham; the affairs of the British Museum and of the Royal Academy. Industrial problems were seldom touched upon at all. The countryside was conceived of as an adjunct to the city or, sometimes, as in the case of Lemon

himself, as a prelude to city life; and the best jokes about the countryside dwelt on the dangers which still lurked there for the well-bred townsman (see overleaf).

It is interesting to compare its 'metropolitanism' with that of the *New Yorker* nearly a century later: like the *New Yorker*, *Punch* was 'avowedly published for a metropolitan audience' and it was believed (rather than just hoped) that it would 'thereby escape an influence which hampers most national publications'.

The masculinity of *Punch* was at least as pervasive as its metropolitanism. The Judies were out. The *Punch* circle was exclusively male, and fun was always derived from the spectacle of any independent-minded woman, whatever the manifestations of her independence. Women's clothes were a perpetual subject of mild satire: so, too, less forgivably, was women's education. A Women's Charter, purported to have been produced in 1848, the year of revolutions (see below, p.114), was deemed to be the funniest document of the year. *Punch* table-talk was all along the same lines. On other subjects there was sometimes a conflict between what was said in private and in public. In the case of women, the only difference was in degrees of frankness and reticence. A wife's place had to be in the home. Mill's dual vote would be a duel vote. One joke did not make its way into the pages of *Punch*. Brooks suggested as a slogan for the supporters of

JONES, who can't sleep well in London during the Hot Weather, goes to have a Quiet Night in a Village!!
Portrait of One *of the Village Cochins, &c.*   (*1853*)

women's right to the franchise 'mis-carriages provided for lady-voters'.

The absence of published jokes of this kind – and doubtless many such were made round the *Punch* table – brings out the final and perhaps the most important general point about *Punch*. It was a family paper when the family, the 'happy family', was the central Victorian institution. Thackeray, who understood all too well the processes of social and cultural censorship, once said in a public lecture that while 'the comic works of past years are sealed to our wives and daughters' this was never true of the jokes in *Punch*. 'For where its editor is,' he explained, 'there is decorous wit, and fun, without the general attendant, coarseness.' *Punch* went out of its way to appeal to children, if they were allowed to see it, to undergraduates – and they were positively encouraged by the multiplicity of references to life in Oxford and Cambridge – and even to daughters. We now know much, at a distance, of the 'other Victorians' and of the 'Victorian underworld'. There was no real place in *Punch* for either. As a medium, for all the vivacity of the team which made it a business success, it was far more prudent and careful than television or even sound radio were to prove in a different kind of century.

The arrangement of this anthology reflects the approach described in this introduction. It is designed to bring out with the minimum of interruption the different facets of *Punch* as a medium of communication. It is divided up, therefore, neither by topics nor by chronology but by aspects of communication, and the titles of the different sections are taken for the most part from *Punch* itself. Its New Year Carol in 1849 ended with the stanza:

And *Punch*, the undrooping, all the public whooping,
Shouting with might and main for joy and mirth,
Rears these new columns on his former volumes,
To teach reform and jollify the earth.

It is not always easy in practice to distinguish between *Punch*'s three self-appointed tasks of 'teaching', 'reforming' and 'jollifying', yet the spectrum has been further extended in this volume, and one chapter deals with *Punch*'s own views of himself.

Chapter I, 'The Watcher', is concerned with *Punch* as a commentator on the changing scene, seldom, however, a 'straight' commentator. The critique was usually only a part of the commentary: so, too, was the fun, since it was an essential part of *Punch*'s view of life that we should

    . . . laugh at all things, for we wish to know
    What, after all, are all things but a show.

Fads and fashions always received as much attention as events or policies, and there was often a strong sense of history in the making, as is shown in the Preface for the year 1859:

XXX

PREFACE

YOU, who would truly be wise, discarding all cant and all humbug;
You, who would know what is what, and also its converse – what isn't;
You, who would see through a millstone without peeping in at the hole;
You, who incline to impart to your grandmothers skill in egg-suction;
You, who would be on a level with *tabac* in pulverisation;
You, who would manifest knowledge concerning the hour on the dial;
Down on the knees of your heart, and thank MR PUNCH for this Volume.

Here you will find the true story, here, and in no other quarter,
(For all the historians but PUNCH are windbags, and blockheads, and boobies,
And further to quote T. CARLYLE, Apes from the Sea called the Dead Sea,)
Of six most eventfullest months, first half of the year Fifty-Nine.
Year of the War in the South, and the winning the Derby by *Musjid*;
Year when the Oxford boat won, and Cambridge was merged in the billows;
Year MR MILLAIS came out with those terrible nuns in the graveyard;
Year the great Ebrew composer, BEER, gave *Le Pardon de Ploermel;*
Year the first fountain for drinking was set up by GURNEY, near Newgate;
Year ALFRED TENNYSON uttered a trumpet-tongued warning to Arm us;
Year that KING BOMBA departed from out of the world he polluted;
Year that the Daughter of England gave a nice baby to Prussia;
Year that MISS CRAIG took the prize for her Ode at the London BURNS Festival;
Year that the young PRINCE OF WALES was received by the POPE in the Vatican;
Year MR PUNCH, the Avenger, kicked MR COX out of Finsbury;
Year that the new Temple chambers were marked with the name of SAM JOHNSON;
Year that the fashion broke out of abusing our wives for bad dinners;
Year QUEEN VICTORIA announced that India, subdued, was HER kingdom;
Year MR OWEN, Professor, expounded the dreadful Gorilla;
Year that the Tories, in office, brought in another Reform Bill;
Year that such Bill was rejected, and DERBY appealed to the Country;
Year when the General Election ejected his Lordship from office;
Year that LORD PALMERSTON found himself Premier again on Whit Sunday;
Year that SAM WARREN the Poet was raised to be Master in Lunacy;
Year that the Westminster Clock began to have thoughts about going;
Year that the gay Floral Hall rose alongside of the Opera House;
Year the Welsh child in the Gallery howled while LORD STANLEY was speaking;
Year that the EMPEROR NAPOLEON THE THIRD entered Milan in triumph;
Year that the Thames smelt as bad as it did in the year antecedent.

Such the events which occurred in one-half of the year Fifty-Nine;
Such, and ten million beside, in the Volume before you are noted.
Noted, but not in the fashion of Apes from the Sea called the Dead Sea;
But made texts for uncountable wealth of wit, ever blended with wisdom.
Down on the knees of your hearts, thanking great PUNCH for this Volume;
Rejoice that you live in a world that He condescends to enlighten;
Shout for your QUEEN and your PUNCH, and then all go and mind your own business:
Leaving Him Watcher, Protector, Censor, Curator, Chastiser.

XXXI

THE BANQUET AT GUILDHALL – TRUE POLITENESS
ALDERMAN GOBBLE. 'Now then, Gals! I've quite done. Can I get you any Grub?'

It is from the end of this Preface that the title of Chapter II, 'Protector, Curator, Chastiser' is taken. The title speaks for itself, as do the titles of the following three chapters, all, in addition, taken direct from *Punch*'s lists of his own attributes – 'The Scalpel of Reform', 'The Lancet of Satire' and 'Lightness of Heart'. Yet already in the year of revolutions, 1848, when *Punch* was proclaiming his 'permanence', he was noting the interchangeability of his roles:

> 'And *Punch* will still his colours wave,
>   And nail them to the mast,
> And battle do with fool and knave,
>   Whilst knaves and fools shall last.
> And *Punch* will still his trumpet blow,
>   In guise of a buffoon;
> But hopes his hearers, high and low,
>   Will own they like the tune.'

It was in the same year that *Punch* produced perhaps the best of its manifestoes 'respectfully addressed to the House of Commons'. 'I laugh at knaves,' Punch declares, 'because the lancet of the satirist may often be a better tool for pricking the world's humours than the scalpel of the reformer, the discipline of the priest, or the sword of the judge. There is always one face of roguery which is purely ridiculous, and as this is the face which least imposes on people, I do some good by turning it towards them.' The same manifesto, contrasting *Punch*'s different brands of laughter with those of the members of

'A bitter and contemptuous chuckle' (*1851*)

the House of Commons (why, he asked, did they laugh whenever the Charter is mentioned or the Chartists?), taps the sources of *Punch*'s own mirth. 'I sometimes, though rarely, laugh at wickedness; but when I do, it is not with a kindly or natural laughter, but a bitter and contemptuous chuckle, which indeed is the only way I have of expressing disgust and indignation. Lastly I laugh a great deal in pure lightness of heart, and this is the laughter I best like the echo of.'

There was, of course, another kind of laughter, not described in this eloquent manifesto, the laughter which was broad rather than light, if the distinction can be drawn. 'The Guffawgraph' was an early term which was only occasionally used in the later history of *Punch*, but there was always this ingredient in its make-up. 'Jolly Old Punch' had promised at the outset that he would provide 'a refuge for destitute wit, an asylum for the thousands of orphan jokes . . . the millions of perishing puns which are now wandering about without so much as a shelf to rest upon'. The punning continued with little respite throughout the whole period covered in this volume, with pictorial punning prominent at the start and fun also being made with statistics as well as with words. 'I hate puns,' says Jerry Chance in Lemon's play *The M.P. for the Rotten*

XXXII

Division of Labour

A Packed Jury

Going against the Grain

Borough (1838); 'they're like ginger beer, all froth, but without stamina.' In fact, they were still revealing all their terrifying stamina in 1861.

THINGS THAT WON'T WASH

IN a recent Trade Report, under the head of Yarns, it is stated that 'Medium wefts have been sold at prices in favour of purchasers.' Surely these wefts must have fetched very little to be sold at prices which were in the purchasers' favour. Medium wefts, considered as spiritual yarns, are tissues of stuff which may be pronounced not worth a rap.

THE CONTRADICTIONS OF LOVE

LOVE is often very contradictory; for instance, Lovers' Knots are frequently made all the tighter by one particular Not meaning a Yes.

Puns had long survived the odd pictorial joke in *Punch* making special fun of them (below). The straight verbal joke took longer to take shape, and one of what became the most famous of all *Punch* jokes was buried away in the middle of a page of the 1848 *Almanack* (reproduced overleaf, under the heading 'Worthy of Attention').

The 'comic-strip' type of joke did not develop during this period, as we have seen, but it is plain that many of the 'funny' themes which *Punch* was to make its own were already prominent during the 1850's. Some of these are picked out in Chapter VIII, 'Plus ça change': they remain themes still. Captions, too, became

The Mere Pun (*1857*)

Of all Foolish Things, the Mere Pun is perhaps the most Foolish. – Now, here's a Fellow (probably a Member of the St—ck Exch—nge) who, in spite of his really Perilous Condition, says 'that he came out for a (W)hole Holiday – and has got it!'

THE POST-OFFICE PANIC

THERE are rumours that the people engaged in the Post-Office are daily in danger of being suffocated, swamped, and smothered, by the enormous quantity of letters pouring in upon them at every chink, hole, corner, and cranny of the establishment. An unhappy clerk was found struggling with a pile of newspapers, to which he had nearly succumbed, when one of the sorters came up, just soon enough to rescue him from an untimely end. An official sitting at one of the windows, very near a receiving-box, was suddenly carried off his stool, and almost completely immersed in a terrific flood of what proved on inquiry to be an ocean of applications for shares in Railway Companies. Another able and respected functionary was found buried under a heap of papers, which had come in suddenly, like a spring tide, and which proved to be a perfect sea of inquiries as to the time fixed for the appearance of '*Punch's Pocket Book*'. To prevent a recurrence of this fearful incident, we beg to announce the

FIRST OF NOVEMBER

as the day when the hopes of millions will be realised, by the publication of the work alluded to.

longer during the 1850's and often more necessary for an understanding of the joke. From the mid-1840's onwards pictures and words were often fully integrated (above).

Chapter VI is a key chapter in this book. It presents *Punch*'s views of himself, and for readers who are already familiar with *Punch* it might even be best to read it first. Chapter VII deals with 'Retrospect and Prospect'. *Punch* had views about both. It is valuable, also, to study alongside this anthology the introductions to each of the volumes prepared for the first collected edition of *Punch*, published, complete with introductory index and notes, after the first hundred volumes. They show how soon after the event it was necessary to provide detailed information about some of the *Punch* pictures and articles: there were to be large numbers of stories dealing with *Punch* on this or that and on him or her.

The last word should be about the selection of this anthology. Having chosen the items, we looked back at each of the six-monthly volumes from 1841 to 1861 to survey what we had left out. We felt then that we could have compiled a second anthology of the period which would be just as revealing. We wondered, too, how our volume would compare with the volume which came out as we were making our *Punch* selection, on '*The Life and Times of Private Eye*'. The compilers of that volume found it difficult to leave *Punch* out, though they made good fun of Mr Punch looking at old *Punch*. *Cap and Bell* is no substitute for *Punch* itself. It is rather an open invitation to go back to the original source, to what *Private Eye* called 'the Rake's Progress', Parts I and II. Part I was simple: 'Born in penury: meagre circulation and impertinent views . . . Queen Victoria not amused'. Part II was even more simple: 'Respectability achieved. Captions lengthened, Savants and foreigners good for a laugh. Queen Victoria amused.' May we admit that some things amused *us* in both Part I and Part II?

SUGGESTIONS FOR FURTHER READING

This brief note covers only a few of the many books which deal briefly or at length with *Punch*.

The best two histories are M. H. Spielmann, *The History of Punch* (1895), London, Cassell and R. G. G. Price, *A History of Punch* (1957), London, Collins.

See also A. Adburgham, *A Punch History of Manners and Modes* (1961), London, Hutchinson; C. L. Graves, *Mr Punch's History of Modern England* (1921), London, Cassell (4 vols. 1921–22); and R. E. Williams, *A Century of Punch* (1956), London, Heinemann.

For biographical information about the members of the *Punch* circle, see A. A. Adrian, *Mark Lemon, First Editor of 'Punch'* (1966), London, O.U.P.; A. W. à Beckett, *The à Becketts of Punch* (1903), London, Constable; D. du Maurier (ed.), *The Young George du Maurier, A Selection of His Letters*, 1860–67 (1951), London, Peter Davies; D. Hudson, *Charles Keene* (1947), London, Pleiades Books; W. C. Jerrold, *Douglas Jerrold and 'Punch'* (1910), London, Macmillan; Gordon N. Ray, *Thackeray, The Uses of Adversity, 1811–1846* (1955), London, O.U.P., *The Age of Wisdom, 1847–1863* (1958), London, O.U.P.; H. Vizetelly, *Glances Back through Seventy Years* (1893), London, Kegan Paul, Trench, Trübner.

There are two useful articles in *Victorian Studies*, Bloomington, University of Indiana Press, an invaluable magazine for an understanding of the problems of the period covered in this anthology – O. Maurer, '"Punch" on Slavery and Civil War in America' (Vol. I, 1957) and E. P. Thompson, 'The Political Education of Henry Mayhew' (Vol. XI, 1967).

The history of press and periodicals is still covered only patchily, but the following books are indispensable – R. D. Altick, *The English Common Reader* (1957), London, C.U.P.; Amy Cruse, *The Englishman and his Books in the early Nineteenth Century* (1930), London, Harrap; H. R. Fox-Bourne, *English Newspapers*, 2 vols. (1887), London, Chatto & Windus; F. K. Hunt, *The Fourth Estate* (1850), London, D. Bogue; J. Gross, *The Rise and Fall of the Man of Letters* (1969), London, Weidenfeld & Nicolson; L. James, *Fiction for the Working Man, 1830–1850* (1963), London, O.U.P., and R. Williams, *The Long Revolution* (1961), London, Chatto & Windus.

For art and caricature in the mid-nineteenth century there are no volumes comparable to M. D. George, *English Political Caricature*, 2 vols. (1959), Oxford, Clarendon Press, which covers the years to 1832, but see G. du Maurier, *Social Pictorial Satire* (1898), N.Y. and London, Harper and Brothers; P. James, *English Book Illustration, 1800–1900* (1947), Harmondsworth, Penguin Books; H. Reitlinger, *From Hogarth to Keene* (1938), London, Methuen; C. Roger-Marx, *Graphic Art of the Nineteenth Century* (1962), London, Thames & Hudson; and F. Reid, *The Illustrators of the Sixties* (1928), London, Faber & Gwyer.

For the history of the period see Asa Briggs, *The Age of Improvement* (1959), London, Longmans, and *Victorian People* (1965 edn), 1st ed. repr. Harmondsworth, Penguin Books; W. L. Burn, *The Age of Equipoise* (1964), London, Allen & Unwin; J. W. Dodds, *The Age of Paradox* (1953), London, Gollancz; and G. M. Young, *Early Victorian England*, 2 vols. (1934), London, O.U.P., which includes his *Victorian England, Portrait of an Age* (1953), 2nd ed. London, O.U.P., and *Last Essays* (1950), London, Hart-Davis.

For a revealing comparison, see R. Ingrams (ed.), *The Life and Times of Private Eye* (1971), Harmondsworth, Penguin Books.

SIGNATURES OF *PUNCH'S* ARTISTS

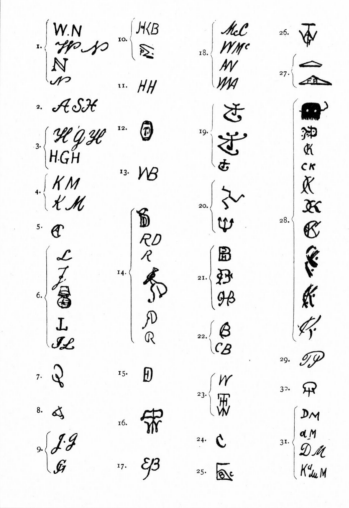

1. William Newman.
2. A. S. Henning.
3. H. G. Hine.
4. Kenny Meadows.
5. Alfred "Crowquill."
6. John Leech.
7. Gavarni.
8. W. M. Thackeray.
9. Sir John Gilbert, R.A.
10. Hablôt K. Browne ("Phiz").
11. H. Heath.
12. R. J. Hamerton.
13. W. Brown.
14. Richard Doyle.
15. Henry Doyle, C.B.
16. A. Watts Phillips.
17. E. J. Burton.
18. W. McConnell.
19. Sir John Tenniel.
20. Capt. H. R. Howard.
21. C. H. Bradley.
22. Rev. Edwd. Bradley ("Cuthbert Bede").
23. T. Harrington Wilson.
24. Rev. W. F. Callaway.
25. Halliday.
26. G. W. Terry.
27. Frank Bellew.
28. Charles Keene.
29. Julian Portch.
30. G. R. Haydon.
31. George du Maurier.

I·THE WATCHER

THE LETTER OF INTRODUCTION

CANDIDATES UNDER DIFFERENT PHASES

ON THE SCIENCE OF ELECTIONEERING

To the progress of science and the rapid march of moral improvement the most effectual spur that has ever been applied was the Reform Bill. Before the introduction of that measure, electioneering was a simple process, hardly deserving the name of an art; it has now arrived at the rank of a science, the great beauty of which is, that, although complicated in practice, it is most easy of acquirement. Under the old system boroughs were bought by wholesale, scot and lot; now the traffic is done by retail. Formerly there was but one seller; at present there must be some thousands at least – all to be bargained with, all to be bought. Thus the 'agency' business of electioneering has wonderfully increased, and so have the expenses.

In fact, an agent is to an election what the main-spring is to a watch; he is, in point of fact, the real returning-officer. His importance is not less than the talents and tact he is obliged to exert. He must take a variety of shapes, must tell a variety of lies, and perform the part of an animated contradiction. He must benevolently pay the taxes of one man who can't vote while in arrear; and cruelly serve notices of ejectment upon another, though he can show his last quarter's receipt – he must attend temperance meetings, and make opposition electors too drunk to vote. He must shake hands with his greatest enemy, and *palm* off upon him lasting proofs of friendship, and silver-paper hints which way to vote. He must make flaming speeches about principle, puns about 'interest,' and promises concerning everything, to everybody. He must never give less than five pounds for being shorn by an honest and independent voter, who never shaves for less than two-pence – nor under ten, for a four-and-ninepenny goss to an uncompromising hatter. He must present ear-rings to wives, bracelets to daughters, and be continually broaching a hogshead for fathers, husbands, and brothers. He must get up fancy balls, and give away fancy dresses to ladies whom he fancies – especially if they fancy his candidate, and their husbands fancy them. He must plan charities, organise mobs, causing free-schools to be knocked up, and opponents to be knocked down. Finally, he must do all these acts, and spend all these sums purely for the good of his country; for, although a select committee of the house tries the validity of the election – though they prove bribery, intimidation, and treating to everybody's satisfaction, yet they always find out that the candidate has had nothing to do with it – that the agent is not *his* agent, but has acted solely on patriotic grounds; by which he is often so completely a martyr, that he is, after all, actually prosecuted for bribery, by order of the very house which he has helped to fill, and by the very man (as a part of the parliament) he has himself returned.

That this great character might not be lost to posterity, we furnish our readers with the portrait of . . .

and the Practice

AN ELECTION AGENT

The Proposer, Seconder, and 900 Free and Independent Electors of Newark.

Whig and Tory

PUNCH'S MONUMENT TO PEEL

LORD JOHN IN A FOG
A SKETCH FOR NOVEMBER, 1847
PEEL. 'A Light, your Honour! I'll show you the way.'

DOMBEY AND SON
'MR DOMBEY was in a difficulty. He would have liked to give him (the boy) some explanation involving the terms circulating-medium, currency, depreciation of currency, paper, bullion, rates of exchange, value of precious metals in the market, and so forth.'

WHIG PROGRESS
JOHN BULL. 'What! wasting your time, as usual. Pray, Master John, what have you been doing all this Session?'
JOHN (whimpering). 'Nothing, Sir.'
JOHN BULL. 'And what have you been about, Master Morpeth?'
MORPETH. 'Helping John, please, Sir.'

6

'THE EDUCATIONAL QUESTION'
'Between two stools he comes to the ground'
– *Old Proverb*

**Dealing with
Ireland (1846) . . .**

'WHERE IGNORANCE IS BLISS,' &c.
(after George Cruikshank)

YOUNG IRELAND IN BUSINESS FOR
HIMSELF

At Home the Radicals want to move faster (1848) . . .

'THE HOUR AND THE MAN'

COBDEN 'Now, Sir, are you going by us?'
RUSSELL. 'No, thank you; you're too fast for me; I shall go by the Parliamentary Train.'

THE
KINGS IN THEIR
COCK-BOATS

Lo, Europe all a-surging with Revolution's sea,
And a dozen cock-boats driving, with breakers on the
  ice;
Each carrying a Caesar and his fortunes – that's to
  say,
Such fortunes as poor Caesars are blest with in our
  day.

A crew of Cockney oarsmen in Chelsea Reach afloat,
And right upon them steaming down a reckless penny
  boat,
A footman in a funny, a lone woman in a wherry,
Compared with these poor sovereigns may be called
  at ease and merry.

What have they not flung overboard, that fling
  overboard they can? –
Pledge, principle, or prejudice, a measure, or a man;
But the breakers still roar nearer, and each sounding
  of the well
Tells how the ship is settling, and how the waters
  swell.

France clings to his umbrella as a sort of safety buoy,
And hails, in desperation, 'The Victoria – ahoy!'
Bavaria plunges overboard, to seek solus cum sola,
For consolation in the arms of his determined Lola.

Poor Austria crouches at the helm in a state of
  helpless snivel,
And military Prussia to his crew grows sudden civil;
And even burly Russia, with his freight of gold and
  tallow,
Whether with rage or retching, looks marvellously
  sallow.

And wistfully they strain their gaze, where thro'
  winds and waters dark,
Scuds, like a sea-bird, taut and trim, the gallant
  British barque,
Close-reefed and snug – her storm-sails set – and rising
  to the seas,
That dash and drench, uncourtly, their foreign
  Majesties.

Her able seamen were at sea, while yours were snug
  on shore;
The shoals that you are driving on she has sounded
  o'er and o'er;
In the gales of Agitation and the white squalls of
  Reform,
She learnt the skill that bears her safe thro'
  Revolution storm.

She was still being caulked and coppered, while your
  lazy keels were shent
With the barnacles of status quo, the worms of
  discontent;
'Tis thus she sails, and mocks the gales that
  threaten to submerge
Your crazy craft and helpless crews under the wild
  sea-verge.

**but the British
note an Object
Lesson across the
Channel**

A PHYSICAL FORCE CHARTIST ARMING FOR THE FIGHT

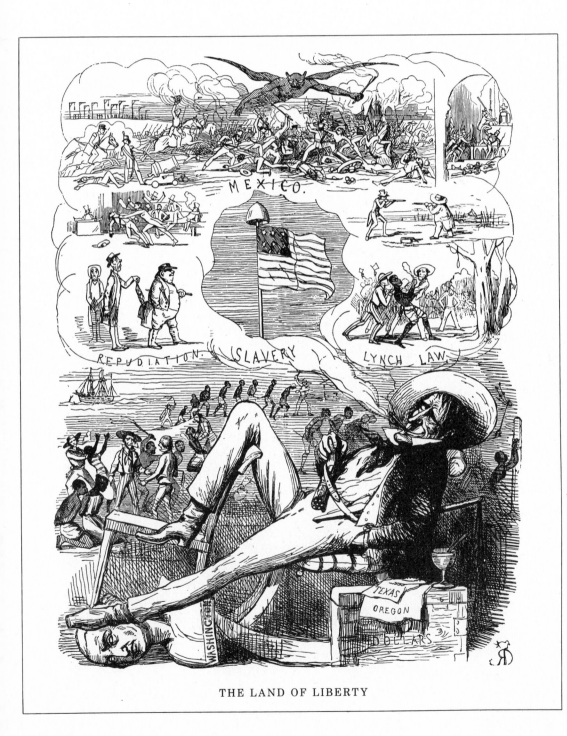

THE LAND OF LIBERTY

At Home there are Avenues of Escape

THE CURRENCY QUESTION

OR, THE STOCK EXCHANGE OUT FOR THE DAY

JONES. 'I say, Brown, things are deuced bad in the City!'

BROWN. 'Then I'm deuced glad I'm at Epsom!'

A PIC-NIC
(IN THE BACKGROUND IS SEEN THE 'ABBEY')

There are, of course, Family Outings, and the Children have their own Social Occasions

A JUVENYLE PARTYE

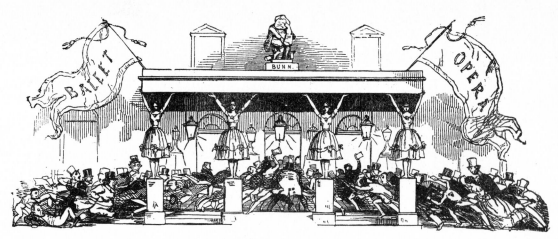

THE THEATRES

Adults go to the Theatre or to Concerts . . .

THE Season has begun! Again do play-bill posters give life to dead walls – again does the neighbour-hood of Drury Lane begin to feel 'music's pulse in all its arteries' – again does the courteous MR ARCHER sit invitingly at the Haymarket Box-Office from ten till four – and MADAME CELESTE, having taken 'more removed ground,' for the first time opens the cleansed and ventilated Adelphi. The theme, however, is too serious to be lightly touched upon. Let us address ourselves to it – for *Punch*, hear it ye green-rooms! purposes to be critical this season – with respectful gravity.

An entirely new portico, under the conscien-tious direction of MR BUNN, has been given to Drury Lane. We present the reader with a faithful representation of the architectural novelty. SHAKSPERE has been removed. We have ALFRED BUNN, vice WILLIAM SHAKSPERE, promoted to Sadler's Wells. This is only as it should be. We have, however, one fault to find with the BUNN statue – it is all white plaster. Now, when we remember those ebon velvet breeches, we would have had, at least half of BUNN, like the Prince in the fairy tale, of black marble. However, let us not

be fastidious. The dancing figures are very taste-fully disposed, and touchingly insinuate what support the manager expects from ballet. . . .

The Haymarket throws open its doors to comedy and farce, and has a company to do them justice. VANBRUGH, with his silver-lace newly cleaned, has already made his bow. At this time, especially, we welcome these revivals. Audiences, nay Hay-market audiences, have had in their time so many pieces without either characters or words, that it is well they should now and then go to school to the old masters.

At the Adelphi we presume we are to have domestic dramas, with spasms of pathos for families. MADAME CELESTE's energy will, we think, be better here than at the Haymarket. . . .

Novelties are, of course, in active preparation. English dramatists have returned from Paris, and now beset the doors of managers with their pieces from the French. Happy the distinguished writer who gets in precedence of his fellow-translator, for vaudevilles, like mackerel, will not keep! Hence, are they often sold at a corresponding price.

A MONSTER CONCERT

ITALIAN OPERA FASHIONS

WHILE we admit, in common with our contemporaries, the merit of most of the musical arrangements at the Royal Italian Opera, Covent Garden, we must (also in common with some of our contemporaries) call attention to the anomalies in fashion and dress that prevail in the new establishment. Decorum is commanded by a printed notice at the door, and violated inside; while 'top-coats, white hats, and umbrellas' are placed under a ban, in a placard, which is wholly set at defiance by those visitors who, armed with the powers of renters, deny the existence of any authority to regulate their costume. They accordingly rush into the house in attire of the most miscellaneous description. Paletots, registered and unregistered, are rife in the pit; while there are two hundred Taglionis among the audience, to make up for the deficiency of one Taglioni in the *ballet*.

The applause bestowed upon the singers very often smacks of the umbrella-ferrule, and we frequently recognise the sound made by the end of an ash stick beating in concert with COSTA'S *bâton*. Many a virtuoso, not content with standing up for his favourite performer in a moderate degree, must needs stand up on the cushions of the pit seats, to show the extent to which his *dilettanteeism* is carried. We do not blame the management of this establishment for the defects of which we complain; if there is an intractable public to be dealt with, there is, of course, no remedy. Every effort is made by the lessees to 'keep the thing respectable;' but if some persons will adopt peculiar notions of a crush hat for what they call 'Common Garden wear,' and if they choose to adopt the early and uncivilised highlow of our ancestors, for the 'patent polish of a brighter age,' it is not the fault of the conductors of this establishment.

We don't see how the rights of the public are to be interfered with, if an attempt should be made to turn the stalls into a Grecian Saloon, or something of the sort, and to intersperse the enjoyment of 'liquid harmony' with indulgence in liquids of a different character. We should be sorry to hear a cry of 'Give your orders, gentlemen: the waiter's in the stalls;' but who knows what it is all tending to? . . .

Opera hat

Opera boots

MELANCHOLY SCENE AT THE OPERA ON A JENNY LIND NIGHT

Whilst Every One goes to the Seaside

NORTH-EAST WIND – THERMOMETER SEVERAL INCHES BELOW
FREEZING
BRIGHTON BOATMAN. 'Did you want a Pleasure-Boat this Morning, Sir? Nice day for a Row!!'

18

HOW TO CALCULATE THE HEIGHT
OF THE SEASON AT THE SEASIDE

WHEN you have to wait an hour for a bathing-machine; when the last new Novel is bespoken ten deep; when donkeys are scarce, and City clerks plentiful; when you have to walk your soles off to get a London Morning Paper; when you meet with an organ-grinder, or a German band, in almost every street; when the Dispensary Ball is given; when chairs are fought for on the sands; when you see more buff slippers in the corridors outside the bed-room doors of hotels than Wellington boots; when one is obliged to send up to town for a piece of salmon; when ice commands a fabulous price; when HERR JONESI, 'from the Nobilities' Concerts,' gives a Grand Musical Festival at the Town Hall; when landladies sleep in the kitchen; when 'One Bed to Let' in a dirty byelane is run after with avidity; when the Sally-lun man makes his tintinnabular perambulations regularly every evening, and wakes up dozing papas with the jingle of his muffin-bell and doggerel rhymes; when the 'Third Robber' from Sadler's Wells shines at the little barn of a theatre with all the effulgence of a Star from Drury Lane; when GUSS FLOUNDERS, the comic singer from EVANS'S (more euphoniously christened 'the Son of MOMUS'), and MRS SALLY FLOUNDERS ('the Daughter of MOMUS') *'Keep a little Farm'* every night at SACKER AND FULLETT'S Library, on the Grand Parade; and, lastly, when prices get so high that they cannot possibly get any higher, then you may be sure that it is the HEIGHT of the SEASON at the SEASIDE!

SEA-SIDE LITERATURE FOR YOUNG LADIES; OR DELIGHTS OF CROCHET

FIRST YOUNG LADY (*reads*). '10th Row – 3 long with 3 chain after each into third small space, 1 long into same space, 5 long with 3 chain after each into middle space, 1 long into same space, 3 long with 3 chain after each into next space, 1 long in same space, 5 chain, ditto in middle of large space, 5 chain, repeat.'
SECOND AND THIRD YOUNG LADIES (*in ecstacies*). 'Oh! how sweetly pretty!!!'

A Cambridge Diversion

A ROW OF HEADS

IT is rumoured that one of the first effects of the royal Chancellorship will be a general Germanising of the costume and appearance of the members of the University. The moustache will become an academical appendage, and 'the tip' will be the distinguishing mark of all the tutors. The Proctors, having already been pretty well bearded by the press, will require nothing additional.

H.R.H. FIELD-MARSHAL CHANCELLOR
PRINCE ALBERT TAKING THE PONS
ASINORUM
After the manner of Napoleon taking the bridge of Arcola

THE UPS AND DOWNS OF KING'S ROAD, EATON SQUARE

TELESCOPIC observation discovers the surface of the moon to be an alternation of tremendously lofty eminences with profound chasms. There is, however, a portion of this planet, the mountains of which top those of the moon, whilst its abysses beat her cavities hollow. We allude to King's Road, Eaton Square, a thoroughfare exhibiting irregularities to which any to be seen on the visage of the Queen of Night are mere fleabites and pimples. King's Road, Eaton Square, in fact, has come to a most formidable pass, not to be forced without extreme peril to man and beast. It is fearful to see, in this chaotic highway, carriages of all descriptions floundering through pools of slush and over mounds of earth, and horses plunging amid rubbish-heaps or sticking in the mud; while fat coachmen are bumped backwards from their boxes; and gentlemen, shot from gigs with the velocity of cannon-balls, illustrate the laws of projectiles.

THE TEN TOWNS

Or, Mr Punch's Complete Handbook to his friend
MR HILL's *New Postal Plan*

ROWLAND HILL has just divided
  London's waste of brick by ten;
Every change, of course, is chided,
  By our stupid 'business-men.'
But the plan has pleased their betters,
  HILL's new boundary rails are cast,
And those nuisances, our Letters,
  Will be brought us twice as fast. . . .

Thus: – **N.W.**'s region's lying
  All around the Regent's Park,
'What **N**ice **W**illas folks are buying
  Round those parts,' is your remark.
W. holds the whole, or nearly,
  Of the Fashionable Squares,
Think of '**W**ealth,' or (more severely)
  Of the **W**anton **W**aste it dares.

Lawyers, and good CORAM's Foundlings,
  All are found in **W.C.**
Theatres delight its groundlings,
  Wicked **C**reatures, is your key.
Pimlico is in **S.W.**,
  Brompton fast, and Chelsea mild,
There the **S**houting **W**retches trouble you
  With the Cries that drive you wild.

E's for **E**ngland, represented
  By her fittest symbol, Docks,
There's her **E**mpire, sea-cemented,
  Throned upon a thousand stocks.
Lady, your **N**ew **E**vening dresses
  Come from yonder scorned **N.E.**,
There the weaving Frenchman blesses
  Nantes' **E**dict. Ah! *mais oui*!

S. for **S**uburbs, neat and cheapish,
  Brixton, Camberwell, Vauxhall,
And one's friend looks rather **S**heepish
  Bidding you to come and call;
Yet that part in turn outhectors
  Yonder dismal hole **S.E.**,
Southwark, where the **S**nob Electors
  Choose SIR CHARLES and APSLEY P.

Under **N.** the map embraces
  Islington and Pentonveal,
Folks who ask you to such places,
  Are a **N**uisance, don't you feel?
While what's ancient, rich, or witty,
  Makes **E.C.** a glorious bunch,
That's our own **E**ternal **C**ity,
  Tower and Bank, St Paul's and *Punch*!

AWFUL DESTITUTION IN LEICESTER SQUARE

In 1850 the Exhibition raises Hopes, and also Fears

[AN IMAGINARY PICTURE OF LONDON IN 1851 BY PUNCH IN 1850]

THE INDUSTRIOUS BOY
'PLEASE TO REMEMBER THE EXPOSITION'

PITY the troubles of a poor young Prince,
Whose costly scheme has borne him to your
   door,
Who's in a fix – the matter not to mince –
Oh, help him out, and Commerce swell your
   store!

This empty hat my awkward case bespeaks,
These blank subscription-lists explain my fear;
Days follow days, and weeks succeed to weeks,
But very few contributors appear. . . .

ALBERT! SPARE THOSE TREES

ALBERT! Spare those trees,
  Mind where you fix your show;
For mercy's sake, don't, please,
  Go spoiling Rotten Row. . . .

Where Fashion rides and drives
  House not industrial Art,
But 'mid the busy hives
  Right in the City's heart.

And is it thy request
  The place that I'd point out?
Then I should say the best
  Were Smithfield, without doubt.

THE POUND AND THE SHILLING
'Whoever Thought of Meeting You Here?'

RATHER ALARMING; Or, HOTELS IN 1851

NO. 7. (*Frenchman*). 'Mademoiselle! Mes bottes, s'il vous plait!'
NO. 10. (*Italian*). 'Signora, avrò io l'acqua calda sta mane?'
NO. 6. (*German*). 'Wo ist mein Soda Wasser?'

PERFIDIOUS ALBION LETS HIS
DRAWING-ROOM FLOOR TO A DISTINGUISHED
FOREIGNER – THE RESULT!!

THE MORALS OF THE GREAT EXHIBITION

THE poet asks,

> 'Is there any moral shut
> Within the bosom of the rose?'

and finds that there are so many, that, to fix on any one is to cramp the use of that which is used to point it. So it is with the Exhibition of the Industry of all Nations. All sorts of morals grow out of it, or are tacked on to it. You overhear them in the Crystal Palace; you pick them up in the Park; they obtrude themselves upon you in leading articles; they oust the weather in casual street-encounters; they beguile the pauses of a quadrille, and set conversation a-going in the railway-carriage. We present a sample to the readers of *Punch*, who will be good enough to select those they like best. All are genuine, and the only fault we have to find with them is, that they cut each other's throats.

The Protectionist's Moral. – Oh! – a pretty benefit to the country to flood us with foreign goods, ruin the home-market, and take all the gold out of the country! However, it will open people's eyes to the humbug of Free Trade.

The Free Trader's Moral. – A wonderful sight: Illustrates admirably the inter-dependence of nation and nation, and proves, to demonstration, that the principles of Free Trade are those of nature and common sense.

The British Manufacturer's Moral. – By JOVE, we must look sharp – or these foreigners will be cutting us out!

The Foreign ditto ditto: –
Sacré!
Potztausend!
Carajo!
Corpo di Bacco!
Mashallah! &c., &c.
} After all, these Englishmen have some notions of their own, beyond machinery and penknives!

SHILLING MORALS

The Artisan's. – I wonder how they'd get on without us? – Or we without them, for that matter.

The Democrat's. – Well, there's something in that chap, PRINCE ALBERT, after all!

The Communist's. – What a grab, if it wasn't for the Policemen!

The Red Republican's. – Confound these English! They don't seem at all ripe for revolt!

The Observer's. – Upon my word, One Shilling seems to make a better use of his time than Five!

MR PUNCH'S MORAL

That the different nations of the world, and the different classes of society, might meet oftener, with much advantage to each other.

SEASON TICKET AND FIVE SHILLING MORALS

The Dandy's. – What a deyvilish pleasant lounge!

The Debutante's. – You know one meets everybody!

Mamma's. – Well-educated girls appear to such advantage; and my girls are so well educated!

The 'Very Remarkable Man's.' – By Jove! How deuced little one knows, after all!

Sir Charles Coldstream's. – A lot of things one doesn't understand, and a host of people one's tired to death of meeting.

MARITAL MORALS

The Husband's. – Avoid the India Shawl and Lace Departments.

The Wife's. – Get the men to take you to see the stupid machinery, and you may get them among those sweet shawls, and those loves of laces!

What are the Lessons?

A Whisper to Prince Albert

MR PUNCH, with extreme deference, begs to whisper one little question to HIS ROYAL HIGHNESS PRINCE ALBERT.

How beautiful is the Palace Crystal! Would not a public dinner, given in Hyde Park to the builders of the aforesaid Palace – the workers in iron and glass – be a dainty sight to set before his Majesty the Sovereign People?

CONSULTATION ABOUT THE
STATE OF TURKEY

'A BEAR WITH A SORE HEAD'

ABERDEEN ON DUTY
A – b – n. 'I shan't interfere till they call murder!'

ENGLAND'S WAR VIGIL

'GENERAL FÉVRIER' TURNED TRAITOR
'Russia has Two Generals in whom she can confide –
Generals Janvier and Février.' – *Speech of the late
Emperor of Russia.*

At Home Victory is extolled, but Punch grows impatient of Mismanagement

ENTHUSIASM OF PATERFAMILIAS
On Reading the Report of the Grand Charge of British
Cavalry on the 25th.

THE QUEEN VISITING THE IMBECILES OF THE CRIMEA

LA BELLE ALLIANCE, 1855

There are mixed Feelings about the Peace

A DISTRESSED AGRICULTURIST

LANDLORD. 'Well, Mr Springwheat, according to the Papers, there seems to be a Probability of a Cessation of Hostilities.'

TENANT (*who strongly approves of War prices*). 'Goodness Gracious! Why you don't mean to say that there's any **DANGER OF PEACE**!'

REJOICINGS FOR PEACE

THANK Heaven the War is ended!
  That is the general voice,
But let us feign no splendid
  Endeavours to rejoice.
To cease from lamentation
  We may contrive – but – pooh!
Can't rise to exultation,
  And cock-a-doodle-doo!

Not glad that War is over? Yes, my boy
But ours is a peculiar kind of joy,
A sort of joy sedate and rather sage,
As when a fever, or a pest,
Has in your dwelling ceased to rage,
  Killed half your family, and left the rest.

It is not now as in those days,
When waists were short, and men wore stays
  We are not so enthusiastic;
We cannot raise a halloo so uproarious,
We're not exactly so vainglorious;
  We are not quite so plastic.
Then, indeed, each of us, eftsoons,
Had donned his tightest pantaloons,
And pumps with monstrous ties,
And capered to the skies,
In wild abandonment of mind,
With swallow coat-tails flying out behind,
  And collars reaching to his eyes.

We can't pass now direct from grief to laughter
  Like supernumeraries on the stage,
  To smiling happiness from settled rage;
We look before and after.
Before, to all those skeletons and corses
Of gallant men and noble horses;
  After – though sordid the consideration –
Unto a certain bill to pay,
Which we shall have for many a day,
  By unrepealable taxation.

Yet never fought we in a better cause,
  Nor conquered yet a nobler peace.
We stood in battle for the eternal laws;
  'Twas an affair of high Police,
Our arms enforced a great arrest of State;
  And now remains – the Rate.

Enough! – be we prepared –
In time of need our good sword shall be bared;
Dry let us keep our powder,
And trust – our cannon yet shall bellow louder;
  And vengeance yet more crushing,
On all who for the Right,
Dare summon us to fight,
  Hurl in the death-bolt on their fire-breath rushing.
Fixed thus in grim resolve,
  We're hardly in the mood for jubilation;
Oh, that brute Force Man's squabbles still must solve.
  Oh, Civilisation!

30

THE TWO GIANTS OF THE TIME

'WHAT can we two great Forces do?'
  Said Steam to Electricity,
'To better the case of the human race,
  And promote mankind's felicity?'

Electricity said, 'From far lands sped,
  Through a wire, with a thought's velocity,
What tidings I bear! – of deeds that were
  Never passed yet for atrocity.'

'Both land and sea,' said Steam, 'by me,
  At the rate of a bird men fly over;
But the quicker they speed to kill and bleed,
  A thought to lament and sigh over.'

'The world, you see,' Electricity
  Remarked, 'thus far is our debtor,
That it faster goes; but, goodness knows,
  It doesn't get on much better.'

'Well, well,' said Steam, with whistle and scream,
  'Herein we help morality;
That means we make to overtake
  Rebellion and rascality.'

'Sure enough, that's true, and so we do,'
  Electricity responded.
'Through us have been caught, and to justice brought,
  Many scoundrels who had absconded.'

Said Steam, 'I hope we shall get the rope
  Round the necks of the Sepoy savages,
In double quick time, to avenge their crime,
  And arrest their murders and ravages.'

'We've been overpraised,' said both; 'we raised
  Too sanguine expectations:
But with all our might, we haven't yet quite
  Regenerated the nations.

'We're afraid we shan't – we suspect we can't
  Cause people to change their courses;
Locomotive powers alone are ours:
  But the world wants motive forces.'

CHIT-CHAT BY TELEGRAPH

Let us express the great delight with which we learn that 'the right to establish an electric telegraph line between France and England, by a sub-marine communication across the Channel,' has been officially conceded. By the aid of a single wire, and of two persons only – one in France and one in England – a message of fifteen words, including address and signature, may be delivered in one minute! These wires will, of course, communicate, via South-Eastern and Boulogne railways, with either capital: thus London and Paris may, when they will, gossip with one another. The amenities produced between the two countries, by this practice, must be of the most rapid growth and of the widest influence. Let us give a few examples of the probable questions and answers put and answered by parties, high and low, of both kingdoms: –

ST JAMES'S TO THE ELYSEE

Q. How d'ye do? Review or shoot this morning?
A. Neither: got to be bothered with Normandy. Compliments to Sa Majesté.

FOREIGN AFFAIRS TO FOREIGN AFFAIRS

Q. What says Russia?
A. Muzzled.
Q. Austria?
A. Mum.
Q. Any arrival from Turkey?
A. Yes: magnificent chibouque, and Circassian shawl for President.
Q. We reduce our army estimates 10,000. Et vous?
A. Will think of it.

WIFE IN LONDON TO HUSBAND IN PARIS

Q. Smith – I say, Smith. Isn't this shameful – abominable – wicked –
A. My life, what is the matter?
Q. Oh, it's just like you men. Been gone ten days, and you said –
A. My dear, bus'ness. Do you think anything but bus'ness could –
Q. Don't talk to me! I wonder you can show your face – I –
A. Now, my love –
Q. Don't 'love' me, and the clerk here laughing –
A. Well, woman, what do you want? This is the last I'll listen to.
Q. Woman, indeed! Want – well, I want – but you know what I want.
A. How can I tell? Now, this is the last time.
Q. I want to know where's the key of the money-box; here you've gone and left me –
A. In my desk – spring-drawer – right. Don't be extravagant.
Q. Extravagant! Here, you can go and spend – now, Smith – my love –
A. Well, this is the last.
Q. Mind you're not cheated, darling; take care that the lace is real Valenciennes.
A. All right.
Q. Make haste home. I blow you – you know what.

Punch already recognises the new Powers of the Time, and their possible Applications

Already (1856) Englishmen are looking West, and there is a strong Feeling against Slavery . . .

THE DIS-UNITED STATES – A BLACK BUSINESS

THE SPLIT IN THE STATES

UNITED STATES, if our good will
  Could but command its way,
You would remain united still,
  For ever and a day.
Does England want to see you split,
United States? – the deuce a bit.

Your North and South dissevered, we
  With less disgust should view
Only than England we should see
  And Scotland cleft in two.
We wish your great Republic whole,
With all our heart and all our soul.

Why who are we? Almost alone,
  With you, upon this Earth,
We bow before no Tyrant's throne.
  Believe us, aught but mirth
Your noble Commonwealth, if cleft,
Would cause us Britons, weaker left.

What head we might, against the wrong,
  Together make, O friends!
We wish you to continue strong,
  On union strength depends.
So, that your States may keep compact
Is our desire – now that's a fact.

By Priest and Soldier's two-fold sway
  The old world groans, opprest.
We, and you only, far away,
  With Liberty are blest.
And may we still example give,
And 'teach the nations how to live.'

How all the Despots would rejoice,
  Should you break up and fail;
How would the flunkeys' echoing voice
  Take up their masters' tale.
'Free institutions will not do'
Would be the cry of all the crew.

The Press is gagged – the mouth is shut –
  None dare their thoughts to name,
In Europe round; and lackeys strut,
  Arrayed in splendid shame;
And creeds are, at the bayonet's point,
Enforced in this time out of joint.

Still be it yours and ours to bear
  Our witness 'gainst these days.
The world, at least will not despair
  Whilst we our free flags raise.
Then may you still your stripes possess,
And may your stars be never less.

Strange it may seem, and yet is not;
  The peril of the Free
All springs from one unhappy blot,
  The taint of Slavery.
That, that is all you have to dread:
Get rid of that and go a-head!

32

although, by
1861, Punch
sympathises with
the President

THE AMERICAN DIFFICULTY
PRESIDENT ABE. 'What a nice **White House** this would be, if it were not for the **Blacks**!'

KNOW'ST THOU THE LAND?

KNOW'ST thou the land where the kangaroos bound,
And the queer-looking ornithorhynci are found?
The land of the South, that lies under our feet,
Deficient in mouths; overburdened with meat;
Know'st thou that land, John Bull, my friend?
Thither, oh! thither, poor people ought to wend.

Know'st thou the land, my dear John Bull,
Where thousands of flocks are reared only for wool,
And sixty-four million good pounds, as they say,
Of mutton, are cast in one twelvemonth away?
Know'st thou that land? Thy starving brood
Thither, oh! thither, should rush in quest of food.

Know'st thou the land where the cattle and sheep,
For the mere want of hands are too many to keep;
And what to do with them their owners know not,
But to slaughter them off for the melting pot?
Know'st thou that land? To save such waste,
Thither, oh! thither, ye hungry creatures haste.

Know'st thou the land where a sheep-shearer's pay,
Or a reaper's, is ten or twelve shillings a day;
Where a labourer may earn thirty pounds by the year,
With a ration, per week, of the best of good cheer?
Know'st thou that land – that jolly land?
Thither should Labour repair to seek Demand.

Know'st thou the land that they paupers may reach
At the trifling expense of six pounds or so each,
There in plenty to live, whilst their gruel and bread
Cost near eight in the workhouse, per annum, a head?
Know'st thou that land? John Bull, if so,
Thither, oh! thither, help those poor souls to go!

Australia is now the Land of Opportunity . . .

NOT A BAD CUSTOMER
FORTUNATE DIGGER (*loq.*) 'Half a hogshead of Port, waiter, and a ton or two of your best Cigars.'

A GOLD FIELD IN THE 'DIGGINS'

though Punch appreciates the social Drawbacks of Emigration; Home is best, after all

DISTRESSING RESULT OF EMIGRATION

LADY. 'Yes, my dear. John left us without any warning, and we can't match the other Footman, because all the tall men are gone to Australia.'

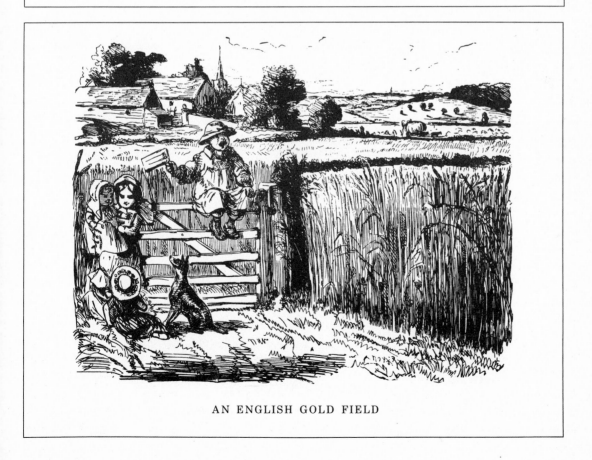

AN ENGLISH GOLD FIELD

WELLINGTON

ALL bring their tribute to his name – from her
   Who wears the crown to him who plies the spade
   Under those windows where his corpse is laid,
Taking its rest at last from all those years of stir.

Years that re-moulded an old world in roar
   And furnace-fires of strife – with hideous clang
   Of battle-hammers; where they loudest rang,
His clear sharp voice was heard that ne'er will be
     heard more.

Courts have a seemly sorrow for such loss;
   Cabinets politic regret: the great
   Will miss his punctual presence at their state –
The shade of such eclipse even lowly hearths will cross.

But I, a jester, what have I to do
   With greatness or the grave? The man and theme
   The comment of my page may ill beseem;
So be it – yet not less do I pay tribute true.

For that in him to which I would bow down
   Comes not of honours heaped upon his head,
   Comes not of orders on his breast outspread –
Nor yet of captain's nor of councillor's renown.

It is that all his life example shews
   Of reverence for duty: where he saw
   Duty commanding word or act, her law
With him was absolute, and brooked no quibbling
     glose.

He followed where she pointed; right ahead –
   Unheeding what might sweep across his path,
   The cannon's volley, or the people's wrath;
No hope, howe'er forlorn, but at her call he led.

Hard as a blade so tempered needs must be,
   And, sometimes, scant of courtesy, as one
   Whose life has dealt with stern things to be done,
Not wide in range of thought, nor deep of subtlety:

Of most distrustful; sparing in discourse;
   Himself untiring, and from all around
   Claiming that force which in himself he found –
He lived, and asked no love, but won respect perforce.

And of respect, at last, came love unsought,
   But not repelled when offered; and we knew
   That this rare sternness had its softness too,
That woman's charm and grace upon his being
     wrought:

That underneath the armour of his breast
   Were springs of tenderness – all quick to flow
   In sympathy with childhood's joy or woe:
That children climbed his knees, and made his arms
     their nest.

For fifty of its eighty years and four
   His life has been before us: who but knew
   The short, spare frame, the eye of piercing blue,
The eagle-beak, the finger reared before

In greeting? – Well he bore his load of years,
   As in his daily walk he paced along
   To early prayer, or, 'mid the admiring throng,
Pass'd through Whitehall to counsel with his Peers.

He was true English – down to the heart's core;
   His sternness and his softness English both:
   Our reverence and love grew with his growth,
Till we are slow to think that he can be no more.

Peace to him! Let him sleep near him who fell
   Victor at Trafalgar; by NELSON's side
   WELLINGTON's ashes fitly may abide.
Great captain – noble heart! Hail to thee, and farewell!

SEEING THE OLD YEAR OUT AND THE NEW YEAR IN

A few Years later (1855–7) Palmerston becomes Punch's Hero

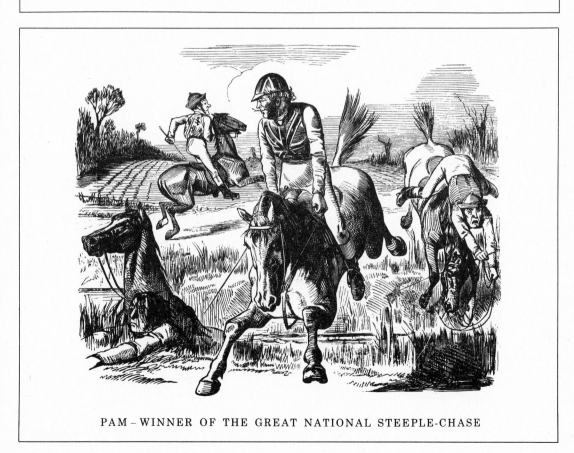

PAM – WINNER OF THE GREAT NATIONAL STEEPLE-CHASE

Patriotism proclaimed (1857)

THE BRITISH LION'S VENGEANCE ON THE BENGAL TIGER

**Another Imperial
Proclamation
(1858)**

THE ACCESSION OF THE QUEEN OF INDIA

FRENCH FASHION

PAM (*To Britannia*). 'Here's a sweet thing in bracelets, Ma'am; worn very generally in Paris.'
BRITANNIA. 'Ah, so I've heard! But it isn't my style.'

MR BULL. 'Invasion, indeed! That's a game two can play at! – Why, to hear these poodles talk, one would think my bull-dog was dead!'

THE VOLUNTEER MOVEMENT

FOREIGN PARTY. 'Mais, Mosieu Bool, I ave all ways thought you vass great Shopkeepare!'
MR BOOL. 'So I am, Moosoo – and these are some of the Boys who mind the Shop! – Comprenny?'

**Punch recognises
his Friends
(1860) . . .**

GARIBALDI THE LIBERATOR
Or, The Modern Perseus

PAPAL ALLOCUTION — SNUFFING OUT MODERN CIVILISATION

At Home the
Radicals are
more interested
in Reform; but
Punch knows
that Reform
means different
Things to
different People

'IT WILL SOON BOIL!'

THE REFORM JANUS

44

MONKEYANA

Am I satyr or man?
Pray tell me who can,
And settle my place in the scale.
A man in ape's shape,
An anthropoid ape,
Or monkey deprived of his tail?

The *Vestiges* taught,
That all came from naught
By 'development,' so called, 'progressive;'
That insects and worms
Assume higher forms
By modification excessive.

Then DARWIN set forth.
In a book of much worth,
The importance of 'Nature's selection;'
How the struggle for life
Is a laudable strife,
And results in 'specific distinction.'

Let pigeons and doves
Select their own loves,
And grant them a million of ages,
Then doubtless you'll find
They've altered their kind,
And changed into prophets and sages.

Zoological Gardens, May, 1861.

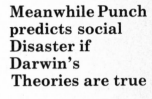

Meanwhile Punch predicts social Disaster if Darwin's Theories are true

THE LION OF THE SEASON
ALARMED FLUNKEY. 'Mr G-g-g-o-o-o-rilla!'

**And on all
Questions Punch
never fails to
give Advice**

'WONDERFUL THINGS'

A NEW weekly periodical was announced a short time since, called *Wonderful Things*. We thought at the time its title was a taking one, and knowing what a large majority of readers are caught by a title quite as readily as a plebeian *millionaire*, we remember that we laid a mental wager with ourselves that our contemporary would soon enjoy a circulation only second to our own. We fear, however, that our bet was pretty nearly as unsafe as if we had made it at a Betting Office; for beyond the publication of the first two numbers, we have seen no advertisement of our predicted rival since. We can hardly think it could have failed from any want of 'copy', for on a subject so prolific almost any pen could write. Here, for instance, are a text or two which might be easily dilated on, and which with our usual philanthropy we freely offer for the use of any used-up contributor. Nobody out of Bedlam will deny, we think, that among 'Wonderful Things' we may fairly class the following:–

A Cab which is not a vehicle of abuse.
A so-called 'Quiet' Street without a barrel-organ in it.
A 'Quart' Bottle of Beer that you can squeeze above a couple of half-pint glasses out of.
A Lodging-house Knife that will cut.

A Government Steamer which can be at sea a whole week without being forced to put back for repairs.
A Dress Circle whose centre is discoverable without a sixpence to the box-keeper.
A Punctual Railway Train.
A Glass of Thames water that you can drink without deodorising.
An 'Alarming Sacrifice' where the process of selling does not invariably include the purchaser.
A Statue which the British Nation need not blush to godfather.
A Carpet-Bag or Omnibus that it is possible to fill.
A Clean Street in the City, or one not under repair.
A 'Warranted Foreign' Cigar which you may not safely bet is cabbaged from a London market-garden.
A New Orleans Paper without the advertisement of a Slave Sale in it.
An Homœopathic Practice which is not quite a *sine-cure*.
An Umbrella which has not been borrowed.
An Area that for four-and-twenty hours has been innocent of a policeman.
A Betting-Office, where whatever horse you wish to back, you may not safely calculate on being 'taken' – in.

We are forced to break off here from our usual 'want of space' – a want that we are always pretty sure to feel whenever we are not inclined to be diffuse. But we think we have already said enough to show that the Catalogue of 'Wonderful Things' would be about as difficult a thing to finish, as the Catalogue of the Library at the British Museum itself.

II
CURATOR,
PROTECTOR,
CHASTISER

SUBSTANCE AND SHADOW
Cartoon No. 1.

THERE are many silly, dissatisfied people in this country, who are continually urging upon Ministers the propriety of considering the wants of the pauper population, under the impression that it is as laudable to feed men as to shelter horses.

To meet the views of such unreasonable people, the Government would have to put its hand into the Treasury money-box. We would ask how the Chancellor of the Exchequer can be required to commit such an act of folly, knowing, as we do, that the balance of the budget was triflingly against him, and that he has such righteous and paramount claims upon him as the Duke of Cumberland's income, the Duchess of Mecklenburg Strelitz's pin-money, and the builder's little account for the Royal stables.

We conceive that Ministers have adopted the very best means to silence this unwarrantable outcry. They have considerately determined that as they cannot afford to give hungry nakedness the *substance* which it covets, at least it shall have the *shadow*.

The poor ask for bread, and the philanthropy of the State accords – an exhibition.

The Sense of Contrast

Punch unwittingly gave the word 'cartoon' a permanent new meaning when in 1843 Leech satirised the grandiose exhibition of cartoons (in the original sense of 'designs for a fresco') for the new Houses of Parliament. He produced a series of six 'cartoons' directed against social abuses in which he contrasted the opulence of the designs in the exhibition with the poverty of the spectators who visited it.

Cartoon, No. 1

SUBSTANCE AND SHADOW

Priorities (1844)

THE GAME LAWS
or, the sacrifice of the peasant to the hare

THE CASE OF MARY FURLEY

SIR JAMES GRAHAM has earned an undying reputation by his conduct in the case of this brokenhearted woman. In the first place, although she was sentenced to death by the honey-tongued MAULE, SIR JAMES GRAHAM knew nothing whatever of the matter. No; when questioned in the House upon the atrocity of the sentence, aggravated as it was by the funereal eloquence of the judge, who doubtless, to teach a great moral lesson, tortured the woman with Tyburn tropes, – even the Home Secretary knew nothing of the circumstances which had sent a shuddering horror through the heart of the kingdom. He would, however, inquire about MARY FURLEY.

A week or so passes, and the country is astounded, horrified at the further barbarity exercised upon the sufferer, who is frenzied, agonised by the official visit of the Sheriff, come with the death-warrant from the Home Office. There is no hope for her! She has, it is true, been driven to madness by accumulated miseries which beggar fiction: she has been tortured into an act of insanity by the cruelty of fortune; it is no matter, says the philosopher at the Home Office – she must die. The woman must be hanged!

For some four-and-twenty hours the doomed creature suffers agony unutterable. SIR JAMES GRAHAM, doubtless, sleeps sweetly in his bed – yes, enjoys that sweet, deep slumber, rewardful of solemn duties solemnly fulfilled. Then, rising, he bethinks himself of the poor wretch in Newgate; the fact is, he is made to think of her by the earnest faces and loud remonstrances of a few Samaritans who beset the Home Office. He is entreated to reconsider the sentence, and the result is – a reprieve for MARY FURLEY. . . .

Then appear in the newspapers comforting paragraphs, indicative of the new tenderness of SIR JAMES GRAHAM. Yes, think we, SIR JAMES has pondered on the history, so complete in all its terrors, of MARY FURLEY, and he will recommend the woman to the royal mercy. A few days, a week or two perhaps, may be the term of her imprisonment in the Penitentiary; and then she will return to the world, to enjoy the active sympathies even of the highest-born of her own sex, who will gather about her, and with Samaritan goodness strive to heal the wounds inflicted by undeserved wretchedness upon her. Such was our daydream.

SIR JAMES GRAHAM *has* recommended MARY FURLEY to the Royal mercy, and the result is – TRANSPORTATION FOR SEVEN YEARS! 'Such is the breath' of Home Secretaries!

The Royal mercy was wont, by a figure of speech, to be called the brightest jewel in the Crown. If it still be so – why then, SIR JAMES, thanks to you, HER MAJESTY, QUEEN VICTORIA, wears at the present moment the dimmest of diadems.

One Law for the Rich : Another for the Poor

FINE OR IMPRISONMENT
Law for the Rich. – The Fine was immediately paid.
Law for the Poor. – The Prisoner, not being able to pay,
was removed in the Van to Prison.

MAN *VERSUS* MACHINE

Punch takes a Stand

LOOKING into the chronicles of the past, this is, perhaps, a greater cause than any yet recorded in the books. The great chancellor of human nature, as Lord BACON is somewhere described, never gave judgment in a weightier, graver case – in one involving so many interests, moral and physical. All England is cited to attend the pleadings; cited in the name of the King of kings, whose suffering creatures, 'made in his image,' invoke the spirit of truth, justice, and humanity, to give judgment on their side. Let us take a single victim.

What a miserable tatterdemalion is the plaintiff! This the 'lord of the creation!' Look at his shrunk and withered anatomy – behold his pallid aspect! Daily hunger has pinched his bloodless cheeks, and utter weariness of spirit has blighted the very look of freeborn man! He is the serf of penury – the bond-slave of want! The birds of the air find food on every bush, and 'the foxes have holes;' but he, invested by his Creator with the majesty of humanity, is famine-stricken, and lodged, if lodged at all, worse than the beast. The earth – this magnificent and prodigal earth – is spread by God one wide banquet for the mouth of man; and the paragon of animals looks with glazing eye and whitening lip upon the feast, forbidden to 'sit down and eat' by his full-gorged master. 'Increase and multiply,' says GOD; and yet, man by man, is deemed the nuisance and the offal of the earth.

However, the plaintiff is upon the floor of the court, and humbly begs, in return for daily sweat, sufficing food and raiment. The evidence of his wrongs is in his withered ghastly face, and the rags that hang about him – his witnesses, his careworn, haggard wife and children; children *without infancy* – the puny, stunted offspring of despairing want; creatures, made prematurely old by daily misery – the doomed of the earth, to whom the world yields no one green and pleasant place, but whose whole journey, from the workhouse-cradle to the workhouse-grave, is over the 'burning waste' of daily privation – of daily barrenness. The plaintiff – poor wretch! – sues, of course, *in forma pauperis*. God help his case!

The defendant employs for counsel that very learned lawyer, Sergeant MAMMON. What a prosperous, full-flushed face he has! How ignominious does the plaintiff look! how vast his insolence – appearing and pleading against such an advocate! The very tones of the plaintiff's voice condemn him; whilst the tongue of the learned Sergeant – oh! it hath brought down angels from their starry homes to soil and stain themselves with earthly dirt. But does MAMMON revile and bully down the plaintiff? Does he call him idler – reprobate? Oh, no! MAMMON has now given up that line of defence; albeit it has long been adopted, and with wished success; namely, to throw the scorn of unbelief upon the plaintiff. Now, MAMMON is become better-hearted. *Now*, the golden Sergeant shakes his apoplectic face, and outweeps crocodile at the misery of the plaintiff. His case is very bad – very bad, indeed: but he has no business in court; the court can do nothing for him. MAMMON is instructed to say that he has a deep sympathy – only a little less deep than his breeches'-pocket – for the plaintiff; and therefore it is in the excess of such feeling that he advises the plaintiff to return to his cellar (if he has one), and, gathering his wife and children about him, since they all must starve, to bolt the door, and, famishing in quiet, not to disturb the neighbourhood. Delivered of this advice, Sergeant MAMMON feels himself, as a good Christian angel, considerably relieved, and goes home to his claret and venison. . . .

[*The plaintiff, however, appeals to 'a body of good Samaritans' who 'speak plain truths to the Prime Minister', Sir Robert Peel. He expresses the fear – among others – that 'an extension of our manufactures . . . would surely bring into play more machinery and not employ manual labour in anything like the rate of the increase in the machine department.'*]

And now for Sir Robert's point – that increased demand for manufactures would only increase machine power. Machinery, in its progress, has doubtless been the origin of terrible calamity: it has made the strong man so much live lumber. But as we cannot go back, and must go on, it is for statesmen and philosophers to prepare for the crisis as surely coming as the morning light. How, when machinery is multiplied – as it will be – a thousandfold? How, when tens of thousand-thousand hands are made idle by the ingenuity of the human mind? How, when, comparatively speaking, there shall be *no* labour for man? Will the multitude lie down and, unrepining, die? We think not – we are sure not. Then will rise – and already we hear the murmur – a cry, a shout for an adjustment of interests; a shout that, hard as it is, will strike upon the heart of Mammon, and make the spoiler tremble.

We put this question to Sir Robert PEEL: if all labour done by man were suddenly performed by machine power, and that power in the possession of some thousand individuals, – what would be the cry of the rest of the race? Would not the shout be – 'Share, share?'

The steam-engine, despite of themselves, must and will carry statesmen back to first principles. As it is, machinery is a fiend to the poor; the time will come when it will be as a beneficent angel.

Q.

'Q' was Douglas Jerrold, radical champion of the poor and oppressed from the earliest days of *Punch*. He was largely responsible for the great political influence which *Punch* enjoyed during its early years.

A ROYAL WIFE OF – £3,000!

READER, when you listen to the bells merrily ringing the birth of a Prince or Princess, what changes do they sound? – Merely the changes of £. s. d.

When you hear the Park and Tower Guns, loaded with harmless powder, roar away at a royal birth, what say their thundering voices? Simply, that to their powder, John Bull must some day add the shot.

Her Majesty has sent down a message to her loving and dutiful Commons. At first our senators believed the whispered communication to be applicable to Ireland. Thoughts of guns, swords, and pistols, conflagrations and hangings, shocked the sensibilities of our law-makers: but soon their latent horror gave way to merriment; for instead of O'CONNELL, decorated with repeal button and riband, and looking dismemberment, – there was HYMEN, gracious Hymen, in his crocus robe, and loves and doves and graces numberless! Sir ROBERT PEEL informed the Commons (many of whom were in ecstacy at the news) that the Princess AUGUSTA was about to be dropt into the cup of bliss (which would then be overflowing) of the Hereditary Duke of MECKLENBURGH STRE-LITZ. The Duke, however, wanted something more in his cup to make the draught palatable; in a word, the wife was very well – but, with the wife he wanted money.

What a pity it is that Majesty and Mendicity are so frequently allied! The Commons were desired to make a suitable provision for German housekeeping, the Duke of CAMBRIDGE, with paternal generosity, having resolved to make an allowance to his daughter during his natural life.

We know that democratic discontent has called the Duke a rich man; and therefore, asks of his Royal Highness why, like any other man who has traded upon the capital of the country – why, he should not at his death (be the day far distant!) leave sufficient means to the child of his affection? These people are foolish, ferocious reasoners. Do they forget that the Duke of CAMBRIDGE is one running conduit of benevolence? He drops gold as he walks for the poor and needy. Look at his constant attendance at charity dinners. Reflect upon his subscriptions thereat. We know that slanderous tongues declare these subscriptions to be apocryphal – we know that they call the gracious Prince of the House of Brunswick no more than a royal decoy duck to plebeian purses. This we do not believe; moreover, we pity the man who can believe it.

The Princess AUGUSTA, after the death of her father (who, there is no doubt, will vindicate his character for active benevolence by dying not worth a single shilling,) will receive £3,000 a year from the taxes. This is moderate – very moderate indeed. How the young couple will be able to get on we know not. To be sure, the court of STRELITZ is not quite so dear as that of St James's, and so they may get fish and pudding for dinner all the year round. Again, when we remember that the immense sum of £10,000 was voted only for the education of the poor of all England, we are surprised at the magnanimity which contents itself with something less than a third of that amount. If Stockport and Paisley do not, with all their rushlights, illuminate when they shall hear the glad tidings, then is the spirit of manufacture dead to gratitude – then have weavers no bowels. (By the way, it would save them much inconvenience if they never had.)

Three thousand per annum! What is it? Why not a drop of water from the ocean of John Bull's funds. But it is the principle – the admirable principle of philanthropy vindicated in the grant – the Christianity, in fact, of the deed. We are suffering cold, hunger, and nakedness; and yet we give away a snip of our blanket – a corner of our penny-loaf – a wristband of our one shirt, to the hereditary Duke of MECKLENBURGH STRELITZ!

Three thousand per annum! We were never great dabs at arithmetic; but, perhaps, there are hard-headed accountants amongst the operatives of Bolton, or in the cellars of Manchester, who will acquaint us with the exact number of their beds, tables, chairs, saucepans, and other house-hold chattels, seized by the Queen's broker, that would be necessary to make up £3,000 – one year's salary for the Hereditary Duchess of MECKLEN-BURGH STRELITZ?

A second Stand

PRINCE ALBERT'S BEES

WE have been favoured by PRINCE ALBERT . . . with a private view of the royal Beehives. They are formed after the most approved political principles, albeit the said principles have not yet come into general fashion. They are so constructed, that the working-bees within, (they are a very curious species of bee, and bear an outward resemblance to British mechanics and artificers,) are carefully deprived of all the honey they elaborate, save the honey that is considered sufficient to afford them ample sustenance in all seasons. Thus, it will be seen, that the Bees pay a very large property-tax; but, unlike too many of their fellow-subjects, they are left enough to eat in return for their labour. *All* is not taken from them. Their hives, we understand, have been expressly fitted up for the instruction of the PRINCE OF WALES, whose dawning mind will, we trust, receive and appreciate the wholesome political and social lesson they so unequivocally convey.

A social Metaphor (1844)

PRINCE ALBERT'S BEE-HIVES
'These Hives are so constructed, that the HONEY may
be removed without DESTROYING THE BEES.'
– *Morning Paper.*

THE POOR MAN'S FRIEND

THE HOME OF THE RICK-BURNER

THE MAYORALTY – THE COMING IN

THE MAYORALTY – THE GOING OUT

DISTRESS
OF THE COUNTRY

MERCIFUL HEAVEN! we shudder as we write! The state of destitution to which the civic authorities are reduced is appalling. Will our readers believe it – there were only five hundred tureens of turtle, or two thousand five hundred pints, or *five thousand* basins, amongst not quite fifteen hundred guests, – only two basins and a half a man, – for the first course! But we print the bill of fare; it will be read with intense interest by the manufacturers of Paisley, inhabitants of poor-law unions, but more especially by the literary community.

'GENERAL BILL OF FARE. – 250 tureens of real turtle, containing five pints each; 200 bottles of sherbet; 6 dishes of fish; 30 entrées; 4 boiled turkeys and oysters; 60 roast pullets; 60 dishes of fowls; 46 ditto of capons; 50 French pies; 60 pigeon pies; 53 hams (ornamented); 43 tongues; 2 quarters of house lamb; 2 barons of beef; 3 rounds of beef; 2 stewed rumps of beef; 13 sirloins, rumps, and ribs of beef; 6 dishes of asparagus; 60 ditto of mashed and other potatoes; 44 ditto of shell-fish; 4 ditto of prawns; 140 jellies; 50 blanc-manges; 40 dishes of tarts (creamed); 30 ditto of orange and other tourtes; 40 ditto of almond pastry; 20 Chantilly baskets; 60 dishes of mince pies; 56 salads; peas and asparagus. The Removes: – 30 roast turkeys; 6 leverets; 80 pheasants; 24 geese; 40 dishes of partridges; 15 dishes of wild fowl; 2 pea-fowls. Dessert: – 100 pineapples, from 2 lb. to 3 lb. each; 200 dishes of hot-house grapes; 250 ice creams; 50 dishes of apples; 100 ditto of pears; 60 ornamented Savoy cakes; 75 plates of walnuts; 80 ditto of dried fruit and preserves; 50 ditto of preserved ginger; 60 ditto of rout cakes and chips; 46 ditto of brandy cherries.

THE PRINCIPAL TABLE (at which the Right Hon. the Lord Mayor presides). – 10 tureens of turtle, 10 bottles of sherbet, 6 dishes of fish, 30 entrées, 1 boiled turkey and oysters, 2 roast pullets, 2 dishes of fowls, 2 ditto of capons, 2 French pies, 2 pigeon pies, 2 hams (ornamented), 2 tongues, 1 quarter of house-lamb, 1 stewed rump of beef, 1 sirloin of beef, 6 dishes of asparagus, 2 dishes of mashed and other potatoes, 3 ditto of shell-fish, 1 dish of prawns, 3 jellies, 3 blanc-manges, 2 dishes of tarts (creamed), 2 dishes of orange and other tourtes, 2 dishes of almond pastry, 4 Chantilly baskets, 2 dishes of mince pies, 4 salads. Removes: – 3 roast turkeys, 1 leveret, 3 pheasants, 2 geese, 2 dishes of partridges, 1 dish of wild fowl, 2 pea-fowls. Dessert: – 6 pineapples, 12 dishes of grapes, 10 ice creams, 2 dishes of apples, 4 dishes of pears, 2 ornamented Savoy cakes, 3 plates of walnuts, 4 plates of dried fruit and preserves, 3 plates of preserved ginger, 3 plates of rout cakes and chips, 3 plates of brandy cherries. . . .

WINES: – Champagne, Hock, Claret, Madeira, Port, and Sherry.'

RAILWAY POLITENESS

THE classification adopted in the management of Railways is not confined to the carriages; but the distinctions of first, second, and third class are scrupulously observed in the degree of politeness shown by the servants of the company to the passengers. The old maxim that civility costs nothing, seems to be utterly repudiated by Railway Directors, who calculate no doubt that politeness at all events takes time; and as time is money, the servants of the company are not justified in giving it without an equivalent. Any one who doubts the fact of the distinction to which we have alluded being drawn, has only to present himself at different times as an applicant for information at a Railway Terminus in the different characters of a first, a second, and a third class passenger.

If he is going by the first class he will get speedy attention from the clerks in the office; bows, and even smiles, from the policemen on the platform; and perhaps a touch of the hat from the guard. The second class passenger will get bare civility, but rather more of the bear than the civility, from the officials who stamp and deliver the checks; and who are very fond of trying to cheat themselves into the belief that they are quite on a par with the 'gentlemen in the public offices,' whom the railway clerks chiefly resemble in an assumed nonchalance, which, however, the plain-speaking of a passenger who *will* be attended to, and who *may* be a shareholder, is pretty sure to dissipate. A second class passenger will get nothing more than a 'Now, Sir,' from the policeman, and a 'Come, jump up!' from the guard; while the third class passenger will experience a poke in the chest from the former with his staff, by way of keeping him back till it is convenient to let him enter the carriage. In fact, there are short answers as well as short trains, and each class has a set of rules of politeness applied to it, which the officers are bound to obey as scrupulously as they do the Railway signals.

THE RAILWAY MONITOR

TO TRAVELLERS

THE existing railway arrangements render it imperative that you should provide yourself with a large stock of philosophy, to enable you to put up with certain inconveniences, which you will be sure, to a greater or less extent, to encounter on most lines, and whereof a classification is hereby appended for your benefit.

FIRST CLASS

THE chief inconvenience peculiar to this class, is, that your fare will be about twice as much as you ought in fairness to pay. You run, perhaps, rather less risk in this class than in the others, of having your neck broken; but you must not be unprepared for such a contingency.

SECOND CLASS

IN travelling by the second class, you will do well to wear a respirator, unless you wish to be choked with dust and ashes from the engine close in front of you. Also, if you are going far, you are recommended to put on a diving-dress, like that used at the Polytechnic; because, if it should rain much during your journey, the sides of the carriage being open, you will have to ride in a pool of water. Your dignity must not be hurt, should you have for next neighbour a ragamuffin in handcuffs, with a policeman next him. The hardness of your seat is a mere trifle; that is the least of the annoyances to which you are judiciously subjected, with the view of driving you into the first class train.

THIRD CLASS

Make up your mind for unmitigated hail, rain, sleet, snow, thunder and lightning. Look out for a double allowance of smoke, dust, dirt, and everything that is disagreeable. Be content to run a twofold risk of loss of life and limb. Do not expect the luxury of a seat. As an individual and a traveller, you are one of the lower classes; a poor, beggarly, contemptible person, and your comfort and convenience are not to be attended to.

ALL THREE CLASSES

Punctuality may be the soul of business, but suppose not that it is the spirit of railways. If you do not care whether you keep an appointment or not, make it on the faith of the Company, by all means; but otherwise by none. Regard starting, or arriving at your destination, only half an hour too late, as luck. You pay nothing extra to attendants for civility, so you must not hope for it. Remember that you are at the mercy of the Company as to where you may stop for refreshments; for which, accordingly, be not surprised if you have to pay through the nose. Beware, if you quit the train for an instant, lest it move on; you have paid your money, the rest is your own look-out, and, you may depend will be no one else's. For loss and damage of luggage, and the like little mishaps, prepare yourself as a matter of course; and if at the end of your journey you find yourself in a whole skin – thank your stars.

The Railway Class System

First Class politeness

Second Class politeness

Third Class politeness

RAILWAY CHARGES

CHARGES on a railway for scalding yourself with a cup of tea or a basin of soup are extraordinary, but still we think they lag far behind those of the railway hotels. The bill is always made out on the principle of never seeing the visitor again. He is therefore charged as much as his patience or his purse will bear, which is a sure plan of never inducing him to return. Our feelings towards Southampton, for instance, are anything but friendly, and the next time we visit that inhospitable town, we shall walk up and down the pier all night, or go to bed in the boiler of the engine, sooner than submit to the atrocious impositions of the railway hotels. We were in one for five minutes, during which time the waiter exchanged just three words with us, when we were asked at the door for 'one shilling.' 'What for?' we indignantly exclaimed. 'Attendance, Sir, one shilling.' It is true we might have stopped all the night conversing with the same attendant for the same amount; still, we thought that fourpence a word was a trifle too dear, even to converse with a waiter at Southampton.

We beg to draw up a small scale of prices, moderate too, for the general use of railway hotels.

	s.	d.
For asking to look at *Bradshaw's*	1	0
For looking at same	1	0
For a wax candle to read the same	1	0
Attendance	1	0

This would do capitally for a casual visitor; but if a person slept there, immense ingenuity might be shown in the high valuation of each separate item, recollecting always that it is not very likely you will ever see the visitor again. The following would not be a poor specimen of its kind: –

	s.	d.
Taking off your boots	1	0
Attendance, lighting you up to bed	1	0
Bed	2	6
Sheets and towels	1	6
Pair of slippers	1	0
Shaving water	1	0
Breakfast, with water-cresses	5	0
The Times, at ditto	1	0
Cleaning your boots	1	0
Attendance	1	0
Cigar, and light for the same	1	0
Attendance	1	0
	18	0

This would not be very bad for one bed and breakfast; but still the thing may be better done. We just throw out the crude hint; and railway hotel proprietors are quite clever enough to improve upon it. What extraordinary notions, by the bye, a railway hotel bill will give an antiquarian of the next century, of the dearness of provisions at the present period!

Railway-mania

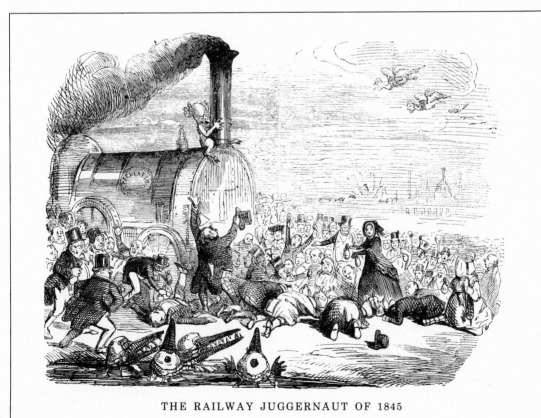

THE RAILWAY JUGGERNAUT OF 1845

WANTED A GOVERNESS BY A 'SMALL FAMILY'

WE have had our attention called to an advertisement which lately appeared in *The Times*, thus commencing: –

WANTED, in a small quiet family, a person about 30 *years of age*, as NURSERY and HOUSE MAID. She must be good tempered and orderly, have some experience as a Nurse, and a good Needlewoman. An active, pious person, would find this a comfortable situation. The duties are not heavy, the children being out of the Nursery in the day time. The salary £13 a-year.

The genteel Oppressed

There is great comfort in a good servant. It is worth at least £13 yearly wages. So think the heads of the 'small and quiet' – possibly 'pious' – family, who would give the labourer his hire, of course.

Stay: the advertisement proceeds: –

'In the same family a Young Lady is wanted to assist in the care and education of three little girls, between the ages of four and seven.'

If £13 a year shall be given for washing children and scrubbing floors, how much for cultivating the youthful intellect, and forming the juvenile mind? Answer – by the advertisement, continued: –

'Accomplishments are not required; but she must write a good hand, and work well at the needle. As opportunity would be afforded for improvement, it is thought that board and washing, with £5 pocket-money, would be a fair remuneration for the first year.' . . .

This 'small quiet family' may be very snug; but *Punch* is afraid it is also dreadfully close.

THE MARCH OF MORALITY

THE following appears in the midst of a linen-draper's advertisement:

'SEVERAL ASSISTANTS WANTED. – None need apply but men of high moral attainments, good abilities, courteous demeanour, determined energies, and strict integrity of character.'

We are not aware that 'high moral attainments' were required to get off 'fifty thousand straw bonnets;' assist at 'alarming sacrifices;' officiate at 'tremendous failures;' help to 'give things away;' and perform the last sad duties of 'clearing off one hundred per cent. under cost price,' by way of climax to 'another awful bankruptcy.' We can comprehend the necessity for 'determined energies' in a linendraper's assistant, for his duty seems to consist in encumbering people with what they do not want; preventing them from getting what they do; and tempting them to the purchase of dozens or half-dozens of an article of which only one is required. The 'high moral attainments' needed for this sort of thing, remain to us a mystery.

SPLENDID OPENING FOR A YOUNG MEDICAL MAN

CHAIRMAN. 'Well, young man. So you wish to be engaged as Parish Doctor?'
DOCTOR. 'Yes, Gentlemen, I am desirous –'
CHAIRMAN. 'Ah! Exactly. Well – It's understood that your wages – salary I should say – is to be twenty pounds per annum; and you find your own tea and sugar – medicines I mean – and, in fact, make yourself generally useful. If you do your duty, and conduct yourself properly, why – ah – you – ah –'
[PUNCH. 'Will probably be bowled out of your situation by some humbug, who will fill it for less money.']

BATTLE OF THE ALPHABET

WHO SHALL EDUCATE? OR,
OUR BABES IN THE WOOD

A DOSE OF CANT

WE hesitate in copying from a contemporary the following advertisement. Words have no substance; yet they can produce a physical effect, and that of these ensuing may be antimonial: –

To PIOUS FAMILIES. – Within a walk of Russell Square. – A respectable lady, who has Christian business to transact in town, WANTS a FURNISHED FLOOR, with plain Board sent from the family table. Offers from £50 a year, payable quarterly. Particulars requested. – H.S., care of H——, &c.

Punch loathes Cant . . .

What can this woman mean by Christian business? The business of a chandler – a dealer in tea, coffee, tobacco, snuff, vinegar, and pepper, is a Christian business, provided it is honestly conducted, and that the person who carries it on does not adulterate his commodities before summoning his establishment to prayers. A linen-draper's business is a Christian one, if he does not overwork his shopmen and cheat his customers. An attorney's or even a barrister's may be a Christian business for that matter – a solicitor need not necessarily seek undue costs, a counsel is not obliged to bully and lie.

The advertiser's requirement of plain board from the family table might seem to indicate that her Christian business was that of a cabinet-maker; but this is an odd occupation for a female, and what a strange fancy does that seem of deriving its material from the domestic mahogany – but some sage will suggest that the board she wants is not raw material.

But seriously, who will answer such an advertisement as the above? Who will dare to say – Mine is a pious family. We are pious people. I am a pious man. Hardly anybody, we should think, but some sanctimonious swindler and member of a Sabbatarian Anti-Recreation Society.

RELIGION FOR THE HIGHER CIRCLES

AN advertisement in *The Times* apprises us of the fact that there is a society established, having for its excessively genteel purpose, the conversion of the higher circles. An article has been prepared by a tract society, which is strongly recommended for fashionable use; and which, of course, is not intended for the mere vulgar votaries of Christianity. We have not met with any of the publications in question, our office being possibly too far east for the elegant efforts of the religious exquisites, whose labours are no doubt bounded on the east by Pall Mall, 'on the south by Spring Gardens, on the north by Grosvenor Square, and on the west by the limits of Belgravia.

We always had an idea that religion knew no distinction of ranks; we know that Christianity repudiates anything like class divisions among its own followers, as far as religion is concerned; but there appears to be a fashionable sect which, refusing to hear of pious *parvenus*, looks upon

'elect' and 'select' as synonymous. We shall not be surprised at any affectation or absurdity in the much abused name of religion after this, nor should we be astonished at finding announcements of a *Thé évangélique*, or a *soirée sérieuse*, or a devotional dinner-party among the 'fashionable arrangements,' and 'further arrangements' of our JENKINSONIAN contemporaries.

Of all the cant to which the fashionable affectation of 'seriousness' has given rise, we know of none more offensive than that which professes to prepare a religion expressly for the use of the 'higher circles' and those frequenting places of 'fashionable resort.' We suppose religion – of this kind – will be expected to leave town for some 'fashionable watering-place' at the ordinary period, and must by no means be seen in London when the season is over. We shall be having a monthly publication of the *Modes Réligieuses*, or Pious Fashions, in which we may expect the revival of the Bishop's sleeves, and for those who are fond of wearing something religious, as a cloak, the restoration of the Cardinal.

CONSEQUENCES FOR CANTERS

THE holier any place is, the greater is any sin committed in it.

Suppose it is wrong to derive pleasure from looking at works of Art on a Sunday.

In that case, anybody who goes, on a Sunday, to church, and experiences gratification from the view of any statues that may be contained in the sacred edifice, is evidently guilty of a greater transgression than he would be, if he enjoyed the same kind of spectacle in the Crystal Palace.

If, then, the people are to be forbidden to rejoice in the contemplation of sculpture at Sydenham on the Sunday, they ought also to be debarred from the more heinous indulgence of gazing on the like objects in church.

Accordingly, if the Crystal Palace is shut up on Sundays, all the monuments in St Paul's and Westminster Abbey ought to be veiled, in order that the public may not incur the guilt of looking round at them.

The necessity for this precaution will be more manifest when it is considered that many, and indeed most, of those particular monuments are of an entirely secular character, as the images of the British Lion, and Britannia, or heathen emblems, and even idols; for instance, the figures of Fame and of Neptune; that several of them represent charges of grenadiers and other transactions which are not edifying: finally, that by far the greater portion of them are calculated to excite emotions of levity, being extremely ludicrous.

The Sabbatarians should consider that to cover up these objects would in one sense be a real charity, which is an additional reason why they should try to get it done, before they seek to close against the working people a more innocent exhibition on their only holiday.

'BRUMMAGEM' PIETY

WE learn that a majority of the Members of the Birmingham Town Council have acted recently in such a manner as to render it desirable to have their portraits taken, and sent in to the Association for wholly closing Sunday, as candidates for the Cant Gallery which we hear is in formation. The act by which they have immortalised themselves has been the prohibition of a concert of purely sacred music, which it was proposed to give in their Town Hall on Christmas Day, at prices that would render it accessible by 'the people.' As a sample of the oratory by which they professed to expound their views, and justify their opposition to the leave which was applied for, we are told that –

'One expressed his opinion, that sacred music was not different from polkas, except that it is played slower. Another observed, that he did not individually object to music of any kind, but he didn't like sacred music blown through a trumpet.'

Had it been proposed at this Christmas Concert to perform the Hallelujah Chorus on a pair of bagpipes, we should think this latter gentleman would have not withheld consent to it. His objection, it would seem, is directed not so much against the music as the instrument; and in instancing the trumpet as his particular aversion, he is probably moved by a spirit of rivalry, as he perhaps is in the habit of blowing his own. Now in the bagpipes he in no way need have had such fear of competition; while its tone might in some measure have 'improved the occasion,' by reminding those who heard it of those sermons in drones which we most of us have listened to.

When ears are stopped with the cotton of Cant, they are rendered deaf not only to reason, but to music. However long a fanatic's auriculars may be, he can hear no difference between a psalm tune and a polka, at least if the former be played out of Church-time. Having 'no music in his soul' all music sounds alike to him, whether it be the Handel of the organ-loft or the handle of the street piano; and having himself 'no mind for' it, he compounds for other sinfulness by condemning that as such.

It is a common phrase to speak of articles of doubtful origin as being 'Brummagem' ones. And we think such spurious sanctity as that which would prevent even the music of the Messiah being played on Christmas Day, may be fittingly set down as 'Brummagem' Piety.

A GREAT SUNDAY EXAMPLE, BY
THE ARCHBISHOP OF CANT

CARTOON FOR THE MERCHANT TAILORS

THE novel of Coningsby clearly discloses
The pride of the world are the children of MOSES.
Mosaic, the bankers – the soldiers, the sailors
The statesmen – and so, by-the-by, are the tailors.
Mosaic, the gold – that is worthless and hollow;
Mosaic, the people – the bailiffs that follow.
The new generation – the party that claim
To take to themselves of Young England the name;
In spite of their waistcoats much whiter than snow,
It seems after all are the tribe of Old Clo!
Then where in the world can Young England repair
To purchase the garments it wishes to wear –
Unless to that mart whose success but discloses
The folly of man, and the cunning of MOSES?

Anti-Semitism

Moses and Son attiring Young England

THE TRIUMPH OF MOSES

So the struggle of MOSES is over at last,
The Jews are no more a disqualified caste,
And MOSES will henceforth in Parliament sit,
If either the Lords or the Commons think fit.

In the Commons 'tis certain that MOSES will meet
With no opposition in taking his seat,
Which he'll firmly endeavour with credit to fill,
For economy, measures, materials, and skill.

He will soon make his way with their Lordships, the
    Peers,
As his high reputation will come to their ears,
And I'll warrant they won't shut their doors in his
    face,
If HER MAJESTY makes him the Duke of Duke's Place.

Only think how 'twould be if they didn't give way;
Consider what England and Europe would say:
The Commons and Lords their old titles would lose,
This called House of Christians, and that House of
    Jews!

Then room for LORD MOSES, ye proud Barons, yield,
With his crest on his carriage, and arms on his shield,
And his pedigree, higher than Norman's can run,
And his business – which he can entail on his son.

A Jew to Canterbury

A LITTLE while ago there prevailed among the clergy of the Church of England a mania for going over to Rome. The Sabbatarian ARCHBISHOP OF CANT appears to be travelling in quite another direction. His GRACE has adopted the views of the Judaising fanatics, and we expect every day to hear that our Primate has gone over to Jerusalem.

CHRISTMAS IN THE MINORIES

'I wish you a Merry Christmas.'

MR NEBUCHADNEZZAR. What is there for Dinner, Waiter?
WAITER. Sir, a nice Leg of Pork is just come up.
[NEBUCHADNEZZAR *sits down, and helps himself to pig, crackling, sage and onions and all.*]

A NATION OF ADVERTISERS

ADVERTISEMENTS are spreading all over England, – they have crept under the bridges – have planted themselves right in the middle of the Thames – have usurped the greatest thoroughfares – and are now just on the point of invading the omnibuses. Advertising is certainly the great vehicle for the age. Go where you will, you are stopped by a monster cart running over with advertisements, or are nearly knocked down by an advertising house put upon wheels, which calls upon you, when too late, not to forget 'Number One.' These vehicles, one would think, were more than enough to satisfy the most greedy lover of advertisements, but it seems there is such an extraordinary run for them that omnibuses are to be lined and stuffed with nothing else. How will you like sitting for an hour opposite to a pleasant list of the wonderful cures by some Professor's Ointment? or how will ladies like being stared in the face all the way from Brentford to the Bank, with an elaborate detail of all the diseases which Old Methusaleh's Pill professes to be a specific for? The testimonials of these gifted gentlemen are as little noted for their delicacy as for their truth, and do not form the kind of reading we should exactly prescribe to the fairer portion of the public which patronise omnibuses. Besides, what kind of advertisement is the conductor to refuse? Has he directions to say, when any objectionable advertisement applies for admission, 'Full inside?' Or are all the quack advertisements to be compelled to get outside, like washerwomen and butchers? It matters very little, for the system of resorting to such a vehicle for advertisements, is in our opinion misplaced altogether. We are haunted with advertisements enough in all shapes, tricks, and disguises. The Penny Post has increased the distribution of them most prolifically. Half of our *billets-doux* end with an eloquent appeal to run to some cheap grocer's, and buy a pound of his best Hyson; and the bill-stickers are indefatigable in making known the virtues of every new discovery in strops, drugs, novels, poisons, and 'poses plastiques.' As we have pantomimes, papers, broadsides, circulars, hand-bills, and fashionable stories, for advertising, do in mercy allow us to ride for a day's pleasure to Richmond, or to go to the Bank to receive our dividends, without compelling us to sit *vis-à-vis* to MOSES & SON, or having ROWLAND's Kalydor perpetually thrown in our faces.

Let us be a nation of shopkeepers as much as we please, but there is no necessity that we should become a nation of advertisers. We say most emphatically to the gentlemen who have announced their advertising omnibuses – 'We prefer your room to your Company.'

A LITTLE ELYSIUM

MR GEORGE ROBINS

HAS been honoured with the instructions of the landlord, who is in under an execution for rent, to offer to public competition

ANOTHER LITTLE PARADISE

comprising what he is fully justified in terming

A love of a Villa,

with all its numerous attractions, which entitle it to the name of the

PET PLACE OF THE COUNTY.

The grounds are not in themselves extensive, but the pleasures of imagination, so beautifully set forth by the

POET AKENSIDE,

will realise any extent of additional ground that the purchaser may require as

A VAST FIELD

for the exercise of his fancy. The Villa is placed in the very centre of a vast manufacturing district, and though it has been said that the propinquity of a factory is not always agreeable to the ol-factories, there can be no doubt that in this age of

Free Trade,

it cannot be objectionable to any one to find himself placed amidst the miraculous

WORKSHOPS OF BRITISH INDUSTRY.

Anti-Advertising

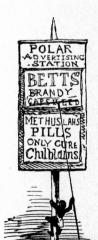

PUSEYITE 'HISTRIONICS'

THEATRE CLERICAL, ST BARNABAS'S, PIMLICO

THE Reverend Proprietor has the honour respectfully to announce that he has established this Temple of the ecclesiastical Drama, with the view, in conjunction with his brother Histrionics, to bring out a SUCCESSION OF NOVELTIES; a designation which it is obviously justifiable to apply to MEDIAEVAL REVIVALS, or the reproduction of MYSTERIES, which, until recently, have never been acted in any AUTHORISED ESTABLISHMENT in this country since the Reformation. To-morrow, and during the week, the Performances will commence with the Farce of

MOCK-MATINS; OR, MONKS IN MASQUERADE

In which the REV. MR BENEDICT BAM *will introduce his celebrated Italian Imitations.*

To be followed by a Grand Romanesque Melodramatic Spectacle, entitled

THE SERVICE IN DISGUISE;
OR, THE MYSTERIOUS MOUNTEBANKS.

With new and startling Effects of Scenery, Dresses and Decorations.

The whole of the Music by PROFESSORS GREGORY AND AMBROSE.

This extraordinary Piece, on the getting up of which no exertion has been spared, will include an imposing display of

SERIOUS PANTOMIME;

as certain portions of the Performance will be gone through in DUMB SHOW, realising to the imagination of the Audience

THE MAGNIFICENCE OF THE ROMAN RITUAL!

and it is confidently asserted that the DELUSION will be COMPLETE. The REV MR BAM will perform the celebrated feat of reading various Passages

WITH HIS BACK TO THE AUDIENCE;

and by way of improving upon ordinary summersets, the REV MR HOAKES will cut a series of right angles in the air. The novel trick of

SHIFTING THE LECTERN,

will be introduced by that celebrated illusionist, the REV MR COZENS, who also, together with the REV MESSRS HUMMALL, CHEEKS, and GREENER will exhibit a variety of

ECCLESIASTICAL POSES PLASTIQUES!!

Fully equal in point of attraction to the most remarkable spectacle of the kind ever witnessed in the genuine

HALL OF ROME!!

The Text, instead of being spoken, will be delivered in recitative, varied by the introduction of solos and choruses, for which latter, an efficient corps of choristers has been engaged; and MR BENEDICT BAM will give his favourite *preghiere* in his admired *sotto voce* style. The Effects will comprise the thrilling incident of a

TERRIFIC APPEARANCE IN THE WHITE SURPLICE,

By a Reverend Gentleman, who will deliver an impressive recitation; and the piece will terminate with a

GRAND CHORAL FINALE.

Religious Capers

THE BISHOP'S WISH

BE mine a modest pension clear
Of just six thousand pounds a-year;
And to complete my humble lot,
Give Fulham Palace for my cot.
Let me enjoy a quiet life,
Away from controversial strife;
My daily meal should ne'er disturb
My tranquil mind! for meat or herb,
Or fish or fowl, I ne'er would look,
But leave it to my foreign cook.
My drink – I ask no better sort,
A bin of six-and-twenty port;
With now and then, to warm my veins,
Some Burgundy or brisk Champagnes.
Of cash I need no large amount,
But at a Bank a good account,
On which – (my tradesmen not to vex) –
To draw from time to time my cheques.
My simple wishes thus supplied,
I into privacy will glide:
My Bishop's mitre I'll resign,
And calm contentment shall be mine,
If they will only give me clear
For life – six thousand pounds a-year.

THE NEW OXFORD COSTUME
An Undergraduate going to Lecture

THE GUY FAWKES OF 1850
Preparing to blow up all England!

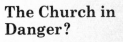

THE THIN END OF THE WEDGE
Daring attempt to break into a church

RELIGION À LA MODE
MR BULL. 'No, no, Mr Jack Priest! After all I have gone through, I'm not such a fool as to stand any of this disgusting nonsense!'

Going to Church

THE TWO CHURCHES

THE NEW

'Tis Sunday at our watering-place by the broad blue
    German Ocean;
The streets are still, the sands are bare, the cliffs
    forlorn and bleak;
The fly-boys and fly-horses have a pause in their
    devotion,
    For if to labour be to pray, they've been praying all
    the week.
A Sabbath stillness reigneth over earth and sea and
    sky,
    All Nature round has gone to Church, so wherefore
    should not I?

The crack Church at our watering-place is very fine
    and new;
Pure Gothic down to *reredos*, and *sedilia*, and *piscina*;
With poppy-heads on open seats – we scorn the
    cushioned pew –
    And our curate he intoneth, so that nothing can be
    finer;
And we've candles on the altar, and occasionally
    flowers –
In short, a small ST BARNABAS is this new Church of
    ours.

'So primitive!' our Curate says – 'so truly Apostolic!
    No Protestant distinctions of private seats and free!
Each portion of the building has significance
    symbolic:'
    Though, save the poppy-heads, nought's significant
    to me.
Their soporific meaning is clearly to be seen,
Thanks to the comment furnished by the sleeping
    heads between.

But finer than our fine new Church – tiles, altar-cloth,
    and all, –
    The gules, and or, and azure on nave and chancel-
    pane, –
And early-English lettering emblazoned on the wall, –
    Are the 'miserable sinners' whom these open seats
    contain:
Oh! the cloud of summer-muslins – oh! the flowered
    and beaded show
Of tiny summer bonnets, in gorgeous row on row!

Oh! cherry lips, and rosy cheeks, and glossy braided
    hair,
    Crowned with dancing, dancing bugles, and flowers
    of myriad dyes!
The Curate he intoneth, but what thought have I for
    prayer,
    'Mid the rustle of the crinolines, the flashing of the
    eyes?
Are these miserable sinners, come for prayer, and
    praise, and psalm,
Or an animated series from *Le Courrier des Dames*?

And the Rector takes his text, and is eloquent upon it –
    How that 'all things here are vanity, and swiftly
    pass away;'
And each lady scans the pattern of her neighbour's
    gown or bonnet,
    And each gentleman's a critic of toilettes for the day.
And out I come, much edified, 'mid the organ's solemn
    swells,
With a lively sense how much I owe to these 'church-
    going belles.'

68

'TIS Sunday at the village that lies three miles away;
  A pleasant morning's walk from our watering-place
    'twill be:
So I'll leave our bran-new Gothic Church, and service
  for the day,
  Our hotels and lodging-houses, with their fine views
    of the sea;
And for watering-place gay toilettes, and watering-
  place church belles,
Content myself with field-flowers – coy beauties of the
  dells.

The Old Church at the village is very damp and small:
  And the house-leek and the moss clothe its low-
    pitched roof with green;
And the inside has no primitive symbolism at all –
  Nor *reredos*, nor *sedilia*, nor *piscina*'s to be seen;
And 'tis blocked up with a gallery, and desecrate with
  pews,
And it shrinks back, grey and shabby, behind its
  churchyard yews.

No painted window casteth a dim religious light:
  No encaustic MINTON-tiling hides the damp and
    broken floor:
The Creed and Ten Commandments are in modern
  letters quite:
  On hard and narrow free-seats, sit the humble
    village poor:
But the 'miserable sinners' those narrow seats within,
Show more misery than our watering-place M.S., if not
  more sin.

But through the open porch comes the sweet, sweet
  summer air,
  And the rustle of the churchyard trees blends
    sweetly with the psalm,
And their ever-moving shadow chequers each
  pavement-square,
  And all about the humble place there broods a holy
    calm;
And crinolines and flounces, beads and bugles are
  unknown:
So I sit and stilly worship, as if I were alone.

Till I hear a sigh beside me and a smothered sound of
  prayer –
  And turning, with bowed head and clasped fingers,
    at my side,
Of a miserable sinner I am suddenly aware –
  An old dame in poke bonnet, and scanty cloak
    new-dyed:
And I thought how such a spectacle, in that New
  Church of ours,
  Would jar with bran new symbols, and bugles, beads,
    and flowers!

And I felt how these two Churches, and their
  worshippers agree;
  Tiles, glass, and chanting curate, flowery altar,
    painted stone,
With rustling crinolines, beads and bugles flashing
  free,
  And this poor old village church with that still and
    stooping crone:
And in spite of pews and gallery, low roof, and
  windows bare,
I was somehow nearer Heaven in that lowly house of
  prayer.

Genteel Christianity

THE dear delicious *Court Circular* contains the
following announcement: –

  'The Bishop of London held a confirmation on
Maunday Thursday, of the *juvenile nobility and gentry*,
in the Chapel Royal, St James's. HIS ROYAL HIGHNESS
THE DUKE OF CAMBRIDGE was present. About thirty of
the juvenile nobility and gentry were confirmed. The
EARL OF RIPON and the COUNTESS OF JERSEY were
among the nobility present.'

Who can say the church is in danger after this?

AGRICULTURAL REVELS

THE *Northampton Herald* reports, that at the late meeting of the Northamptonshire Agricultural Association, MR STAFFORD, in proposing the health of 'The Agricultural Labourers of England,' made the following candid remarks:—

'The labourer asked as much for his labour as he could get for it, and the employer engaged that labour for as small a sum as he could. That was a hard bargain in which there was no question of feeling cherished, but simply a transaction of commerce and barter; but undeterred by that severe bargain, the agriculturists still drank to the prosperity of the agricultural labourer.'

According to the journal just quoted, the toast was received with loud cheers; the reporter, however, does not state that it was succeeded by a song, with the appropriate title of

DRINK THE LABOURER!

Drink the labourer; drink the swain,
Through whose toil we reap our grain,
Rear our oxen, sheep, and swine,
By whose means we've got this wine.

Drink him; and observe that he
Should be drunk with three times three,
Of the labourer's hire a sign,
Meaning weekly shillings nine.

Drink him; in a sense 'tis true
That we absolutely do;
That, whereby we cut him short,
Forms a portion of our port.

Claret too, champagne, and hock:
Drink the fellow in the smock!
Drink him; nay you must do so
If you drink his health or no.

Drink him, farmers, in your wealth,
Shall we say we drink his health?
Yes; for toil and scanty fare
Do the labourer's health impair.

Drink his health; but, as we do,
Let him drink his own health too,
Health, imbibed with wholesome beer,
Lest we drink it all out here.

THE COTTAGE

MR PUNCH (*to Landlord*). 'Your stable arrangements are excellent! Suppose you try something of the sort here! Eh?'

THE STRIKE, A SUBJECT FOR THE CONSIDERATION
OF THE REAL WORKING MAN

COMMITTEE MAN AND GENERAL TALKER. 'What I say, my boy, is – Hold out! Hold out – and we'll soon bring the Masters to their Senses!'

WORKER. 'Ah! It's all very well for *you* to hold out – *you* live at a Public House, and get plenty to eat and to drink – meantime, *we* are next to *Starving*!'

but he warns
Strikers that
they will hurt
only themselves,
and criticises
their Leaders

EFFECTS OF A STRIKE
upon the Capitalist and upon the Working Man

PITY THE GREAT UNEMPLOYED

GOOD people here thus to appear exposed to public view,
Ashamed, indeed, we feel; but need compels us so to do.
Sad is our case, we're out of place, of salary devoid,
Commiserate our painful state, and pity the Unemployed.

We hope and pray you never may know what it is to go
Without a berth in times of dearth, whereby we are brought low.
Work could we find we should not mind; we should be overjoyed.
We would turn to, we promise you; then pity the Unemployed.

'Tis near five years since we poor Peers, and Commoners distressed,
Have touched red tape in any shape, of office dispossessed;
'Tis long to wait in such a state, with hope almost destroyed.
Which way to turn we can't discern, so pity the Unemployed.

We gladly would take what we could, although the smallest job;
The truth we speak, we do not seek the public purse to rob.
There is a lot by that garotte that people have annoyed:
But don't suppose we're such as those; and pity the Unemployed.

Of elbows out we go about and toes come through our boots:
We only ask to have a task, according as it suits,
Dishonesty is that which we are anxious to avoid.
Then labour give that we may live, and pity the Unemployed.

A Premier good there's one you could, to your advantage make;
Another for the Chancellor of your Exchequer take.
Affairs to mend we do intend, and by the hope we're buoyed,
That you will try us by and by, and pity the Unemployed.

THE HOMELESS POOR
'Ah! We're badly off – but just think of the poor middle classes, who are obliged to eat roast mutton and boiled fowl every day!'

III
THE SCALPEL
OF REFORM

'Our once Facetious Contemporary is by no means
Funny this Week.' [*Vide* BRIGHT, *in his Great Political
Organ, the* 'Morning Star.'

THE 'MILK' OF POOR-LAW 'KINDNESS'

THE 'BRITISH LABOURER'
AT ANDOVER

**A Poor Law
Case History**

I'M STEPHEN WITCHER, labouring man – of Andover I
   be,
A pauper of the workhouse, and a cripple in the knee;
The Guardians there have sent me out, here, in the
   cold and rain,
To zit all day, a breakin' stones in agony and pain.

I've arn'd my living honestly and fairly all my life,
And zo, till lately, did suppoort a vamily and wife;
I broke my thigh some time agoo, but still I struggled
   on,
Notwithstandun that 'a left me wi' a 'largement o' the
   bone.

But, twelvemonths gone come Christmas, I was cuttin'
   of a tree,
When, by ill luck, my axe did slip, and open laid my
   knee;
The neighbours put me in a cart and took me whoam
   to bed,
Wherefrom 'twas full five months afore I lifted up my
   head.

Lame as I was, I couldn't work; zo what was I to do?
Unto the Boord o' Guardians I at last was foced to goo.
'Oh! WITCHER,' says the Chairman – he's a parson, I
   should say –
'We'll relieve you for a vortnight, but no longer – not
   one day.

'For when that time is up, you must turn to at breakun'
   stones.'
'Why, Sir,' says I, 'you can't tell what I suffers in my
   bones;
If I do but put my foot to ground it pierces to the
   heart.'
'We aint got nought to do wi' that,' he says, and bids
   me start.

Then I went unto the Doctor, for to beg and pray of he
For to spake a word o' kindness to the gentlemen for
   me –
For my wife and little children's sake some pity to
   beseech:
He said he shouldn't alter. That was MR DOCTOR'S
   speech.

Zo then I went to CAPTAIN POORE, an order for to beg
For the Hospital at Winchester, to cure my dreadful
   leg:
The Captain – thank him kindly – took and wrote un
   then and there,
By which means I got admitted under MUSTER MAYO'S
   care.

Five weeks I bid in hospital, and there I had, I'll own,
The very best o' tendance and o' skill as could be
   shown;
But, erysip'las breakin' out, as I was ill and wake
They zent me whoam again, for fear the 'fection I
   should take.

I left wi' a certificat from DOCTOR MAYO'S hand
(Long life to un), which gave the Union Boord to
   understand
I wanted warmth and nourishment, in clothin' and in
   food,
If ever they expected for to do me any good.

To the workhouse on my crutches then I hobbled back
   again,
And begg'd and pray'd for mercy, but my words was
   all in vain;
So here be I a crackin' stones in misery and grief,
And this here treatment's what they calls their
   'System of Relief.'

Oh! gentle folks, I don't purtend to be a larned man,
But I've lately had the newspeapers read to me now
   and tan,
Them goins on in Vrance, I thinks, should tache ye to
   beware
How ye drives the lower classes, as ye calls us, to
   despair.

Think well upon't, ye Lords and Squires, and rulers o'
   the land:
As 'tis, there baint much love that's lost between us,
   understand;
The time may come when you may wish that you had
   know'd afore,
That kindness is the only means of keepun down the
   poor.

SEVENPENCE IN THE POUND

THERE were many long faces on Saturday morning. Thousands of respectable philanthropic folks, who had long felt their hearts bleeding and breaking for the distress of their fellow-creatures – who had groaned at the miseries of Bolton, shuddered at the horrors of Paisley, and with the most animated benevolence declared that something must be done for the poor – thousands of these Good Samaritans, whose faith was in Sir ROBERT PEEL and the 'elastic resources of the country,' might be seen on Saturday morning with astonishment in their faces, their jaws dropped down to their waistcoats, and their breeches-pockets gaping with horror! Sir ROBERT had been already burnt in effigy in a hundred parts of the country; but on Saturday morning there were thousands of worshippers who degraded the Minister from the pedestal of their affections – who reviled him as the arch-enemy of all their creature-comforts, all their 'most domestic' happiness. It was very true that something must be done for the poor; but then not at the expense of the 'respectable' middle classes. . . .

'No, no – *now* I give up Sir ROBERT PEEL – I've done with him for ever,' cried many a staunch Tory on Saturday, as he felt the sevenpence oozing away from every sovereign in his pocket – 'I thought he was a great man – a very great man – an *honest* man; – but – an income tax! – I've done with him!' Friday's sun rose upon Sir Robert as the tutelary genius of England: in his right hand he held the golden key of abundance. Saturday came, and the Prime Minister was the despoiler of men's cupboards; for the key had fallen from his grasp, and in his hand was a mortal pistol, whereon was written – *Income Tax!*

We must at least give Sir ROBERT PEEL this praise: he has looked a great evil boldly in the face, and has proposed an unpopular but sufficing remedy. We know it is asked – Why should we not have a Property Tax? Why should the burden fall disproportionately on the man of limited means, the rich being in comparison free of taxation? Let us suppose the Bishop of EXETER (modern apostle as he is) had in the House of Lords moved that his brother Peers, spiritual and temporal, should sell all they have, and give the money to the poor: by what majority does the reader imagine the motion would have been agreed to? We believe, by precisely the same majority that would agree to a Property Tax.

When we consider the present constitution of the House of Commons – when we know that it in no way represents the feelings of the people; that it is as much the emanation of the will and sympathies of the citizens of Timbuctoo as of the men of England – when we find an assembly of lawgivers, by their very education and social prejudices, insensible of the rights of an enlarged humanity, – all of them resolved into petty knots, cut up into small sections, intent and vigorous upon the advocacy of the selfishness of a conflicting few to the disadvantage of all else beside; – when we are daily and hourly taught this melancholy, sordid truth, by the acts of our so-called representatives, can any one – not worthy of a cell in Bedlam – hope a Property Tax from the wisdom and self-devotion of the House of Commons?

Awaiting the advent of this golden time, we are disposed to hail the measure of Sir ROBERT PEEL as one of enlarged statesmanship – as one calculated to lessen an evil, from the contemplation of which humanity turns away sickened and humiliated. There is much blundering selfishness abroad, whose 'horny eyes' will see nothing in the measure save the spoliation of 'respectability' for the questionable benevolence of permanently relieving the lower classes. We can perfectly understand Respectability, seated in his back parlour, with rump-steak and foaming pot of porter, in his disappointment of PEEL, calling down all sorts of mischief on the head of the traitor Minister. We can understand how the said Respectability really believes the national distress to be 'very much over-rated, and that things would right themselves, without any such abominable measure as an Income Tax.' . . .

We take the Income Tax as a portion of the whole – a tax on Property must follow; but then we must have a different House of Commons, a much-reformed House of Peers. We may return to this subject in our next. In the mean time, in the name of suffering thousands, we thank Sir ROBERT PEEL. We thank him, and are not ashamed to own that he has disappointed us, and that most agreeably.   Q.

AN INCOME-TAX APOLOGIST (WANTED)

THE income-tax for ever! We do not mean this for a shout, but a groan. SIR ROBERT PEEL means to try it on for three more years, and assuredly he will never try it off. As certainly as the hump of *Mr Punch* will remain a fixture on his shoulders till doomsday, so will this burden on those of MR JOHN BULL. Well; it is a necessary evil, and we must submit to it. There is nothing like content and resignation. No; and unfortunately there will be nothing like them in the community as long as Industry and Capital pay sevenpence a-piece. A deplorable opinion prevails, that to tax the poor man's earnings equally with the rich man's wealth, is an unjust, wicked, villanous, abominable shame; a gross, intolerable, monstrous imposition. Such are the hard words which the people, in their ignorance, apply to this mode of taxation. . . .

The Income Tax: a necessary Evil

THE SONG OF THE SHIRT

**A famous Page
by Thomas Hood
(1843)**

WITH fingers weary and worn,
   With eyelids heavy and red,
A Woman sat, in unwomanly rags,
   Plying her needle and thread –
      Stitch! stitch! stitch!
In poverty, hunger, and dirt,
   And still with a voice of dolorous pitch
She sang the 'Song of the Shirt!'

   'Work! work! work!
While the cock is crowing aloof!
   And work – work – work,
Till the stars shine through the roof!
   It's O! to be a slave
      Along with the barbarous Turk,
Where woman has never a soul to save,
   If this is Christian work!

   'Work – work – work
Till the brain begins to swim;
   Work – work – work
Till the eyes are heavy and dim!
   Seam, and gusset, and band,
      Band, and gusset, and seam,
         Till over the buttons I fall asleep,
And sew them on in a dream!

"O! Men, with Sisters dear!
   O! men! with Mothers and Wives!
It is not linen you're wearing out,
   But human creatures' lives!
      Stitch – stitch – stitch,
   In poverty, hunger, and dirt,
Sewing at once, with a double thread,
   A Shroud as well as a Shirt.

'But why do I talk of Death?
   That Phantom of grisly bone,
I hardly fear his terrible shape,
   It seems so like my own –
      It seems so like my own,
      Because of the fasts I keep,
Oh! God! that bread should be so dear,
   And flesh and blood so cheap!

'Work – work – work!
   My labour never flags;
And what are its wages? A bed of straw,
   A crust of bread – and rags.

That shatter'd roof – and this naked floor –
   A table – a broken chair –
And a wall so blank, my shadow I thank
   For sometimes falling there!

   'Work – work – work!
From weary chime to chime,
   Work – work – work –
As prisoners work for crime!
   Band, and gusset, and seam,
      Seam, and gusset, and band,
Till the heart is sick, and the brain benumb'd,
   As well as the weary hand.

   'Work – work – work,
In the dull December light,
   And work – work – work,
When the weather is warm and bright –
While underneath the eaves
   The brooding swallows cling
As if to show me their sunny backs
   And twit me with the spring.

   'Oh! but to breathe the breath
Of the cowslip and primrose sweet –
   With the sky above my head,
And the grass beneath my feet,
For only one short hour
   To feel as I used to feel,
Before I knew the woes of want
   And the walk that costs a meal!

'Oh but for one short hour!
   A respite however brief!
No blessed leisure for Love or Hope,
   But only time for Grief!
A little weeping would ease my heart,
   But in their briny bed
My tears must stop, for every drop
   Hinders needle and thread!'

With fingers weary and worn,
   With eyelids heavy and red,
A Woman sate in unwomanly rags,
   Plying her needle and thread –
      Stitch! stitch! stitch!
   In poverty, hunger, and dirt,
And still with a voice of dolorous pitch,
Would that its tone could reach the Rich!
   She sang this 'Song of the Shirt!'

A 'WARM, WOOLLEN PRISON DRESS'

JOHN MATTHEWS was recently discharged from Brinkworth Gaol, Wiltshire; he having been committed there for two months for desertion of his wife and children. That is, the man went to Wales, to obtain work, leaving his wife and children in the workhouse. He was unsuccessful in his attempt to be employed – no shirking idler, be it remembered – he returned to the workhouse, and was sent to gaol. In this way, in some places in merry England, does Justice play the grim mountebank! The man was discharged in the late bitter cold weather.

'He was most miserably clad, having exchanged his *warm, woollen prison dress* for his own clothes – mere rags; the upper garments consisting of an old waistcoat and a thin slop. He was also suffering from a diseased heart, a complaint of long standing!'

The end is soon told. He had no money; he took shelter in a hovel near the road, where there happened to be some straw.

'Here, according to his own account, he remained from the *Wednesday evening till the Monday morning,* during a most intense frost, and having nothing to eat except the remaining portion of the loaf which was given him on leaving the prison.'

On the Wednesday afternoon the man was conveyed to the Malmesbury Union, his feet being so badly frost-bitten, that the surgeon declared he *must lose them!* The man died on the Saturday. His wife, on the inquest, said that he 'had always been kind towards her and the child, *was a sober man,* and brought his earnings home, when able to work.' The jury returned the following verdict:—

'That deceased died from the inclemency of the weather, and the jury are of opinion, that disease of the heart, *and sudden exposure to cold on leaving the prison with insufficient clothing,* rendered him peculiarly susceptible to its effects.'

And thus it is proved to a bold peasantry, a country's pride, that it is better to endure, with all its ignominy, 'a warm, woollen *prison dress,'* than to seek, by the honest employment of their energies, the comfortable clothing of a free labourer. In the one case he is well-fed, and well-clothed; in the other, he is starved, and dies with gangrened legs, the victim of 'bitter weather.'

A TRIFLE FROM BRIGHTON

I TOOK the train to Brighton – I walked beside the sea,
And thirty thousand Londoners were there along with me.
We crowded every lodging, and we lumbered each hotel,
Sniff'd the briny for an appetite, and dined extremely well.

The Cliff it shows like Regent Street come down for the sea-air;
Not in Hyde Park's self do ladies more becoming bonnets wear;
In enchanted 'upper circles' one seems to move about,
When the sunshine brings the flies and private equipages out.

To Brighton the Pavilion lends a lath-and-plaster grace –
Fit shrine for fittest God of this pleasant watering place;
And against the show and shallowness, the vanity and glee,
With his hollow, hushless murmur, comes up the solemn Sea.

I sat there in the Bedford, and in the *Times* I read
Of the West Riding Canvass, and a thought came in my head:
How England's one Great Brighton – we all so rich and gay,
While at our feet and in our face a sea comes up alway.

Our wealth is vast, our gains grow fast, we are dealers fair and free;
Our goods tempt every market, our ships plough every sea;
Our lords are great, our traders true, our priests good men and grave,
Our women fair, our sailors staunch, our soldiers blunt and brave.

We have a brilliant lot for some, a bustling lot for all;
Our hold on life seems manful, our fear of evil small;
But underneath this surface, with all its strength and shine,
The hoarse and heaving sea of toil doth chafe, and moan, and mine.

For I saw how in that Canvass, were it Whig or were it Tory
That talked to the Electors, it was always the same story:
Whate'er the hustings said in praise, or self-congratulation,
Produced a comment from the crowd of aught but approbation.

It was Capital a-preaching, out of plump and prosperous men,
And Labour's hundred hungry throats refusing their 'Amen:'
When Riches mentioned 'Industry,' Rags answered with 'Despair,'
And Fustian rapp'd a curse out, when Broadcloth talked of prayer.

I dropped the *Times* to look upon the Cliff with all its life,
And that stern sea, that now 'gan curl its white waves as for strife –
And I felt to seek for appetite from the briny, 'twas in vain,
And so took my place for London by the earliest fast train.

PUNCH'S COMMISSION TO INQUIRE INTO THE GENERAL DISTRESS

Punch calls himself the Commissioner for Everywhere

I. – *Copy of a Letter from the Under Secretary of State to Punch.*

Downing-street.

SIR, – Knowing that you are everywhere, the Secretary of State has desired me to request you will inquire into the alleged distress, and particularly into the fact of people who it is alleged are so unreasonable in their expectations of food, as to die because they cannot get any. I have the honour to be, &c.

HORATIO FITZ-SPOONY

II. – *Copy of Punch's Letter to the Under Secretary of State.*

SIR, – I have received your note. I am everywhere; but as everything is gay when I make my appearance, I have not seen much of the distress you speak of. I shall, however, make it my business to look the subject up, and will convey my report to the Government.

I think it no honour to be yours, &c.; but I have the very great honour to be myself without any &c. PUNCH

In compliance with the above correspondence, Punch proceeded to make the necessary inquiries, and very soon was enabled to forward the following

REPORT ON THE PUBLIC DISTRESS
To Her Majesty's Secretary of State for the Home Department.

SIR, – In compliance with my undertaking to inquire into the public distress, I went into the manufacturing districts, where I had heard that several families were living in one room with nothing to eat, and no bed to lie upon. Now, though it is true that there are in some places as many as thirty people in one apartment, I do not think their case very distressing, because, at all events, they have the advantage of society, which could not be the case if they were residing in separate apartments. It is clear that their living together must be a matter of choice, because I found in the same town several extensive mansions inhabited by one or two people and few servants; and there are also some hundreds of houses wholly untenanted. Now, if we multiply the houses by the rooms in them, and then divide by the number of the population, we should find that there will be an average of three attics and two-sitting-rooms for each family of five persons, or an attic and a half with one parlour for every two and a half individuals; and though one person and a half would find it inconvenient to occupy a sleeping room and three-quarters, I think my calculation will show you that the accounts of the insufficiency of lodging are gross and wicked exaggerations, only spread by designing persons to embarrass the Government.

With regard to the starvation part of the question, I have made every possible inquiry, and it is true that several people have died because they would not eat food; for the facts I shall bring to your notice will prove that no one can have perished from the *want* of it. Now, after visiting a family, which I was told were in a famishing state, what was my surprise to observe a baker's shop exactly opposite their lodging, whilst a short way down the street there was a butcher's also! The family consisted of a husband and wife, four girls, eight boys, and an infant of three weeks old, making in all fifteen individuals. They told me they were literally dying of hunger, and that they had applied to the vestry, who had referred them to the guardians, who had referred them to the overseer, who had referred them to the relieving officer, who had gone out of town, and would be back in a week or two. Now even supposing there were a brief delay in attending to their case, at least by the proper authorities, you will perceive that I have already alluded to a baker's and a butcher's, *both* (it will scarcely be believed at the Home-office) in the *very street* the family were residing in. Being determined to judge for myself, I counted personally the number of four-pound loaves in the baker's window, which amounted to thirty-six, while there were twenty-five two-pound loaves on the shelves, to say nothing of fancy-bread and flour *ad libitum*. But let us take the loaves alone.

pounds, multiplied by | 36 loaves, each weighing four
4

will give | 144 pounds of wheaten bread;
To which must be added | 50 pounds (the weight of the 25 half-qtns.),

Making a total of | 194 pounds of good wholesome bread,

which, if divided amongst a family of fifteen, would give 12 pounds and 14 fractions of a pound to each individual. Knocking off the baby, for the sake of uniformity, and striking out the mother, both of whom might be supposed to take the fancy bread and the flour, which I have not included in my calculation, and in order to get even numbers, supposing that 194 pounds of bread might become 195 pounds by over weight, we should get the enormous quantity of fifteen full pounds weight of bread, or a stone and one-fourteenth, (more, positively, than anybody ought to eat), for the husband and each of the children (except the baby, who gets a moiety of the rolls) belonging to this *starving family!!!* You will see, Sir, how shamefully matters have been misrepresented by the Anti-Corn-Law demagogues; but let us now come to the butcher's meat.

It will hardly be credited that I counted no less than fourteen sheep hanging up in the shop I have alluded to, while there was a bullock being skinned in the back yard, and a countless quantity of liver and lights all over the premises. Knocking off the infant again for the sake of uniformity, you will perceive that the fourteen sheep would be one sheep each for every member of this family, including the mother, to whom we gave half the rolls and flour in the former case, and there still remains (to say nothing of the entire bullock for the baby of three weeks, which no one will deny to be sufficient) a large quantity of lights, et cetera, for the cat or dog, if there should be such a wilful extravagance in the family. With these facts I close my report, and I trust that you will see how thoroughly I have proved the assertion of the Duke of Wellington – that if there is distress, it must be in some way quite unconnected with a want of food, for there is plenty to eat in every part of the country.

I shall be happy to undertake further inquiries, and shall have no objection to consider myself regularly under Government.

Yours obediently,   PUNCH.

FUSTIAN JACKETS!

IN merry England, labour is ignominy. Your only man is the man with white hands and filbert nails. Adam himself, though soiled with the sweat of Paradise, loses his dignity in his labour. This is a doctrine preached from all the high places of England; enforced by public door-keepers and small park rangers. True respectability lives and grows fat upon the labour of others; it being the more respectable in proportion to the number of hands that feed it. He who digs, or hews, or spins, is a varlet; he who profits by the work, the true man.

In the House of Commons, only a night or two since, Mr C. BULLER adduced a new illustration of this truth. He said the keepers of St James's Park were particularly ordered 'not to admit persons who wore fustian jackets.'

The Earl of LINCOLN replied: 'Men *in their working-dresses* might very well go along the Birdcage-walk.'

Surely, here is a sufficient provision for the pedestrian wants of labour; it may not, if in its working dress, intrude upon the greensward of St James's, but it may, 'like a guilty thing,' slink along the Birdcage-walk; or, as the Earl humanely added, 'the other outer passages.' The fustian jacket is a social abomination – the livery of ignominious labour, and only to be suffered with due discretion to approach the precincts of the royal palace. Is it the Earl of LINCOLN's fault if labouring men will persist in wearing the objectionable habit? Is the Earl to be blamed if carpenters, plumbers, house-painters, and others, will obstinately refuse to do their daily work in superfine Saxony?

However, it is gratifying to know that the labouring man has sometimes his honours. At the recent Agricultural Meeting, held at Bristol, the 'health of the labourer' was drunk. There was no one labourer present – not even a sample of the animal at a side-table. Neither do we hear that any dinner has been provided for him by the meeting in his own county. Of this, however, we are assured – his health was drunk!

A FRONT FOR A WORKHOUSE

THE Guardians of the Highworth and Swindon Union, Wiltshire, have advertised for tenders for the erection of a new Workhouse. There is much wit in this announcement; for the word Tender, in connexion with the word Workhouse, is an apt association of incongruous ideas. Anybody who can build a Gaol can also build a Workhouse; but *Punch*, not having devoted his attention to Prison-Architecture, is afraid that he could hardly plan one that would be sufficiently uncomfortable. As far, however, as a façade goes, of a fanciful and ornamental character, he has a few hints, available in the erection of any such edifice, which are quite at the advertisers' service:–

Let the façade be of the plainest Doric pillars supporting an entablature. Instead of ox-skulls, let the frieze be decorated with sheep-skulls – to express the richest order of broth to be expected within. Above these let there be certain sculptures, emblematical of the nature and internal economy – which is very strict – of the building. For conspicuousness' sake, these might be carved in high relief; notwithstanding the objection that the relief given to the inmates is the reverse of high. As to subjects, those which present themselves most strongly to the mind of *Punch*, are, – Discipline as a Beadle, allowancing Poverty with gruel; Mercy shaving a pauper's head; and Political Economy, in the form of the Home Secretary, separating man and wife.

HINTS TO VISITING AND RELIEF SOCIETIES

HAVING entered a poor person's dwelling, behave as if it were your own. Do not wait to be asked to sit down. If you are a gentleman keep your hat on.

Address the male occupant of the house as 'My Good Man,' and his wife as 'My Good Woman;' or if you find it necessary to assert your dignity, omit the 'Good' altogether. Say 'Boy,' and 'Girl,' to the children, as the case may be. Your first object is, to impress the visited with a due sense of their distance from yourself. For this reason, if they remain standing in your presence, never suggest that they should sit. . . .

Make them tell you what they do with their rags; and how they are situated in regard to soap. Insist on being minutely informed how each of the family spends every portion of his or her time; and animadvert strongly on any application thereof to rest or recreation.

Having read the whole round of them a severe homily on any imprudence or mismanagement of their household and affairs that you may have elicited, give them, provided they appear sufficiently abashed, a ticket for sixpennyworth of relief, accompanied by a penny tract. Let your gift be made with an air of lofty condescension; retire majestically, and go home to your three courses and dessert.

Fustian

Superfine Saxon

CAPITAL AND LABOUR

CARTOON NO. V

The Social System

It is gratifying to know that though there is much misery in the coalmines, where the 'labourers are obliged to go on all-fours like dogs,' there is a great deal of luxury results from it. The public mind has been a good deal shocked by very offensive representations of certain underground operations, carried on by an inferior race of human beings, employed in working the mines, but *Punch's* artist has endeavoured to do away with the disagreeable impression, by showing the very refined and elegant result that happily arises from the labours of these inferior creatures. The works being performed wholly under ground, ought never to have been intruded on the notice of the public. They are not intended for the light of day, and it is therefore unfair to make them the subject of illustration. When taken in conjunction with the very pleasing picture of aristocratic ease to which they give rise, the labours in the mines must have a very different aspect from that which some injudicious writers have endeavoured to attach to them.

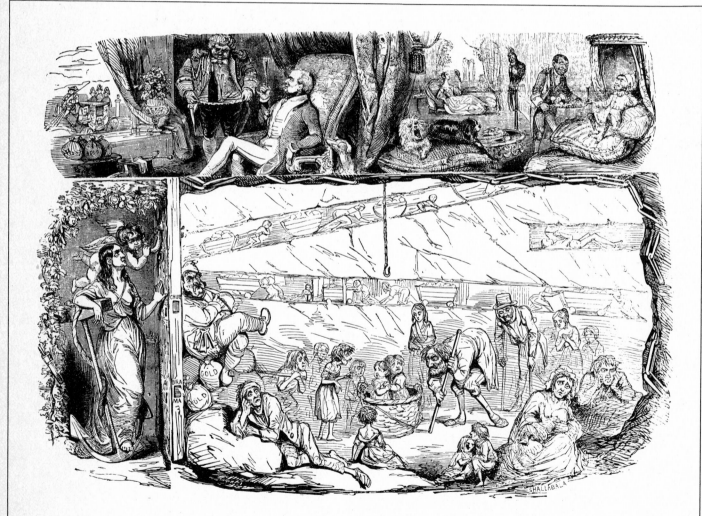

CAPITAL AND LABOUR

ELBOW-ROOM

Listen, and mark you press that wedged in close
    discomfort stands,
Where Labour thrusts on Capital a crowd of craving
    hands,
Where Capital itself is cramped, till stagnant stands
    the gold,
That thro' its limbs, with room to stir, a living tide
    had rolled.

No air to breathe, but at the price – a buffet for a
    breath;
No space to spare, but what lays bare the scythe of
    Mower Death.
Each foot must tread some fellow's head, or heart, or
    heel, at best,
With smiting hands for helpful, and restlessness for
    rest.

'Tis England, full and over full! True – fertile is her
    soil,
But all its growth, trod out by those that have no room
    to toil:
Hearts may be oak, and sinews steel, and arms of
    Saxon pith:
There's work enow for these to win bare standing-room
    therewith.

Look, where a steam of filthy life the breath of
    summer taints,
Where o'er day and night-long shuttle the hand-loom
    weaver faints;
Where plies the skinny stockinger his labour till he
    drops;
And the grinder drinks Consumption from the wheel
    that never stops;

Where mothers turn from mothers' cares to earn a
    niggard dole;
Where Infancy must toil to eke the household's scanty
    whole;
Where for hours the little trapper crouches darkling
    in the mine,
Nor, save when comes the Sabbath, sees the blessed
    daylight shine;

Where diggers and where delvers, with due sweat of
    the brow,
May scantly earn their meed of bread from acres that
    they plough;
Whereon outworn Labour, gloomily to close a life of
    gloom,
Waits, certain, Workhouse dotage, Parish-shell, and
    Pauper tomb.

Or this the only wretchedness of field, or mine, or mill:
There's starvation that must smite and wear its black
    coat bravely still;
The thread-bare Usher, hawking all about his useless
    store,
Glad, for the sorriest mess, to sell his heritage of lore.

The Barrister who thro' the Courts, sore pinched and
    ill at ease,
Hollow of cheek and bag alike, still hopes for hopeless
    fees;
The College-bred Physician, heart-sick, and poor, and
    prim,
Patient as patients waiting, that never wait on him.

And the poor Scribe, that to a film spins out his sorry
    brains,
As spider spins its web – but his, alas! no prey detains;

The worn Inventor, adding still new engines to the old,
Starving himself on the device shall breed for others
    gold.

So Mind and Matter pine alike in this eternal press,
The kindly seed of pity choked with rank growth of
    distress;
Hearts drown with all their freight of hopes, as on
    life's ocean rolls,
Sapping our bodies of their strength, and of their
    grasp our souls.

Yet earth is wide enough for all, and England holds in
    fee
Rich prairies – broad savannas – o'er South or Western
    sea,
Where virgin soils are offering their riches to the hand
That withers for pure lack of work, in this o'er-peopled
    land.

Unopened mines, ports shipless, loam innocent of
    grain,
Gardens unpruned, wild vineyards, happy islands,
    happy main;
The banquet spread, the guests unfed, that jostle here
    and jar,
Plenty that runs, unblessed, to waste, while want here
    breedeth war.

Then raise the cry, till loud and high it rise from lathe
    and loom,
From forge and field, from hut and hall, the cry of
    'Elbow-room!'
Of elbow-room for labour, of elbow-room for life,
For mind, for means, that so may come some calm
    upon our strife.

That we may have some pause for thought, may find
    some breathing-space,
To look, not as a foeman looks, upon our neighbour's
    face;
That we may hold our hold on life, not like poor
    drowning souls,
Where each that grasps the plank, to death some
    weaker comrade rolls.

And then how many a swimmer, now struggling with
    the tide,
Will find that he was grappling with a brother at his
    side! –
What Right may grow where Wrong is now, what
    Concord from Debate,
What Knowledge out of Ignorance, what Loving out
    of Hate!

CRIME AND IGNORANCE

JOHN SMITH, aged 21; WILLIAM SMITH, 19; THOMAS BURROWS, 18; and GEORGE LEES, 18, were a few days since tried at Appleby, for a most heinous offence. A poor girl was the outraged victim of their combined brutality. The culprits – who would have been hanged under the old law – were sentenced by MR JUSTICE CRESWELL to transportation for life. He said in his address: –

'They were all still very young, and yet apparently, from their previous conduct, and their present demeanor in the dock, so hardened and devoid of shame, that it could scarcely be expected that punishment with them would operate in any other way than as an example for others. They had been well employed here, working like free men in a free country, for masters of their own choosing, and well paid for their labour. But his Lordship would tell them, that they would now have to go where there would be no freedom, and no such wages – where there would be labour, indeed, as that of a slave, but without any pay-day, and where a holiday would never come round.'

Why, this is true – terribly true: and the benighted condition of these men – the hideous state of moral darkness that renders them, like the brute, the mere creatures of the lowest animal instinct – is to be answered for, surely not alone by the culprits, but by a Government that assumes to itself the title of maternal – (for is not the QUEEN, by the gentle fiction of the law, the Mother of her People?) – by the State that suffers thousands and tens of thousands to grow up, with no more self-respect taught them than is taught their contemporary cattle. A hideous, shocking spectacle is it to contemplate the condition of these wretched men – as yet upon the threshold of manhood – doomed to a life-long slavery, in which 'a holiday never comes round.' Nevertheless, disgust of the culprits must not make us forgetful of the terrible truth that, had the State fulfilled its first duty to them, they might not have so grievously failed in their duties to a fellow-creature. They were brought up as brutes, and society reaps the terrible fruit of their rearing.

HINTS FOR CALLING
A SPADE A SPADE

WE perceive from the last report of the Inspectors of Prison for Scotland, that it is the practice in Edinburgh to commit girls to prison for beating carpets at wrong hours, and boys for playing at marbles, boxing each other's ears, or plucking a few pods of beans.

Now, such cases ought to be peculiarly entered on the prison registers. The mere announcement of ten days' or a fortnight's imprisonment conveys no adequate notion of the way these heinous offences are really visited in Scotland, that eminently virtuous and pious country. The entry should be made after some such fashion as the following: –

Name and Description	Offence	Punishment
John M'K., a dirty little boy, aged 11.	Fighting with another dirty little boy.	To be taught to lie, steal, and swear.
Mary M'C., little girl, aged 12.	Throwing a pail of water into the street, and wetting a policeman's boots.	To be contaminated by street walkers, and taught to pick pockets.
John M'F., aged 9.	Stealing a turnip.	To be made a finished area-sneak.

And so on, specifying the punishment, not by its duration but its effects. People would then see the admirable effects of our present prison arrangements.

A CRY FROM THE
CONDEMNED CELL

[THE CASE OF MARY ANN HUNT. – It having been satisfactorily ascertained, after a proper medical examination, that there is every reason to believe that this wretched woman is quick with child, her execution is stayed by order of the Sheriffs of London and Middlesex. – *Times*.]

Two prisoners in a cell
  Where felons, doom'd to die .
Are garner'd for the gibbet, dwell;
  The time of each is nigh:
A murderess and a babe unborn within that dungeon lie.

Ere this the wretch had died,
  But that the law abstains
From taking human life, whose tide
  Doth flow in guiltless veins.
The hangman therefore waits till she hath pass'd her travail's pains.

Prepare the bed, and see
  The woman that ye tend;
And then prepare the gallows-tree,
  To be the felon's end,
Soon as a mother's anguish shall have ceased her frame to rend.

Prepare the swathing-bands,
  The hempen cord prepare;
Alike ye need the hangman's hands,
  The nurse's tender care:
The infant to the cradle – to the drop the mother bear. . . .

Think on the anguish dread
  That hath aveng'd her deed;
Think how that woman's heart hath bled,
  If 'blood for blood' you need,
And 'eye for eye, and tooth for tooth,' be still your law and creed.

OLD BAILEY HOLIDAYS

'*You will not leave one behind you who will not think a good deed done when your life is put an end to.*'

THUS spoke LORD DENMAN from the judgment-seat of the Old Bailey to a convicted murderer; and the mob assembled outside of Newgate sent forth many and joyous hurrahs, as they became assured of another Old Bailey holiday! A man was to be hanged – a good thing was to be done, – and the wise, and humane, and contemplative of this huge metropolis, would be gathered together to bear solemn witness to the merits and the great social utility of the deed. However, before the crowning sacrifice ordained by law to vindicate humanity was performed, it was necessary, most necessary to the ends of justice, that there should be acted a prefatory ceremony: the wretch should be made a *warning show* to the public – or, at least, to that happy and delighted section thereof with Newgate interest, or, better still, with private influence with the wife of London's Mayor. The 'condemned sermon,' with the real murderer, racked and torn, and convulsed with agony, was a great moral lesson not to be neglected by any who could command the enjoyment of so rare an excitement; and, therefore, many were the applicants, great was the knocking at the doors of Newgate, on the long-expected Sabbath!

However, '*at ten o'clock all were accommodated in the most satisfactory manner in the different parts of the chapel allotted to visitors. At about that hour the Lady Mayoress and some of her ladyship's friends entered the governor's pew!*'

They have all, in a few heartfelt sentences, addressed themselves to God, imploring that what they are about to hear *and see* that day may work to their soul's health. This duty done, the benevolence of the law, that on such occasions shows a murderer

' – as men show an ape,'

is made manifest, for the real assassin – (and, oh! what a fluttering of hearts among the Mayoress's friends!) – is brought in by real turnkeys, and placed in a chair!

'His appearance indicated extreme mental suffering. He clasped his hands together sometimes, and sometimes he raised them up and pressed them against *his breast in great agony*, *the tears streaming from his eyes*, whilst he endeavoured to catch a glimpse of some old acquaintance or friend amongst the surrounding multitude. So strong *was the expression of horror* in his face and demeanour, that a *respectable female*, who was prompted by the curiosity which will induce even persons of the weakest nerves to witness the "condemned sermon" once in their lives, *shrieked and fainted*. The culprit looked with evident anxiety towards the spot from which the alarm proceeded; but, finding that a stranger was the cause of it, he seemed to retire *within the awful circle of his own meditations*, and to struggle with feelings beyond the power of any human being to describe.'

Now, was not this a spectacle worthy of the curiosity of refined, gentle, sight-seeking woman! Who would seek the vulgar play-house, and pay their money to witness only ideal woe, when – with Newgate interest – ladies may be on the free list for all condemned sermons? – when they may witness real agony – may see the scalding tears of hopeless remorse – may behold a real murderer, dyed from crown to sole in human blood, writhing in all the hell of horror and despair! Is not this a sight worthy of meek, soft-hearted woman?

We think, however, that the great social good arising from the exhibition made at condemned sermons would certainly be increased by further carrying out the sentiment that induces ladies to attend them. Hence, they certainly should be present at the galvanic experiment; and more, what a wholesome, moral fillip it would give them, if, at midnight, they were to attend the burial of the assassin, and, to show their horror of his deeds, were to cast within his unblest, unsanctified grave, a handful or so of lime, duly provided on these occasions to consume the murderer's bones! . . .

But the 'condemned sermon' is over; the Lady Mayoress's friends and other visitors having wept and shrieked, and gazed upon the livid, tortured brow of homicide, feel their Christianity and their morals mightily refreshed by the discipline, and not being of those

'Who think they're pious when they're only bilious,'

they retire to their homes, more than ever odorous from the sanctity of the 'governor's pew.' They have seen a murderer – have stared at him – have seen his whole frame convulsed and tortured – have gazed upon his flesh-quakes as they would have watched an exquisite piece of mechanism, – and the sight has done them all 'a world of good!'

The knell of the murderer sounds, and the dying wretch mounts the scaffold. How hushed the mob! Each man may hear his fellow's heart beat in that terrible moment of silence and suspense. The bolt is drawn, and as the culprit falls, thousands gasp as one man, and lock their palsied hands in breathless horror. A few minutes pass, and the enormous multitude, awe-stricken by what they have beheld, and casting terrified looks at the corpse yet turning in the air, silently disperse, and for that day at least are never seen to smile. Their daily labour done, they seek their early homes, and having read their bibles, pray *not* to be led 'into temptation.'

Moreover, throughout the Old Bailey, no man loses snuffbox, purse, or pocket-handkerchief!

And 'this is the moral influence!' and it is with delight we quote these words from *The Times* – 'this is the moral influence of capital punishments!'

Q.

A Plea for Mercy

85

A COLLOQUY BETWEEN
THE INVALIDS

SAYS Leeds to Nottingham, 'Ah! how d'ye do?'
'So, so,' says Nottingham, 'and how are you?'
Says Leeds, 'I'm with an epidemic troubled,
And fear my hospitals must soon be doubled.'
'How's Liverpool?' says Manchester. 'Oh dear!'
Says Liverpool, 'I'm going fast, I fear;
I'm with contagion positively teeming,
And you, I think, are very poorly seeming.'
'I am,' says Manchester, 'extremely ailing;
In all my quarters typhus is prevailing.
And how is Birmingham?' 'I'm doing badly,'
Says Birmingham; 'my breathing plagues me sadly;
I sometimes almost fear my heart's cessation;
I know what's killing me – bad ventilation.
How are you, London, rolling in your wealth?'
'Alas!' says London, 'money isn't health.
'Tis true I roll in wealth, as in a flood,
But, also, I'm compelled to roll in mud.
My cesspools, sinks, and sewers are neglected,
Hence by all kinds of ailments I'm affected:
I'm devastated by a host of fevers,
Which rage in Spitalfields amongst my weavers.
In Clerkenwell, and Houndsditch, and about
My filthy ward of Farringdon. Without,
Measles and small-pox – spite of vaccination –

Are thinning fast my crowded population;
Consumption, too, for want of air and water,
Amid my denizens spreads wholesale slaughter.
Then I've pneumonia, pleurisy, gastritis,
Mumps and marasmus, jaundice, enteritis.
Forth from my reeking courts and noisome alleys
Breaks fatal pestilence in frequent sallies;
Lurking meanwhile, like fire in smouldering embers.
I've erysipelas about my members.
My children, too, have ricketty affections,
And strumous constitutions and complexions.
I'm always ill, in every kind of weather:
In fact, I've all your ailments put together.
Of physic I despair: I want ablution;
My system needs a thorough revolution –
At least, a very sweeping reformation,
Not only of my streets, but Corporation.'
Quoth all the other towns, 'That's our condition;
We want the scavenger – not the physician.'

Pollution: on Land and Water

A COURT FOR KING CHOLERA

DIRTY FATHER THAMES

FILTHY river, filthy river,
   Foul from London to the Nore,
What art thou but one vast gutter,
   One tremendous common shore?

All beside thy sludgy waters,
   All beside thy reeking ooze,
Christian folks inhale mephitis,
   Which thy bubbly bosom brews.

All her foul abominations
   Into thee the City throws;
These pollutions, ever churning,
   To and fro thy current flows.

And from thee is brew'd our porter –
   Thee, thou gully, puddle, sink!
Thou, vile cesspool, art the liquor
   Whence is made the beer we drink!

Thou, too, hast a Conservator,
   He who fills the civic chair;
Well does he conserve thee, truly,
   Does he not, my good LORD MAYOR?

TO THE THAMES

(After TENNYSON*)*

BAKE, bake, bake,
   O Thames, on thy way to the sea!
And I would that thy stink could poison
   A Bishop, Peer, or M.P.

Oh, well for the Rotherhithe boy
   That he shouts with the mudlarks at play!
Oh, well, for the Greenwich lad,
   That he dives for the browns in thy clay!

And the swoln dead dogs go down
   Through the bridges, past Tow'r Hill;
But, oh, for the touch of a despot's hand
   To the works of a Board that is *nil!*

Bake, bake, bake,
   O Thames, on thy way to the sea!
But the appetite which thy stink strikes dead
   Will never come back to me.

THE 'SILENT HIGHWAY'-MAN
'Your Money or your Life!'

AN ELEGY, WRITTEN IN A
LONDON CHURCHYARD

By a tradesman in the vicinity

Cemeteries, and Homes . . .

THE sexton tolls the knell till parting day,
  The latest funeral train has paid its fee,
The mourners homeward take their dreary way
  And leave the scene to Typhus and to me.

Now fades the crowded graveyard on the sight,
  But all, its air who scent, their nostrils hold,
Save where the beadle drones, contented quite,
  And drowsy mutes their arms in slumber fold.

Save where, hard by yon soot-incrusted tower,
  A Reverend Man does o'er his port complain,
Of such as would, by sanitary power,
  Invade his ancient customary gain.

Beneath those arid mounds, that dead wall's shade,
  Where grows no turf above the mouldering heap,
All in their narrow cells together laid,
  The former people of the parish sleep.

The queasy call of sewage-breathing morn,
  The ox, urg'd bellowing to the butcher's shed,
The crowd's loud clamouring at his threatening horn,
  No more shall rouse them from their loathly bed.

For them no more the chamber-light shall burn,
  The busy doctor ply his daily care,
Nor children to their sire from school return,
  And climb his knees the dreaded pest to share.

Good folks, impute not to their friends the fault,
  If memory o'er their bones no tombstone raise;
Where there lie dozens huddled in one vault,
  No art can mark the spot where each decays.

No doubt, in this revolting place are laid,
  Hearts lately pregnant with infectious fire;
Hands, by whose grasp contagion was conveyed,
  As sure as electricity by wire.

Full many a gas of direst power unclean,
  The dark o'erpeopled graves of London bear,
Full many a poison, born to kill unseen,
  And spread its rankness in the neighbouring air.

Some district Surgeon, that with dauntless breast
  The epidemic 'mongst the poor withstood,
Some brave, humane Physician here may rest,
  Some Curate, martyrs to infected blood.

To some doom'd breast the noxious vapour flies,
  Some luckless lung the deadly reek inspires,
Ev'n from the tomb morbific fumes arise,
  Ev'n in men's ashes live Disorder's fires.

For thee, who, shock'd to see th' unhonoured dead,
  Dost in these lines their shameful plight relate
If, chance, by sanitary musings led,
  Some graveyard-gleaner shall inquire thy fate.

Haply some muddle-headed clerk will say,
  We used to see him at the peep of dawn,
Shaving with hasty strokes his beard away,
  Whene'er his window-curtains were undrawn.

There would he stand o'erlooking yonder shed,
  That hides those relics from the public eye,
And watch what we were doing with the dead,
  And count the funerals daily going by.

One morn we miss'd him in the 'custom'd shop;
  Behind the counter where he used to be,
Another serv'd; nor at his early chop,
  Nor at the 'Cock,' nor at the 'Cheese,' was he.

The next, by special wish, with small array,
  To Kensall Green we saw our neighbour borne,
Thither go read (if thou canst read) the lay
  With which a chum his headstone did adorn.

THE EPITAPH

Here rest with decency the bones in earth,
  Of one to Comfort and to Health unknown,
Miasma ever plagued his humble hearth,
  And Scarlatina mark'd him for her own.

Long was his illness, tedious, and severe,
  Hard by a London Churchyard dwelt our friend;
He follow'd to the grave a neighbour's bier,
  He met thereby ('twas what he fear'd) his end.

No longer seek Corruption to enclose
  Within the places of mankind's abode;
But far from cities let our dust repose,
  Where daisies blossom on the verdant clod.

THE MODEL COURT

PUBLIC attention having been at length in some degree attracted to the long-since mooted, and daily more and more important question of providing the poor with a better class of dwellings, we understand that the directors of the Crystal Palace intend fitting up a Court to represent the now existing state of architecture, and internal house economy of our lower London and provincial city districts.

The directors conceive that by so doing they will most likely bring the matter to the notice of a number of people, by whom it may have hitherto been considered quite beneath it; and will also stand a chance of introducing it to certain duly salaried officials, who in their capacity of overseers have completely overlooked it. . . .

Accordingly, a quantity of casts have been taken by certain duly qualified employés of the Company, who have lately, at a great expense to health, been exploring what are generally alluded to as the 'back slums' of Spitalfields, Lambeth, Soho, and Bethnal Green: and, as the result of their self-sacrificing labours, a Court at Sydenham is being now constructed, which it is expected will present a faithful copy of the courts that still exist in those so long-infected districts.

To represent the gutter which generally runs down the middle of our courts, there will be a fountain placed in the centre of this, to play alternately with Thames water and liquid manure; and it is expected that but few eyes, or noses, will be found sufficiently acute to detect the difference.

In order to assimilate the atmosphere of the Court as closely as possible with that of its originals, engagements have been made with some of our most eminent bone-boilers and gut-dressers for a continual supply of those highly noxious gases, which have so long kept in such bad odour the districts where their trade establishments are situate. This arrangement, and that of the fountains afore-mentioned, will, it is expected, form the chief (nasal) attractions of the court: and will obviate the need of any guides or finger-posts, as the visitor who may wish to be directed to it, will simply find it necessary to follow his nose.

In order to ensure the most perfect mismanagement, we learn that the general superintendence of the Court will be entrusted to certain duly constituted parish authorities, who have had great experience in local government, and are now fully competent to administer its defects. When we add that all the sanitary arrangements have been placed under the control of a regularly organised Board of Health, our readers will feel satisfied that no pains will be spared to keep it in the most unhealthy state possible.

a more salubrious London

OUR MEAN METROPOLIS

PARIS making such a movement in her buildings and her streets,
  How is it that all improvement here with opposition meets?
Hear the Corporation clamour; hear the Parish Vestries' row:
  How they bark and how they hammer, Centralisation, bow wow wow!
        Centralisation! Centralisation!
        Centralisation! Centralisation!

Paramount some power is wanted, noble schemes to carry out,
  Not to be withstood or daunted; nothing can be done without:
Which, when Vested Interests muster, can their sordid spirits cow,
  And put down their worships' bluster, and their bark of bow wow wow!
        Centralisation! Centralisation!
        Centralisation! bow wow wow!

When the Seine is as the Derwent limpid, if not yet more pure,
  Of the Thames why does the current run with liquid (pah!) manure?
Oh! no proper drainage measure will the stingy snobs allow,
  Whilst they bark in gruff displeasure, Centralisation, bow wow wow!
        Centralisation! Centralisation!
        Centralisation! bow wow wow!

Wherefore do those clouds appalling still the sky above us cloak,
  And the blacks continue falling; when we might consume our smoke?
We forbidden are to do it, though we very well know how,
  By that cry – confusion to it! Centralisation! bow wow wow!
        Centralisation! Centralisation!
        Centralisation! bow wow wow!

In the name of all that's gracious, let our streets be wider made,
  Why should not they be as spacious as is meet for health and trade?
Narrow ways to views are owing, narrower still, which they avow,
  Barking, grunting, puffing, blowing, Centralisation! bow wow wow!
        Centralisation! Centralisation!
        Centralisation! bow wow wow!

THE USE OF ADULTERATION
LITTLE GIRL. 'If you please, Sir, Mother says,
will you let her have a quarter of a pound of
your best tea to kill the rats with, and a ounce
of chocolate as would get rid of the black beadles.'

THE GREAT LOZENGE-MAKER
A Hint to Paterfamilias

THE ADULTERATOR'S
ALPHABET

BY AN APPRENTICE OF THE LAUREL

A's the Mock Auction – go buy, if you choose,
The trash palm'd upon you by duffers and Jews.

B is the Baker, whose loaves sell the faster
When made up of alum, potatoes, and plaster.

C is the Clergyman – mind he don't mix
His Rubric with PUSEY's or Claphamite tricks.

D is the Druggist – the *Lancet* explains
How he poisons each drug, and increases your pains.

E 's the Excise, that affixes its locks –
But very queer mixtures are made in the docks.

F is the Fellow whose Furniture falls
To pieces as soon as it's set round your walls.

G is the Grocer – the rascal is he
Who puts sand in your sugar, and sticks in your tea.

H is the Hatter – his hats (which you bet)
Turn shamefully brown the first time they get wet.

I is the Ink-maker, he's a nice fellow –
His deepest Jet black in a week becomes yellow.

J is the Jeweller – I know who is sold
When you've bought his sham gems neatly set in
    sham gold.

K is K.G., and a title debased
Since NICK and Nurse AB in the Chapel were graced.

L is the Laureate, who tenders us *for* song
A lachrymose whine when we wanted a war-song.

M is the Member, the place-hunting elf,
Selling rubbish he's no right to sell – that's himself.

N is the Nurse who your suffering insults –
Who gives GODFREY to babies, and plunders adults.

O is the Omnibus cad, who deceives
Concerning his route, and who lets in the thieves.

P is the Publican, neck deep in sin,
With salt in his beer, and with turps in his gin.

Q 's the QUEEN'S GOVERNMENT (that's but a phrase)
Who delude their good Mistress in all kinds of ways.

R 's the Romance writer, read with a groan,
What's good he has prigg'd, and what's stupid's his
    own.

S is the Stockjobber – none can dispute
That a bull or a bear is a low kind of brute.

T is the Tailor, who makes us all wroth
With his skimping bad fits, and his rotten old cloth.

U is your Uncle, the Usurer POP,
And legalised cheating goes on at his shop.

V is the Vintner, you trace, when you dine,
His crimes in the mess that is brought you for wine.

W 's the Watchmaker, nine times a-week
His 'warrants' should bring up himself to the Beak.

X (with an *e*)'s the EXCHEQUER, which axes
All sorts of unjust and irrational taxes.

Y is a Yokel – when *he* meets your eyes,
Look out – he's most likely a thief in disguise.

Z 's ZADKIEL, the quack who, with 'Venus' and 'Mars,'
Diddles Zanies, by lying reports from the stars.

THE ROADSIDE INN
A Mouthful of Dust and a Pull at the Pump

THE CLUB
Just a Sandwich and a Nice Glass of Hock and
Seltzer Water

**The Licensing
Laws: Some
Contrasts**

A DROP OF GIN!

GIN! Gin! a Drop of Gin!
What magnified Monsters circle therein!
Ragged, and stained with filth and mud,
Some plague-spotted, and some with blood!
Shapes of Misery, Shame, and Sin!
Figures that make us loathe and tremble,
Creatures scarce human, that more resemble
Broods of diabolical kin,
Ghoule and Vampyre, Demon and Jin!

Gin! Gin! a Drop of Gin!
The dram of Satan! the liquor of Sin!
When darkly Adversity's day's set in,
   And the friends and peers
   Of earlier years
Prove warm without, but cold within, –
   And cannot retrace
   A familiar face
That's steep'd in poverty up to the chin; –
But snub, neglect, cold-shoulder and cut
The ragged pauper, misfortune's butt,
Hardly acknowledg'd by kith and kin –
   Because, poor rat!
   He has no cravat;
A seedy coat, and a hole in that! –
No sole to his shoe, and no brim to his hat;
Nor a change of linen – except his skin: –
   No gloves – no vest,
   Either second or best;
And what is worse than all the rest,
No light heart, tho' his breeches are thin, –
   While Time elopes
   With all golden hopes,

And even with those of pewter and tin, –
   The brightest dreams,
   And the best of schemes,
All knock'd down, like a wicket by Mynn, –
   Each castle in air
   Seized by Giant Despair,
No prospect in life worth a minikin pin, –
   No credit – no cash,
   No cold mutton to hash,
   No bread – not even potatoes to mash;
No coal in the cellar, no wine in the binn, –
   Smash'd, broken to bits,
   With judgments and writs,
Bonds, bills, and cognovits, distracting the wits,
In the webs that the spiders of Chancery spin, –
   Till weary of life, its worry and strife;
   Black visions are rife of a razor, a knife,
Of poison – a rope – 'louping over a linn.' –
Gin! Gin! a Drop of Gin!
Oh! then its tremendous temptations begin,
   To take, alas!
   To the fatal glass, –
And happy the wretch that it does not win
   To change the black hue
   Of his ruin to blue –
While Angels sorrow, and Demons grin –
   And lose the rheumatic
   Chill of his attic
By plunging into the Palace of Gin!

SAUCE FOR THE GANDER
PUSEY – PUSEY – Gander,
Whither would he wander,
Up-stairs, down-stairs,
And to My Lady's Chamber.
But BULL and *Punch* declared they wouldn't
Stand such priestly airs –
So took him by his shoulders,
And kicked him down-stairs.

A PROPER CHARGE
B-P OF L-D-N. 'You must not bring your playthings into Church, my little men.'

CHRISTMAS IN THE CHURCH

MR HUME is always picking a hole in the black silk apron of Mistress Church. He has just procured a return, containing 'abstracts of the number and classes of non-resident incumbents, and the number of resident incumbents' – in a word, the number of drones and the number of working bees, of the Established Hive. The *Times* publishes an abstract of the abstract: –

'The gross total number of non-residents amounted to 3,366, including 1,635 cases of 'exemption,' and 781 of 'license,' whilst there were no less than 950 (nearly 1,000!) ordained clergymen of the Church of England, *munificently remunerated* for their *sinecure 'services,'* who were *altogether absent* from the sphere of their important and sacred duties without either license or exemption!'

And wherefore are many of these exempt? The reason – the orthodox reason? Why, some are pluralists and cannot – like Noah's dove – be in two places at the same time. Some preach to Royalty, having the cure of Royal souls; wherefore souls not royal must look to themselves. From the diocese of Exeter alone, there are fifty absentees; BISHOP PHILPOTTS being so rapt in divine meditation that he, doubtless, never misses the truants: otherwise, would he not put forth his crook, and bring back the shepherds to their bleating sheep?

And now for the Curates – the light porters of the Church – what of their salaries? Why –

'There are nearly 1000 Curates whose stipends are all under 100*l.*; and 113 receive less than 50*l.* a year! The total number of assistant Curates to incumbents who are resident on their benefices amounted (in 1846) to 2642, and the number licensed to 2094. Of these 1192 receive stipends *under* 100*l.* a year, and 173 *less* than 50*l.* a year.'

Poor Curates! How many footmen, warm in ardent plush, cosey in cerulean blue, must look down upon your shabby rusty black, and be thankful that their care is the care of the hats and coats and canes of men, – and not of their immortal souls!

Christmas is coming. We should like – were it possible – to have the heroes of the above 'abstract' assembled round some mighty Mahogony Tree. Would the pluralists take soup with six hands – feeding six mouths? Would he take six slices of plum-pudding – six legs of turkies – six mince-pies? Surely, yes; for as he takes the toil and the remuneration of six men, he must needs have sextuple sustenance to strengthen him for his labours.

An Episcopal Sum

GIVEN – a bishop of £8000 a year, with an outlay of £28,000 for a palace. How many curates, at £75 per annum, will it require to feed and house him?

A VISION OF THE REPEAL OF
THE WINDOW-TAX
'Hollo! Old Fellow; we're glad to see You here.'

The Repeal of the
Window Tax, and
a Call for
Saturday
Half-Holidays

THE SATURDAY EARLY CLOSING MOVEMENT

THOUGH we have done much to economise labour, we have done as yet little towards economising the labourer. We sometimes forget that though worn-out machinery may be re-placed, the wear and tear of the human machine may lead to mischief beyond the power of remedy. Men should not be 'used up' as if flesh and blood were mere clay and water, or as if the human frame, like the knitting or any other mechanical frame, was to be regarded simply as the means of doing the largest possible amount of work in the shortest possible period. If a man is to be treated as so much mere material, we are apt to lose sight of the fact that his composition includes the immaterial, which by the way, some employers have been in the habit of looking at in its first and lowest sense, regarding it as so thoroughly immaterial, as to be not worth noticing. A clerk or an assistant has been considered merely as a medium for making money, and the person employed may have been intellectually a lump of lead, so that the employer could 'turn all his lead to gold,' by keeping him from morning till night at the desk or the counter.

Something has happily been done towards the shortening of the hours of business, and the copying lawyers' clerk, who formerly was kept so continually face to face with parchment that 'to that complexion did he come at last,' is now able to reach his suburban home soon enough to enjoy an hour in that medley of infantine screams, jingling tea-cups, and conjugal complaints, which constitute what is called 'the bosom of his family.' The 'assistant' may now escape an hour or two earlier from the atmosphere of gas, and may seek some more wholesome enlightenment.

The Early Closing Movement has been followed by a rather general motion, which we have much pleasure in seconding, for a half-holiday on Saturday. Now that the Crystal Palace has opened, it is evident that places of mere business must be occasionally shut if the industrious classes are to benefit by an institution which will do more for popular education than anything that the world has yet been able to boast of. The People's Palace will become a misnomer if the people are so confined in workshops, warehouses, counting-houses, and offices, that none but the comparatively idle can visit what is expressly designed for the appreciation of the industrious. We cordially join in the demand for a half-holiday once at least in the week, and we hope to see the time when there may be a still greater curtailment of the hours devoted to mere money-making purposes. . . .

THE SORROWS OF 'THE STAR'

In vain I spend my eloquence,
  My arguments let fly,
To teach the people how to be
  Dissatisfied, and why.
I poke the British Lion up –
  In his dull ear I scream;
I stir the fire, I blow the coals,
  But can't get up the steam!

There's flogging in the Army;
  There's jobbing in the Fleet;
Corruption in the Treasury;
  Intrigue in Downing Street!
That horrid Volunteering –
  For sarcasm what a theme!
But vain my skill, do what I will,
  I can't get up the steam!

Vain, morning after morning,
  My preaching up Reform;
The more I beat the iron
  The more it won't get warm:
On indirect Taxation
  My attacks would fill a ream,
Yet none will buy or back my cry, –
  I can't get up the steam!

At all the age's vices
  I've gone in left and right;
I've written down TOM SAYERS –
  I've written up JOHN BRIGHT;
'Gainst cakes and ale in general
  I've turned my vitriol stream;
But cakes and ale do still prevail;
  I can't get up the steam!

It's awful to contemplate
  A nation like our own,
Going headlong to perdition
  (As the *Star* has often shown).
They tread the flowery pathway,
  Wrapped in their fatal dream,
And turn deaf ears to all my fears, –
  I can't get up the steam!

When, our Commons' rights invading,
  The Peers' presumptuous vote
Keeps up the excise on paper,
  In vain I swell my throat, –
Vain an 'outraged constitution'
  And a 'down-trod people' seem,
E'en a 'bloated aristocracy'
  Will not get up the steam!

In short, the country's apathy
  To *Times*, Peers, Church, and Crown;
Must sicken one who fain would see
  All things turned upside down;
Who'd make the *Star* its country's guide,
  For the *Times*' delusive beam –
But the more I preach the fewer I reach –
  And I can't get up the steam!

Oh, what this England yet might be,
  If BRIGHT were at the helm,
With a graduated Income-Tax
  All taxes to o'erwhelm –
And Universal Suffrage –
  But hence too pleasing dream,
For that bright page – that Golden Age –
  I can't get up the steam!

The Scalpel laid down – by all Classes

TOO FULL OF BEER

A SONG OF THE WORKING CLASSES

AIR – '*Poor Mary Anne*'

FOR Reform we feels too lazy;
  Too full o' beer.
Much malt liquor makes us hazy,
  Too full o' beer.
We don't want no alteration
Of the present Legislation,
'Twon't affect our sittiwation,
  Too full o' beer.

We've the means to bile our kettles,
  Too full o' beer.
Not bad off for drink and wittles,
  Too full o' beer.
When we've got no work nor wages,
Politics our minds engages,
Till such time we never rages,
  Too full o' beer.

Will this here Reform, we axes,
  Too full o' beer?
Clear us quite of rates and taxes,
  Too full o' beer.
Income-Tax the middlin' classes
Loads unequal – patient asses! –
But it don't oppress the masses,
  Too full o' beer.

We be willin' to be quiet,
  Too full o' beer.
Not a bit inclined to riot,
  Too full o' beer.
From the ale that's sound and nappy,
Him as wants a change is sappy,
Wot's the odds so long's you're happy,
  Too full o' beer?

94

IV
THE LANCET
OF SATIRE

JOHN BULL'S IDOL!

CATECHISMS FOR THE HUSTINGS

WE have serious thoughts of publishing a series of little manuals, under the above title, that should contain a summary of questions likely and unlikely to be asked of Candidates, with answers calculated not to satisfy the minds, but to stop the mouths of the querists, the latter being the great object in such cases. Of course, there should be separate manuals for different parties. The following may serve as a specimen: –

TORY MANUAL

Q. How do you define our glorious Constitution in Church and State?

A. That state of things dictated by the wisdom of our ancestors, for the advantage of ourselves and the amazement of posterity.

Q. Are you prepared to stand upon the old paths?

A. I am; and to keep off all trespassers.

Q. What are the old paths?

A. Those which begin, like charity, at home, and lead, like officers of the army, to glory. The Nobility, Gentry, and Dignified Clergy are their trustees; they are paved with good intentions; their 'pikes' must be paid, and therefore none but those with a money qualification can travel along them.

Q. Who pays for keeping up those paths?

A. The Public.

Q. Who has the administration of the road fund?

A. The Aristocracy.

Q. Will you maintain the Church?

A. I will – comfortably.

Q. Will you keep up the Exclusion of the Dissenters from the Universities?

A. I will. Churchmen don't ask for admission to Coward College, or Highbury – Why should Dissenters to Oxford or Cambridge?

Q. What do you understand by *meum* and *tuum*?

A. *Meum*, is all I can get. *Tuum*, is all others can prevent me from getting.

Q. What would you teach the poor?

A. Their duties.

Q. What would you teach the rich?

A. Their rights.

Q. What is your object in seeking for a seat in the House of Commons?

A. To advocate your interests and push my own.

Q. What is your opinion of the Ballot?

A. That it is un-English, as tending to withdraw the voter from the influence of his natural superiors.

Q. Will you oppose any Extension of the Suffrage?

A. I will. If votes were given to all, they would cease to command any price in the market.

BRIBERY IS DETESTABLE; BUT POLITENESS COSTS NOTHING

CANVASSER. 'Pray, Gentlemen, don't think of walking to the Polling Booth; I am sure your time must be valuable, and here's a Carriage quite at your service.'

INTELLIGENCE OF THE PEOPLE

Rothschild for ever!

EMIGRATION FOR THE UPPER CLASSES

The Electorate

WHEN there is talk of any Extension of the Suffrage, it is naturally enough usual to inquire how far the Intelligence of the People would justify their being entrusted with the right of voting for Members of Parliament. As far as the amount of intelligence can be gathered from the conduct of the people at public meetings of a political character, we regret to say the account is somewhat beggarly. The late election for the City of London presented a very poor result with reference to the wisdom of the masses, who had nothing better than bellowing and roaring to offer, by way of criticism, on the merits of the respective candidates. One of our staff of private reporters attended at the nomination, but he was compelled to furnish us with a pictorial sketch of the proceedings, which consisted of the emission, from several hundred open mouths, of a quantity of 'sound and fury, signifying nothing.' Nothing else was audible during the attempts of LORD JOHN MANNERS to address the multitude, whose intelligence never reached beyond such a remark as 'Go home,' 'It won't do here,' or some other observation of about equal profundity. Such ejaculations do not say very much for the sagacity of the people from whom they emanate, and who can scarcely lay claim to a voice in the representation, when the only use to which the voice appears to be put is such as the election for the City of London has just exemplified.

THE Lords have been complaining bitterly of having nothing to do in their own House, in consequence of the little work that has been cut out for them this Session by the Commons. LORD BROUGHAM has done his utmost to find a vent for his superfluous energy, and has been trying Legal Reform as a safety-valve, though without much effect, for he has been almost constantly on the fiz and fume without being able to go a-head by the aid of his vapour. We recommend their Lordships to try emigration, the great remedy of the day, which, during the recess, they might resort to very beneficially. They have been lately merely dummies in the game of life; but if they were to suit themselves with spades, they might turn up regular trumps in some distant colony. We do not recommend permanent expatriation to the peers; but after the *ennui* of this do-nothing Session, we are sure they might find both health and amusement abroad, in the exercise of a little manual labour.

No Manners!

THE POLITICAL EUCLID.

WHEREIN ARE CONSIDERED

THE RELATIONS OF PLACE;

OR,

THE BEST MODE OF

GETTING A PLACE FOR YOUR RELATIONS:

Being a complete Guide to the Art of

LEGISLATIVE MENSURATION,

OR,

How to estimate the value of a Vote upon

WHIG AND TORY MEASURES.

THE WHOLE ADAPTED TO

THE USE OF HONOURABLE MEMBERS.

BY

LORD PALMERSTON,

Late Professor of Toryism, but now Lecturer on Whiggery to the College of St. Stephen's.

A point in politics is that which always has *place* (in view,) but no particular party.

A line in politics is interest without principle.

The extremities of a line are loaves and fishes.

A right line is that which lies evenly between the Ministerial and Opposition benches.

A plain angle is the evident inclination, and consequent piscation, of a member for a certain place; or it is the meeting together of two members who are not in the same line of politics.

When a member sits on the cross benches, and shows no particular inclination to one side or the other, it is called a right angle.

An obtuse angle is that in which the inclination is *evidently* to the Treasury.

An acute angle is that in which the inclination is *apparently* to the Opposition benches.

A boundary is the extremity or whipper-in of any party.

A party is that which is kept together by one or more whippers-in.

A circular member is a rum figure, produced by turning round; and is such that all lines of politics centre in himself, and are the same to him.

The diameter of a circular member is a line drawn on the Treasury, and terminating in both pockets.

Trilateral members, or waverers, are those which have three sides.

Of three-sided members an equilateral or independent member is that to which all sides are the same.

An isosceles or vacillating member is that to which two sides only are the same.

Parallel lines of politics are such as are in the same direction – say Downing-street; but which, being produced ever so far – say to Windsor – do not meet.

A political problem is a Tory proposition, showing that the country is to be done.

A theorem is a Whig proposition – the benefit of which to any one but the Whigs always requires to be demonstrated.

HINTS TO NEW MEMBERS

BY AN OLD TRIMMER

It being now an established axiom that every member goes into Parliament for the sole purpose of advancing his own private interest, and not, as has been ignorantly believed, for the benefit of his country or the constituency he represents, it becomes a matter of vast importance to those individuals who have not had the advantage of long experience in the house, to be informed of the mode usually adopted by honourable members in the discharge of their legislative duties. . . .

HINT 1. – It is a vulgar error to imagine that a man, to be a member of Parliament, requires either education, talents, or honesty: all that it is necessary for him to possess is – impudence and humbug!

HINT 2. – When a candidate addresses a constituency, he should promise everything. Some men will only pledge themselves to what their conscience considers right. Fools of this sort can never hope to be →

HINT 3. – Oratory is a showy, but by no means necessary, accomplishment in the house. If a member knows when to say 'Ay' or 'No,' it is quite sufficient for all useful purposes.

HINT 4. – If, however, a young member should be seized with the desire of speaking in Parliament, he may do so without the slightest regard to sense, as the reporters in the gallery are paid for the purpose of making speeches for honourable members; and on the following morning he may calculate on seeing, in the columns of the daily papers, a full report of his splendid →

HINT 5. – A knowledge of the exact time to cry 'Hear, hear!' is absolutely necessary. A severe cough, when a member of the opposite side of the house is speaking, is greatly to be commended; cock-crowing is also a desirable qualification for a young legislator, and, if judiciously practised, cannot fail to bring the possessor into the notice of his party.

HINT 6. – The back seats in the gallery are considered, by several members, as the most comfortable for taking a nap on.

HINT 7. – If one honourable member wishes to tell another honourable member that he is anything but a gentleman, he should be particular to do so within the walls of the house – as, in that case, the Speaker will put him under arrest, to prevent any unpleasant consequences arising from his hasty expressions.

HINT 8. – If a member promise to give his vote to the minister, he must in honour do so – unless he happen to fall asleep in the smoking-room, and so gets shut out from the division of the house.

HINT 9. – No independent member need trouble himself to understand the merits of any question before the house. He may, therefore, amuse himself at Bellamy's until five minutes before the Speaker's bell rings for a division.

Political Theory

returned by a large majority.

maiden speech.

and Practice

YOUNG ENGLAND'S 'OLD NOBILITY'

Political Romance

LORD JOHN MANNERS, the Home Secretary *in posse*, when Young England shall reign in Downing Street, has published a volume of verse called '*England's Trust, and other Poems.*' In this volume there are – let the reader prepare for a gasp – the following lines: –

> 'Though I *could bear* to view our crowded towns
> Sink into hamlets, *or unpeopled downs;*'

he could *not* bear that any decay should fall upon the ancient peerage. No, says LORD JOHN –

> '*Let wealth and commerce, laws and learning die,*
> BUT LEAVE US STILL OUR OLD NOBILITY.'

These lines were quoted by EARL DUCIE at the last Anti-Corn-Law meeting, but their authorship, and the book that enshrines them, were not given. We supply the information for the benefit of the curious. And now, with every wished respect for the ancient aristocracy of England, we must own we were not aware of its surpassing worth in comparison with wealth and commerce, laws and learning. We were evidently in darkness. Yes; put all the wealth of Britain – all the labours of its law-makers – all the inspiration, as bequeathed in books to us, of its God-gifted men into one scale, and clap an Earl's coronet into the other, and that little ornament shall make all things else kick the beam; that is, when the balance shall be held by the pure and just hands of – Young England!

But, after all, would not this said old nobility be a poor, plucked, very shabby thing indeed, divested of all the refinements, all the graces of life? With no wealth, no commerce, no laws to restrict its ferocity, – no learning to soften it, – would it be little other than a BARON RAWHEAD AND BLOODYBONES – an EARL GOGMAGOG, living on lordly pillage? Let us imagine this old nobility, spared amidst the wreck of all the commerce, all the arts of life.

Our 'crowded towns' exist no longer. No: Liverpool is a mere village; Birmingham, a hamlet; Manchester, a place where two or three old women ply the spinning-wheel; Sheffield, a casual home for wandering tinker or knife-grinder; all Yarmouth shrunk into the huts of a few fishermen who cure herrings; and where Hull, and Paisley, and Glasgow stood, are swamps and unpeopled downs. Bitterns boom and hares squat, where merchants trafficked and baillies judged. Thousands of men have withered from the face of the earth – whole towns are but empty sepulchres; but let us clap our hands, and utter hallelujahs for the mercy; there remains to us what is dearer than all – for very dear, indeed, it sometimes has been – 'our old nobility.'

Well, in this new state of things, let us inquire what Old Nobility would do for itself? All wealth and commerce annihilated, Old Nobility would of course set about subjugating the rest of society into hordes of serfs and villains. The sword of Old Nobility would exact from Serfdom labour unrecompensed, brutal vassalage, and those sweet privileges of the by-gone day, – the *droits du seigneur*. As for laws, Old Nobility, as of yore, would make its own; a stout, significant code of timber, easily comprehended by the meanest capacity – namely, a gallows at every castle-gate.

And then for learning, why should Old Nobility care to spell even the monosyllable *sword*, so that Old Nobility had its own sweet will to make its mark with it?

'Oh, no!' cries the spirit of Young England, 'there is such an instinctive refinement, such an inborn benevolence in Old Nobility, that without any other laws or learning than those fashioned and acquired by its own pure heart, it would work the unqualified good of the meaner millions placed by Providence at its disposal.' Of course, all history proves the truth of this. We have no doubt that if all the social arts should suddenly perish, and Old Nobility, to distinguish itself from vulgar flesh and blood, should dye its body with its armorial bearings – that in this forked and naked state its first anxieties would be for its unpainted brotherhood. . . .

It must, however, be a great consolation to the people of England to know in what consist their happiness and refinement as a nation. Not in their wealth; not in their laws; not in the wisdom of their buried sages. Oh, no! Let them despise their colonies – their fleets of ships – their literature, with its wings of light for distant nations – let them look upon all these things as cumbrous vanities, and with thankfulness pulling at their hamstrings, reverently drop down upon their knees before the House of Lords!

The House of Lords! Yea, that is Nature's prime laboratory; there, indeed, she toils and labours to 'give the world assurance' of her best article. Indeed, the eye of the philosopher – borrowing the glass of Young England – sees painted on the outside of the House of Lords – '*Real men to be had only within. All elsewhere are spurious. No connexion with any other House.*'

Thus, all that we have to do, is to pray for the procreation of Peers. With an Old Nobility, let 'crowded towns,' with all their wealth, sink and perish – the true national property is in the Lords!

Thus, if Bristol should be again assailed by a devastating mob, let them burn every stick. Why should we care, if Bristol's Earl be safe?

If all Westminster should catch fire, let it blaze away; for have we not a nobleman of that ilk dearer than all Westminster put together?

And, lastly; if an earthquake should swallow the entire city of LONDONDERRY, ought we to mourn over the desolation, – seeing that Providence has benignly preserved to us a wise and gentle Marquess of that glorious name? Yes! –

> 'Let wealth and commerce, laws and learning die,
> BUT LEAVE US STILL OUR OLD NOBILITY.'

YOUNG ENGLAND'S LAMENT

[YOUNG ENGLAND *discovered sitting dolorously before his parlour-fire: he grievously waileth as follows: –*]

I REALLY can't imagine why,
　With my confess'd ability –
From the ungrateful Tories, I
　Get nothing – but civility.

The 'independent' dodge I've tried,
　I've also tried servility; –
It's all the same, – they *won't* provide, –
　I only get – civility.

I've flattered PEEL; he smiles back thanks
　With Belial's own tranquillity;
But still he keeps me in 'the ranks,'
　And pays me – with civility.

If not the birth, at least I've now
　The *manners* of nobility;
But yet SIR ROBERT scorns to bow
　With more than mere civility.

Well, I've been pretty mild as yet,
　But now I'll try scurrility;
It's very hard if *that* don't get
　Me more than mere civility.

A NICE YOUNG MAN FOR A SMALL PARTY

YOUNG BEN he was a nice young man,
　An author by his trade;
He fell in love with Polly-Tics,
　And was an M.P. made.

He was a Radical one day,
　But met a Tory crew;
His Polly-Tics he cast away,
　And then turned Tory too.

But when he called on ROBERT PEEL,
　His talents to employ,
His answer was, 'Young Englander,
　For me you're not the boy.'

Oh, ROBERT PEEL! Oh, ROBERT PEEL!
　How could you serve me so?
I've met with Whig rebuffs before,
　But not a Tory blow.

Young England died when in its birth:
　In forty-five it fell;
The papers told the public, but
　None for it toll'd the bell.

The Body Politic

POISONS

As Poisons are claiming, or likely to claim, the attention of Parliament, the following, with appropriate tests, are drawn up, that the public may also pay attention to them before any election: –

Poisons	Mode of Action	Antidotes	Tests	Where to be looked for	Colour of the Precipitate
ROUTINE	Stagnates the blood and generally carries off half its victims.	Cut away all the clothing and diminish the bulk of the Offices by purging in the most speedy manner.	Any emergency requiring common sense and alertness.	In Downing Street and the Government Offices generally.	Pinky red, with a mouldy appearance in places.
COMMISSIONS PURCHASE	Causes irregular action, feverish excitement, and paralysis.	Promotion for services and good conduct, accompanied by competent examinations.	The trenches in winter. – N.B. The Cossack test recommended by a noble Lord does not answer.	Whitehall.	Scarlet.
FALSEHOOD	Seems to exhilarate at first, afterwards runs into mortification.	Bleed with the truth copiously, then send the patient to Austria.	Time and circumstances.	Amongst Emperors & Kings in the despatch-box and high places generally, a good deal in the Church, not much in a *free* press.	At first rose, afterwards running rapidly through brown to black.
HYPOCRISY	Lowers and stretches out the voice, gives a downlook, and other symptoms too *deceptive* for description.	Try hydropathy; do not wait for any doctor, but use the nearest pond or pump.	Tastes soft and sweet at first, suddenly changing to an intense bitter if exposed to light.	Amongst confirmed saints and the long cloth a good deal; may be found in Lincoln's Inn also.	Sable, with a velvety appearance.

POLITICAL RAILWAY ACCIDENT

THE POLITICAL PECKSNIFF

WE have heard that MR CHARLES DICKENS is about to apply to the Court of Chancery for an injunction to prevent SIR ROBERT PEEL continuing any longer to personate, in his capacity of Premier, the character of MR PECKSNIFF, as delineated in *Martin Chuzzlewit*, that character being copyright. We hope this rumour is unfounded, as the injunction would certainly be refused. SIR ROBERT PEEL is in a condition to prove that the part in question has been enacted by him for a long series of years, and was so, long before any of MR DICKENS's works appeared; in short, that he, SIR ROBERT PEEL, is the original PECKSNIFF.

WE regret to have to record an accident which happened to one PEEL, the driver of the engine 'Expediency,' belonging to the express train on the government line of railway. It is well known that this line is exceedingly crooked, and the ins and outs have always been considered very dangerous. PEEL, who is a reckless fellow, and who has lost his place once or twice for improper conduct, put the engine at full speed, though it had got an enormous weight to pull against in the shape of an article for Maynooth, which was very awkwardly placed, and if it had fallen down must inevitably have crushed him.

Regardless of consequences, he urged the engine on; and if it had not happened to be 'Expediency,' which he is in the habit of driving, the result would probably have been fatal. It was however by keeping up the speed that he succeeded in keeping clear of the dead-weight at his back; and there being fortunately nothing in his way to cause a collision, he arrived in safety at the end of his journey.

PEEL'S MECHANICAL MEMBERS

WE understand that SIR ROBERT PEEL intends taking out a patent for a new method of working a sort of political fantoccini, which he has applied with considerable success during the present session to the members of the House of Commons. The puppets are all got together in a line, and by means of a small revolving wheel, they are made to assume such attitudes as may be desired by the person working them. They are thrown into postures of attention, admiration, or enthusiasm, without the smallest difficulty; and, as they all go upon a pivot, they can be turned round to any extent or in any direction at a moment's notice. The invention requires some skill in using it at first, but the PREMIER has brought it to perfection by long experience. We have no doubt the invention will be hailed as a boon by 'PEEL's pocket majority.'

THE GOVERNMENT OFFICES

Are the temporary residences of numerous patriotic gentlemen who are anxious to serve their country – at from 75*l.* to 5000*l.* per annum. They are generally very snug berths, and are pleasantly situated in the vicinity of the parks, thus rendering one of the duties of the *employés* – that of looking out of window – less arduous and irksome. The interiors are usually fitted up in the 'severe style of classic coldness;' but the fireplaces are admirably constructed for imparting a grateful warmth to the dorsal part of the body when the coat-tails are officially expanded. The chairs are

of that peculiar style of upholstery which, partaking of the character of the employment, is appropriately denominated 'easy,' and are so constructed as not to induce positive sleep, nor to disturb those valuable reveries in which government clerks are in the habit of indulging for the benefit of their country. The desks are of mahogany, elaborately embellished with initial letters and peculiar cyphers in office ink. They are found to be highly suggestive to a negligent correspondent; and from the beauty of the paper and pliability of the quills with which they are furnished, the delinquent has no excuse for any further neglect; they also lend an air of dignified condescension to the acceptance of a polite invitation to dinner, and render impressive and indisputable a downright refusal to aid your tailor in 'meeting a bill which he has to take up.'

The paper is of that superior quality known as 'Government post,' and from the smoothness of its surface forms an admirable cartoon, whereon the Raphaeline Clerk can delineate the portraits of his superiors, heightened by those playful touches of fancy which always characterise the early productions of the imaginative school of artists. The 'office-pen' is so well known, that any lengthened description would be supererogatory; but in order to detect the spurious from the genuine, it must be observed that the true government goosequill is selected from that class of pinion-feathers which admit of its being instantly converted into a tooth-pick.

Government offices are liberally supplied with

A Government clerk's cartoon

the daily papers, the careful perusal of which constitutes one of the principal duties of the Clerk whose glorious privilege it is to assist in the regulation of the affairs of his native land.

The most direct road to the government offices is through a member of parliament who supports the party in power. The independent elector may with confidence look to the Excise-office for the reward which he naturally expects as the consequence of voting according to his conscience. The liberal and faithful butler, who procures discount for his master's bills, may certainly consider the Customs as the Ararat of his old age, while the member of parliament may honestly expect an honourable provision for his younger sons, as a trifling equivalent for the many hours that he has slumbered in the cause of the Ministry in the House of Commons.

A NEW CABINET LIBRARY

MINISTERS intend shortly, we understand, issuing a series of volumes on various subjects, for the purpose of enlightening the people, to be called the New Cabinet Library. The work will be written chiefly by the Ministers themselves, so that there will be great variety in the style, and in the mode of treating the various topics handled.

The following will be a few of the volumes that will shortly appear:–

1. The Curiosities of Literature, chiefly selected from intercepted correspondence. By SIR JAMES GRAHAM.

2. How to Live on Fourteen Thousand a year. By the LORD CHANCELLOR.

3. Three Experiments of Living; or, Three Livings at Once, by way of Experiment. By the BISHOP OF EXETER.

4. The Outcast; The Exile's Return; and other Poems. By LORD ELLENBOROUGH.

5. Natural Magic, including several new tricks; with an Essay on Gammon and Backgammon. By SIR R. PEEL.

6. Miscellaneous Essays. By LORD BROUGHAM.

7. The Pauper's Cookery Book; including ten thousand economical recipes, amongst which will be found five hundred different modes of dressing oatmeal, and a plan for roasting a fowl before the fire, in such a way as to make chicken-broth of the shadow. By the POOR LAW COMMISSIONERS.

8. Confessions of an English Opium-Eater. By One who has swallowed all the dull speeches that have been spoken in the House of Commons for the last ten years.

The Fabric of Society

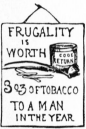

HOW TO LIVE ON
NINE SHILLINGS A WEEK

EVERY man's income is limited more or less; and he must limit his expenditure accordingly. Thus, he may be forced to content himself with a house of a rent not exceeding two thousand a year, with no greater number of servants than a dozen, with six horses and no more; with but two carriages; with turtle, venison, champagne, and burgundy, only now and then; with a middling box at the opera, and so on.

Nine shillings a week is a decidedly limited income. To live upon it a man must first cut down his expenditure to the fewest possible branches, and secondly apply the closest shaving to each. They can hardly be reduced below three: food, clothes, and lodging; but if anybody could do without one of these, the difficulty would be much simplified. As to lodging. The cheapest to be had must be chosen: the more unpleasant the situation the better, as the rent will then be more reasonable. A road-side hovel, or a ruinous old house up a court, may be recommended. A single room, however small, must suffice for a whole family, however large. Chairs, tables, bedsteads, and other moveables, may be dispensed with; the entire furniture should consist of a few blankets and some straw; and the blankets ought to be begged. Coals and candles are too expensive; and it is extravagant to have any fire at all, except to cook a few potatoes, or to avoid being frozen to death.

With regard to clothes. These must be obtained, if possible, through charity: there is another way of getting them, which it would be hardly right to hint at. By a proper economy they may be made to last till they fall to pieces, which they will not altogether do for years. If it is necessary to buy clothes, they must be bought; but the purchase should only include indispensables. Shirts and stockings are superfluities; and the younger children may always, and the whole family at times, manage to do without shoes. Food must be confined, in general, to bread and potatoes; but perhaps, with management, a little bacon may be indulged in now and then. It will be out of the question to think of any other drink than the plain water; and tea and sugar are luxuries not to be dreamt of.

By following the above rules it is perhaps possible to live honestly on nine shillings a week, with a wife and family. Medical attendance is out of the question. What are called comforts must be considered unattainable; for any man, even though starving and perishing, to help himself to a meal, a handful of wood, or anything of the kind, is highly immoral; the law respects not persons but property, and severely visits such wickedness.

The City Article
A well-known Alderman was taken to see the Hippopotamus. He looked at it intently for a quarter of an hour, and then burst out of his reverie with the following remark: – 'I wonder what sort of soup it would make!'

ADVICE GRATIS TO THE POOR

DOCTOR. 'Yes, Mrs Brown! You must give her plenty of nice puddings, some calves' foot jelly – a little wine – a fowl or two – take her to the seaside, and, if possible, go with her to Baden-Baden.'

DOCTORS' BILLS

A GENTLEMAN, the other day, wrote a letter to the *Times*, complaining of a bill which had been sent in to him by his medical man. His grievance was, that the items of professional service had, therein, been generalised under the two heads of 'Medicine and Attendance' simply, instead of being set forth severally and at large. He wished the Account had been drawn up according to the good old formula, which was a specific enumeration of the different pills, draughts, boluses, and other matters and articles, constituting the 'value received.'

This gentleman evidently prided himself upon his common sense, which told him that it would have been satisfactory to know what he had to pay for. The same faculty, perhaps, informed him that medicine has a marketable value, like tea or sugar; and that skill and science can be sold by weight and measure.

We hope the gentleman will approve of the following model of a bill, which we drew up for the guidance of those medical men who may have patients of his way of thinking to deal with.

——— ———, *Esq.*
To ——— ———, *Surgeon, Apothecary, &c.*

	£	s.	d.
Jan. 11, 1844. – To attending you at your own house, at your request, at a distance of five miles	0	5	0
To listening for half an hour to a detail of your symptoms	0	4	2
To asking you to put out your tongue	0	1	0
To feeling your pulse	0	1	0
To inquiring whether you had slept well on the previous night	0	1	0
To replying, in the negative, to your question, Whether oyster-sauce was good for you?	0	6	8
To answer to your question, Whether I considered you consumptive? by telling you to make your own mind easy, for that your lungs were as sound as my own	0	6	8
To saying 'Yes,' when you inquired, Whether you were bilious?	0	6	8
To telling you, in answer to your question, What I thought was the matter with you? 'that you had got a common cold'	0	6	8
To recommending you to put your feet into warm water, and take a basin of hot gruel, going to bed	0	3	4
To calomel pill	0	0	6
To black dose	0	1	0
Total	£2	3	8

That bill was settled long ago

The above is the sort of bill to please your sensible man of business, who looks upon medical attendance as journey-work, and medicine as merchandise. For those who, in their simplicity, think that one question prompted by skill and science, which in a moment elicits the nature of a disorder, is worth as much as a thousand; and that the value of physic depends rather upon its efficiency than its quantity, the charge of 'Medicine and Attendance,' if reasonable in amount, may suffice.

Bubbles of the Year – Patent Life Pills

Romance and Reality of the Railways

VIEWS ON RAILROADS

SINCE we never go anywhere without having an eye to the picturesque, we took our sketch-book with us, intending to make views of the scenery during one of our recent trips by railroad. Seeing the country, we know, is one of the chief delights of travelling, and we supplied ourselves therefore with a telescope, as well as drawing materials, for the purpose of fully enjoying the beauties of nature, and transferring them on the instant to the immortal pasteboard. Unfortunately, whenever we succeeded in catching a glimpse of any thing that we thought worthy of the imperishable lead, it was whisked away from our vision; and just as we had commenced foreshortening something thirty miles off, some fresh object was suddenly brought close up to the window of the carriage, to the exclusion of everything else that our eyes had been resting on. A castle in a momentary perspective was suddenly blotted out by a policeman's hat, and a hanging wood was abruptly curtained in by a flying signal. A background of peaceful meadows was broken, as if by magic, with the smoking chimney of a screeching engine, and sheds seemed sliding past on a groove, like a moving panorama, going at the rate of sixty miles an hour.

Having heard that there was a beautiful bit of still life at about twenty miles from London, we determined to make a desperate effort to catch the favourable moment for sketching it. The sun was shining brilliantly, and we thought the weather had conspired with Nature to add loveliness to the spot; but alas! the express train was proceeding at such a rapid rate, that the following was the only sketch we had an opportunity of taking. Though it scarcely gives an adequate idea of the beauty of the spot, the picture will not be contemptible in the eye of a true admirer of the beauties of Nature.

The mile-post in the foreground, standing bravely up under the intense heat of a July sun, has its story prettily told by the shadow that proceeds from it. A rich background of wild grass shows the reckless luxuriance of Nature, and the whole scene is one of delicious calm, which will be found very soothing to the spirit.

The next view we were enabled to take is of another character, and indicates the presence of agricultural industry. It shows the labourer – or, at least, his legs – walking to his work; and there is an expression in the foot – a fine manly tone in the heel – a determined activity in the toe, which tells the characteristic energy of the British Yeoman. That foot, in the hands of PICKERSGILL, might have taken its place by the side of that great effort of art – the bone in his picture of PROFESSOR OWEN.

We had not the time to throw into the foot all the soul we could desire; but such as it is, and such as it appeared to us in our rapid transit by the rail, we have no hesitation in giving it. But it was in the Tunnel that the true artistical feeling came over us. We there fancied we were going through some of those subterranean passages through which the Sibyls used to pass before the invention of sewers provided them with a fitting thoroughfare.

There was something sublime in the emotion with which, amid the roar of the engine, the rattle of the rails, the screams of the whistle, the choking sensation from the smoke, and the tingling of the cheeks and eyes from the ashes, we made the annexed sketch of what we saw in our passage through the Tunnel.

We were so pleased with that last result, that we determined on proceeding again by night through the same Tunnel; and we were rewarded by witnessing a figure that the pencil of MACLISE could alone do justice to. We are still haunted by the demoniac glare of the policeman under the strong lurid light of a bull's-eye.

Description would, however, faint quite away in any exertion it might make to describe the awful object; and we therefore give the sketch exactly as we made it.

Our readers will perceive that genius can draw beauties from the most unpromising subjects: and as the gentlemen described by SHAKSPERE drew 'sermons from stones' – rather hard reading, by the way, those sermons must have been – so have we been able to elicit a series of sketches of scenery taken during a trip by railroad.

PANORAMA OF THE BLACKWALL RAILWAY

ENJOYMENT of the scenery constitutes more than half the pleasure of travelling; and in order that the voyager along the Blackwall Railway may know what to expect, we have had a panorama prepared by a first-rate artist of the scene that will greet the eye and sink into the heart of the passenger from Fenchurch Street.

Talk of the 'feast of reason and the flow of soul,' what are they compared with 'the feast of chimneys and the flow of smoke,' on the line alluded to? There is something elevating in the idea of running for miles on a level with the weathercock and the cowl, while we mark the fierce cat revelling uncontrolled along the sky-piercing parapet. The chamois hopping and skipping over rocky peaks, or the goat frisking about in the caves of the Colosseum, are both objects of grandeur; but the unfettered cat, roaming at ease through the lofty gutters of Limehouse and Poplar, is a sight which none but the passenger on the Blackwall Railway is privileged to contemplate.

But we are growing sentimental, and the teardrop is trickling down the cedar pen-holder, till, mingling with the murky ink, it becomes darkened with that it mixes with; like the gushing dewdrop, which – but we are losing sight of the Panorama of the Blackwall Railway, to which we entreat the serious attention of all lovers of the beautiful.

RAILWAY PASTORALS

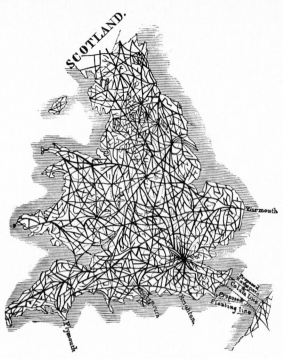

THE iron hand of Railway enterprise is fast tearing up by the roots all the pastoral and poetical associations of our youth, and cottages near woods, as well as mossy cells or leafy nooks, are being superseded by Railway termini. Where the cow once lowed, the engine now screams, and the pipe of the gentle CORYDON is completely put out by the funnel of the locomotive. PHILLIS is sent flying by the power of steam, and the hermit of the dale is compelled to break his staff or cut his stick, to make way for the immense staff of officials required on the Railways.

What is to become of those long accustomed to a pastoral state of existence, we are quite incapable of conjecturing. They cannot remove themselves by *certiorari* to the woodlands wild or the vale sequestered from the hum of men; for it would indeed be a hum of the most grievous kind to encourage them in the hope that anything in the shape of sylvan seclusion is now open to them. As we perceive that the Isle of Dogs is to be sold right out, we recommend its being taken as a colony for the pastorally-disposed population, where the shepherd might still play variations on the flageolet to a flock of sheep, undisturbed by the row incidental to every Railway. PHILLIS might also 'go a-milking,' with a cage containing a couple of turtle-doves in her hand, which, according to the poets, appears to have been the old pastoral practice. As to the gentle hermit of the dale, we see nothing left for him but Herne Bay, or the toll-house on Waterloo Bridge, where, since the opening of Hungerford, an anchorite with fifteen shillings a week might make himself very comfortable.

A RAILWAY MAP OF ENGLAND

WE are not among those who like going on with the March of Intellect at the old jog-trot pace, for we rather prefer running on before to loitering by the side, and we have consequently taken a few strides in advance with Geography, by furnishing a Map of England, as it will be in another year or two. Our country will, of course, never be in chains, for there would be such a general bubbling up of heart's blood, and such a bounding of British bosoms, as would effectually prevent that; but though England will never be in chains, she will pretty soon be in irons, as a glance at the numerous new Railway prospectuses will testify. It is boasted that the spread of Railways will shorten time and labour of travelling; but we shall soon be unable to go anywhere without crossing the line, – which once used to be considered a very formidable undertaking. We can only say that we ought to be going on very smoothly, considering that our country is being regularly ironed from one end of it to the other.

RAILWAY MAXIMS

(Perfectly at the Service of any Railway Company)

Delays are dangerous.
A Train in time saves nine.
Live and let Live.
After a Railway excursion, the Doctor.
Do not halloo till you are out of the Train.
Between two Trains we fall to the ground.
Fire and Water make good Servants but bad Masters.
A Director is known by the Company he keeps.
A Railway Train is the Thief of Time.

There is no place like Home – but the difficulty is to get there.
The farther you go, the worse is your fare.
It's the Railway pace that kills.
The great charm about a Railway accident is that, no matter how many lives are lost, 'no blame is ever attached to any one.'
A Railway is long, but Life is short – and generally the longer a railway, the shorter your life.

THE ROYAL
RHYTHMICAL ALPHABET

The Romance (and Reality?) of Royalty

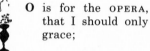

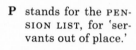

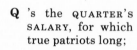

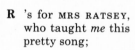

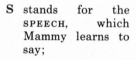

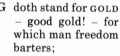

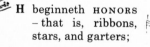

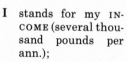

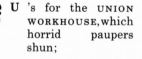

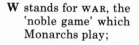

A stands for ARISTO-CRACY, a thing I should admire;

B stands for a BISHOP, who is clothed in soft attire;

C beginneth CABINET, where Mamma keeps her *tools;*

D doth stand for DOWNING-STREET, the 'Paradise of Fools;'

E beginneth ENG-LAND, that granteth the supplies;

F doth stand for FOREIGNERS, whom I should patronise;

G doth stand for GOLD – good gold! – for which man freedom barters;

H beginneth HONORS – that is, ribbons, stars, and garters;

I stands for my IN-COME (several thousand pounds per ann.);

J stands for JOHNNY BULL, a soft and easy kind of man;

K beginneth KING, who rules the land by 'right divine;'

L 's for MRS LILLY, who was once a nurse of mine.

M beginneth MEL-BOURNE, who rules *the roast* and State;

N stands for a NOBLE-MAN, who's *always* good and great.

O is for the OPERA, that I should only grace;

P stands for the PEN-SION LIST, for 'servants out of place.'

Q 's the QUARTER'S SALARY, for which true patriots long;

R 's for MRS RATSEY, who taught *me* this pretty song;

S stands for the SPEECH, which Mammy learns to say;

T doth stand for TAXES, which the people ought to pay;

U 's for the UNION WORKHOUSE, which horrid paupers shun;

V is for VICTORIA, 'the Bess of forty-one;'

W stands for WAR, the 'noble game' which Monarchs play;

X is for the TREBLE X – Lilly drank three times a day;

And **Y Z**'s for the WISE HEADS, who admire all I say.

108

PREPARATIONS AT BRIGHTON

In consequence of the contemplated arrival of the Royal Children, the Pavilion has been for the last fortnight in a state of confusion, in order to complete the necessary preparations. The Royal carpet-beater was sent for, and entrusted with the hearth-rug of the Pavilion play-room; and MR SANDERS, the Inspector of Palaces, was sent down expressly from London to see to the lighting of the fires, the airing of the beds, and the other domestic arrangements. The Comptroller of the Congreve Lights, attended by Stick in Waiting carrying a bundle of fire-wood, proceeded up stairs; and the Steward of the Clothes-horse held a consultation with Warming-pan in Ordinary as to the airing of the sheets and blankets.

We are happy to say that the whole of the arrangements are now in a state of forwardness, and it is expected that in about a week they will be completed.

ROYAL SPORT

It will be in the recollection of our readers that a handsome rod (which turns out to be really a fishing-rod after all), was a little while ago presented to the Prince of WALES. His Royal Highness has lately had some capital sport with this rod, having succeeded in capturing several of his Mamma's gold fish, one of which was as big as a dace and weighed six ounces. It was very nearly pulling the Prince in.

COSTUMES OF THE ROYAL CHILDREN

At the celebration of a birth-day of one of the Royal Family, the two little Princes were dressed in the costume of true British sailors, after a well-known design in a former number of *Punch*. We perfectly approve of HER MAJESTY's desire to keep up in her own family the naval glories of England, by making hearts of oak out of those interesting little acorns already to be found in the Royal abode. We have heard, however, that other classes object to the preference given to the navy by HER MAJESTY's choice; and the poor Protectionists are crying out for the adoption of their costume, by the conversion of one at least of the little Princes into a diminutive 'one of spades.' The complaint of exclusiveness might be carried to a considerable length, for there is no profession that would not have a right to cry out against the adoption of the navy to the prejudice of all the rest. The civil engineer might solicit the dressing up of one at least of the young Princes in the costume of the craft, with a theodolite for a walking-stick, a 'dumpy level' for an eye-glass, and a few of the other symbolical badges of the profession about him, to render the making up complete.

JUVENILE COURT CIRCULAR

WE have always regarded it as a singular omission on the part of the Court newsman, that he makes a point of saying nothing whatever of the movements of the junior branches of the Royal Family. By a judicious system of bribery, added to an adroitness only to be equalled by the Boy Jones, 'the Maniac,' and other uninvited guests at Buckingham Palace, we have succeeded in introducing a reporter of our own, who will put us in possession of the news, the doings, and the small-talk, of the Royal Nursery; which we proceed to lay before our readers, under the head of

NURSERY COURT CIRCULAR

The Princess Royal took a short skip with the rope, and subsequently swung for half an hour, attended – or held on to the swing – by the Dowager Lady Littleton.

His Royal Highness the Prince of Wales played for some minutes a number of variations on the glass harmonicon. His Royal Highness was subsequently taken, for change of scene – and change of pinafore – to the Nursery dressing-room.

The Princess Royal honoured a hoop with a short trundle during the afternoon.

The Royal Infants yawned for a few minutes in the evening; and a representation having been made as to the approach of the Dustmen, the Princess Royal left for Beds by the Marrowbone stage, and was soon followed by her brother and sister.

109

**National
Attitudes to
Manners and
Morals across
the Channel . . .**

SMALL CHANGE FOR PERSONS GOING ON THE CONTINENT

PERSONS of importance being in the habit, at this season of the year, of rushing to the Continent, we have drawn up the following rules, after six trips up and down the Danube and Rhine, to enable travellers to support the character of Englishmen with that degree of pride and gentlemanly spirit for which they are noted abroad.

1. Write your name in large letters, with date and address, wherever you go. For this purpose, you had better carry about with you a bottle of WARREN's blacking and a large brush, and you can then lay it on as thick as you please.

2. If you go into a cathedral when service is going on, never mind talking, or staring, or pointing, as much as you like; for it stands to reason, if the people are really as intent on their devotions as they pretend to be, they cannot hear or see you. The best way to test this, is to walk down the aisles with your hat on.

3. Always suspect you are being imposed upon. It is well known that the innumerable small foreign coins were expressly invented to puzzle the English. To guard against giving too much bargain for everything you have, and try to beat down every item in your bill. Recollect it is the notion of foreigners that every Englishman is stuffed full of money. The sooner you disabuse them of this notion the better.

4. Laugh at everything you do not understand, and never fail to ridicule anything that appears strange to you. The habits of the lower class will afford you abundant entertainment, if you have the proper talent to mimic them. Their religious ceremonies you will also find to be an endless source of amusement.

5. Never mind what damage you do, as long as you can afford to pay for it. Your brothers and sisters will naturally expect some remembrance of your *tour*, so do not scruple to carry off a *souvenir* of every monument you visit. A saint's finger, or a collection of king's noses, if cleverly taken from the statues, or a whole statue itself taken during the night from its consecrated niche in some lonely street, will convince your relations you have not forgotten them, besides affording you capital sport and healthy excitement in making the collection.

6. Recollect very few people talk English on the Continent, so you may be perfectly at your ease in abusing foreigners before their faces, and talking any modest nonsense you like, in the presence of ladies, at a *table d'hôte*. Do not care what you say about the government of any particular state you may be visiting, and show your national spirit by boasting, on every possible occasion, of the superiority of England and everything English.

7. If you go to a theatre and do not know a word of the language of the pieces, do not hesitate to talk as loudly as you can, or to laugh preposterously at the gibberish, which it is a marvel to you anybody can understand.

8. If foreign states will have foolish laws about passports, it is not to be expected that you, as a free-born Englishman, will tamely submit to them, so always move about as independently as if you were in your own country. If, by a stretch of despotism, you are taken up or sent back, you have your redress by complaining to the British ambassador, or else by sending your case to be laid before Parliament as a *casus belli*, to any distinguished member of the opposition of the time being.

9. Be particular about your diet. Avoid foreign dishes; be sure that the wines are poison; and grumble at everything you get. Recollect that beefsteaks and bottled porter are always kept in the smallest villages for the use of the English.

10. Swear, if you have a mind for it, at the smallest provocation; and, if a fellow is insolent, thrash him, and if any one interferes, thrash him also. Recollect you can indulge in any violence you please, as long as you have the means to pay for it.

11. Be sure to take English servants with you. They are useful in speaking the language, settling the bills, and taking you to see the most remarkable sights of the country. . . .

12. Buy something at every place you stop at. The foreign articles are not only so much cheaper and better than any you can get in England, but there is also the pleasure of looking at them, and the pride of displaying them before other people, every time your boxes are examined at a custom-house. If you are asked to pay anything extra for them, on the ground of duty, sooner allow every article to be confiscated, than submit to the imposition.

13. Take all your wardrobe with you. Extra luggage is never charged for on the continent, and it would be very foolish to miss an important ceremony, or a royal invitation, for the want of a proper gown, coat, bonnet, cocked hat, pelisse, or regimentals. . . .

14. Be sure to cultivate your moustachios the very day you start for the continent, and allow your hair to grow down your back. Buy a dialogue-book, and, if you study it attentively all the way up the Rhine, and at all the places you visit, you will be able, by the time you reach London, to ask, 'Which is the nearest way to Cologne?' in no less than eight different languages.

Attend most scrupulously to the above golden rules, and you will never find any difficulty in getting on with the small change with which we have provided you for your trip. Disburse it liberally wherever you go, and you will certainly succeed in making the name of an Englishman respected and beloved all over the continent, and will impress foreigners with the belief that England is without a doubt – what you must always be boasting she is – the most civilised country in the world.

110

A YANKEE NOTION

'REPUDIATION' is a Yankee notion – so is slavery, so is Lynch law, so is annexation, so is Mormonism, so is chewing tobacco. But the Yankee notion which we are about to develop is the notion of a Yankee; and if the reader does not own it to be a considerable one, we are pretty particularly mistaken.

All foreigners, whether counts and barons, or fiddlers and dancing-masters, are distinguished by peculiarities of dress and person. This assertion includes the Yankee, who thus, though untitled, may be ranked among distinguished foreigners.

The Yankee, in the first place, is distinguished by

His hat,

which is something like that devised for the military by our gracious Prince, ALBERTUS PARVUS, so named by us in contradistinction to ALBERTUS MAGNUS, who, as everybody knows, was a conjuror. The brim, however, turns up more at the sides: so that there is much less of the flat about it than there is about the Royal invention; a difference, perhaps, depending on the different minds of which respectively the two hats were emanations.

In the second place, the Yankee may be discriminated by

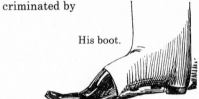

His boot.

Wherefore *ex pede Jonathanum* is as sound an axiom as *ex pede Herculem;* since JONATHAN, like HERCULES, may be guessed at, or calculated, by his foot – with the boot on it. The boot of the Yankee in shape very strongly resembles the ox's tongue, as exhibited in the last cut.

Thirdly, the Yankee is denoted by

His phiz,

in which lankness of feature may be said to vie with sallowness of complexion. The mouth, to speak with mathematical precision, is curvilinear, like that of a steel purse: his nose is as plain as that on your face; probably plainer, whoever you are. It may be defined an incipient aquiline, terminating in a goose-bill. His eye is of the gimlet order; the crow lending its tint to the pupil, and its foot to the outer angle. The same bird, or its first cousin, the raven, affords, in its wing, a comparison to the dye of his hair, of which the mode of growth is typified by the tail of the rat.

The Yankee has also divers moral peculiarities. Of these, one of the most remarkable is his devotion to

His idol.

There is a hole in his head where veneration, according to phrenology, ought to be; but there is nothing in it. We allude to phrenology, as well as the hole; for his veneration for dollars is immense.

and across the Atlantic

YANKEE DOODLE
IN 1851

According to the 'New York Weekly Herald'

YANKEE DOODLE's come to town,
  To see the Exhibition
And strike a blow at England's Crown,
  By stirring up sedition.
The *New York Weekly Herald* see,
  Whose Editor's a noodle,
Or QUEEN VICTORIA's throne will be
  Upset by YANKEE DOODLE.
    Chorus. – YANKEE DOODLE, doodle, &c.

YANKEE DOODLE is no fool,
  He's up to all that's doing,
Full well he knows what Liverpool
  And Manchester are brewing;
Their own republic they're to form,
  And cut the QUEEN's connexion;
And he intends to guide the storm,
  And lead the insurrection.
    Chorus. – YANKEE DOODLE, &c. . . .

YANKEE DOODLE's come to town,
  In all his force and power,
He means to burn the Abbey down,
  Bank, Parliament, and Tower.
Oh! yes – and fire the Thames as well,
  Or, my! what fibs e-tarnal
That catawampous print do tell!
  Our screamin' New York jarnal.
    Chorus. – YANKEE DOODLE, &c.

The Californian outfit

NATIONAL CHARACTERISTICS

National Likes and Dislikes

FRANCE is the land of sober common sense,
And Spain, of intellectual eminence;
Unbounded liberty is Austria's boast,
And Prussia's kingdom is as free – almost;
In Russia there are no such things as chains,
Supreme in Rome enlightened Reason reigns;
America – that stationary clime –
Holds to Tradition and the Olden Time;
England, the light, the thoughtless, and the gay,
Rejoices in theatrical display;
The sons of Scotland are impulsive, rash,
Infirm of purpose, prodigal of cash;
Whilst PADDY's are the lips that know no guile,
For truth has fixed her throne in Erin's isle.

Superiority of British Labour

As a proof that the English are quicker and better workmen than the French, we may mention the fact, that whereas it will take three Frenchmen a week to write a farce, one Englishman will translate it in a day.

OLD GENT. 'You see, my Dear, that the Earth turns on its own Axis, and makes one Revolution round the Sun each Year.'
YOUNG REVOLVER. 'Then, Pa, Does France turn on its own Axis when it makes its Revolutions?'
OLD GENT. 'No, my Dear, it turns on its bayonets. However, that's not a Question in Astronomy.'

TOO CIVIL BY HALF!

ENGLISH COOK. 'Oh, dear! Here, James, come and take this Roast Beef and Plum Pudding out of the window. It Hurts the Feelings of the foreign gents as they walk by!'

Christmas in Ireland

CHRISTMAS-DAY was kept a complete holiday throughout all Ireland. No business whatever was transacted. Not even a single landlord was shot.

Irish Game Laws

1st January. Landlord shooting begins.
31st December. Landlord shooting ends.

Certificates may be had from JOHN ARCHBISHOP OF TUAM, and FATHER MCDERMOTT.

112

LA PRESSE EST MORTE; VIVE LA PRESSE

How newspapers are published in France

FRANCE enjoys, since its last Revolution, a most curious Liberty of the Press. This Liberty seems to be the Liberty of saying anything that is agreeable to the Government, and nothing more. The freedom of thought is allowed to the greatest extent, providing the National Assembly is most freely praised. One word of censure, and the poor Editor is called upon by the President 'to excuse the freedom, but will he take the liberty to walk this way?' – and he is escorted in the politest manner to Vincennes, or shown into some private apartment, where he may study at his leisure the profound mysteries of *Locke on the Understanding*. In England, 'open and advised speaking' is forbidden; in France, it is open and advised writing. In Paris, a journal is suppressed, the Rédacteur imprisoned, and a whole printing establishment stopped, and perhaps ruined in a day, without the smallest public resistance or sensation; in London, such an event would almost cause a Revolution, if Revolutions were not fortunately so unpopular. Imagine the editor of the *Times* being carried off to-morrow morning to the Tower, and Martial Law being proclaimed in Printing-House Square! Why, the stoppage of the Bank would scarcely create a greater panic. The whole country would rush to the rescue, the united Press would nobly league together and forget their little jealousies in the defence of their injured brother, and *Punch* would wield his *bâton* with the force of a pocket thunderbolt. But in Paris there is a regular *battue* of newspapers, and not a murmur is raised to inveigh against the slaughter. . . .

THE FRENCH CONSTITUTION

THE President of the Republic is responsible (to the Republic's President).

Being responsible to the President, the President will do as he deems fit.

The President will have Ministers, who will and must be honoured by thinking as the President shall cogitate.

The higher the President is placed, the more has he the need of faithful councillors; and the greater the need the President may have of them, the less the call the President proposes to make upon them.

Thus, the Government is free in its movements, and enlightened in its progress.

A Chamber, to be called 'the Legislative body,' will vote laws and taxes. This Chamber, to begin with, will be of about 260 members; but the fewer the better, in order to guarantee the calmness of deliberation. History and philosophy having proved that the fewer the number, the less the mobility and ardour of the deliberative body; hence, 60 may be better than 260; 6 better than 60, and 1 better than 6.

The deliberations of the Assembly will not, henceforth, be allowed to run verbosely riot in the public prints, but will be given with drumhead brevity in the President's own newspaper.

The Legislative body will pass laws, but will neither originate nor amend them.

Much time having been lost in vain interpellations, no questions will be asked; or if asked, none answered.

Another assembly bears the name of the Senate. It will be its function to deliberate according to the direction of the President; and will contain all the illustrious names and talent that may not have been transported.

Thus, the people remains master of its destiny.

Such are the ideas, such the principles, that you have authorised me to apply.

A *Te Deum* will be performed in aid of the blessings promised by the Constitution. *Amen.*

LOUIS NAPOLEON BONAPARTE.
Palace of the Tuileries, Jan. 14, 1852.

A Question Questionably Answered

WHEN will France find repose? It will, mayhap,
If it resolves at once to take a NAP.

NOBLE LORD. 'Here's this Confounded Newspaper Speaking the Truth again. Ah! They Manage these Things better in France.'

French
Demonstrations
of Democracy

113

**Women's Rights
and Duties**

CLUB DES FEMMES

At a time when the gentlemen of France are asserting the 'Rights of Man,' no wonder the ladies are protesting against the 'Wrongs of Woman.' Amongst the many Clubs, which the temporary triumph of Club-law has engendered in Paris, there was lately opened a 'Club des Femmes.' At its first sitting much confusion was created by the criticisms of a number of the Lords of the Creation, who had intruded themselves upon the assemblage. This is unfair. What would be the result if a corps of ladies was let loose to criticise the House of Commons? The 'Club des Femmes' has promulgated the following

CODE OF RIGHTS

1. Woman naturally is superior to man. The rule of the husband by the wife is in the order of nature.
2. The wife is the natural guardian of her husband's secrets.
3. To the wife belongs the absolute control of her own milliners' bills.
4. The extreme age of woman is thirty years. She may be below this age, but cannot pass beyond it.
5. Woman has a right to her opinions. It is an odious tyranny which enforces the reasons of them.

CODE OF DUTIES

1. It is the duty of the woman to insist on her own way. This duty is paramount. The end justifies the means.
2. It is the duty of the wife to love and honour her husband. The word 'obey' is abolished except as a duty of husbands.
3. It is the duty of every woman to set off those advantages with which Nature has provided her. Dress is thus invested with the sanctity of a religious observance.
4. The human species is the only one which clothes itself, amuses itself, and cooks its food. Woman, as the highest being in the scale of the human species, has exclusive sovereignty in the three domains of – the Table, the Toilet, and Society.

PROJECTS OF LAWS

1. A law rendering it penal in husbands to grumble at cold meat.
2. A law imposing various terms of imprisonment on the husband who complains of a deficiency of shirt-buttons, struggles for the last word, or exhibits impatience while his wife is dressing.
3. A law to constitute and punish the offence of *lèze-marriage*, or conjugal treason – of which shall be adjudged guilty,
   a. Every husband found in possession of a latch-key, without written permission of his wife:
   b. Every husband bringing home friends to dinner, without a notice of at least twenty-four hours, and an adjudication thereon by the proper authority:
   c. Every husband paying attention to any other woman in the presence of his wife:
   d. Every husband convicted of smoking, unless when the wife smokes also.

THE WOMEN'S CHARTER

We believe in the speedy freedom of the female sex. That beautiful half of the creation – and, like the rosy side of a peach, the much better half – has too long been in bonds. The cunning, the selfishness, and the cowardice of man have, apart and together, operated for many thousand years to crush the lovely flower, or at best that he might wear it – as one may say, in his button-hole as little more than a fragrant, blooming ornament for a brief holiday. These days are fast going – dying upon the save-all of Time. At length women are beginning to know their own strength, at length the hour of equality is about to strike; and when it *has* struck, the world will really for the first time know what's o'clock.

The women, be it known then, have resolved upon a Charter; a triple Charter, for Maid – Wife – and Widow. Each condition of life is to rest upon its seven points. At present, we are only enabled to give them: but we are happy to inform our readers (Women, of course) that a magnificent meeting has been determined upon; it will take place in Kensington Gardens, under the very eye of the military – within the very smell of gunpowder – to show the world that Women, at least, are not afraid of soldiers.

We have, as the earnest and uncompromising advocate both of the Rights of Woman, and of setting Woman to Rights, been favoured with a placard, printed in gold letters upon white satin (which placard it is our intention to have worked up into a waistcoat); and of which the subjoined is an ink-and-paper copy: –

'WOMEN OF THE UNIVERSE!

'Every woman – who is henceforth to be considered every woman's sister – is invited to hold herself in readiness to meet in Kensington Gardens on a day to be hereafter privately appointed.

'As the enemy [it is needless further to particularise] may muster in great force, every sister is entreated to come armed; yes, armed – to the teeth. She will therefore see it expedient to wear new bonnet strings, (if possible, a new bonnet). She must further not fail to dress in her best gown; and further, to bring with her any bonnet or shawl that she may consider to have the most fatal effect upon the enemy!

'Every woman will also provide herself with a serviceable parasol: which – for sharpshooting – is occasionally found of the most efficient use.

'It is moreover expressly required of every single woman, and of every widow, that she do not appear upon the ground without bringing with her a stout substantial wedding-ring (with unmistakeable Hallmark), to the effect that, should the enemy attack us – the single captives may instantly be tried by martial law, and with the speediest benefit of clergy be condemned to a settlement for life. (A parson will be in attendance.)

'Women, – Be ready to appear in full dress (if possible) at six hours' notice!'

HOW TO TREAT THE FEMALE CHARTISTS

LONDON is threatened with an irruption of female Chartists, and every man of experience is naturally alarmed, for he knows that the *vox fœminæ* is the *vox diaboli* when it is once set going. We confess we are much more alarmed about the threatened rising of the ladies than we should be by the revolt of half the scamps in the metropolis. The women must be put down, as any unfortunate victim to female dominion can testify. How, then, are we to deal with the female Chartists? The police will never be got to act against them; for that gallant force knows how much the kitchens are in the hands of the gentler sex, and there is no member of the force who would willingly make himself an outcast from the hearth of the British basement. We have, however, something to propose that will easily meet the emergency. A heroine who would never run from a man, would fly in dismay before an industrious flea or a burly black-beetle. We have only to collect together a good supply of cockroaches, with a fair sprinkling of rats, and a muster of mice, in order to disperse the largest and most ferocious crowd of females that ever was collected.

A new Runnymede

A POSER FOR A BLOOMER

OLD GENTLEMAN. 'Before I can Entertain your Proposal, and Give my Consent to your Marrying my Son, I must ask you, Whether you are in a Position – a – to – a – Keep him in the Style to which – a – I may say – He has always been Accustomed? Ahem!'

SPECIAL CONSTABLE. 'I beg your pardon, Young Ladies, but yours is a very dangerous Procession, and we must take you in Charge – we must indeed.'

A 'BLOOMER.' – A MRS BLOOMER, editress of the *Lily*, as an advance from the weakness of her sex, has – according to the *New York Post* – adopted 'the short dress and trousers.' So far so good. When does the lady begin to shave?

115

BLOOMERIANA. A DREAM

ARTICLES AND ART

NOTHING can be finer than the exhibition of the Royal Academy, except the articles upon it in the newspapers. They are storehouses of critical maxims; and, by a diligent study of them, *Punch* has arrived at a thorough knowledge of art, and, what is more, of the principles of criticism thereof. Anxious to extend this acquisition to others gifted with less analytical acumen than himself, he has digested his results into the following apothegms:

GENERAL MAXIMS

Maxims on Art Criticism

I. The power of criticism is a gift, and requires no previous education.

II. The critic is greater than the artist.

III. The artist cannot know his own meaning. The critic's office is to inform him of it.

IV. Painting is a mystery. The language of pictorial criticism, like its subject, should be mysterious and unintelligible to the vulgar. It is a mistake to classify it as ordinary English, the rules of which it does not recognise.

V. Approbation should be sparingly given: it should be bestowed in preference on what the general eye condemns. The critical dignity must never be lowered by any explanation why a work of art is good or bad.

VI. Never use the word '*picture*,' say '*canvas*:' it looks technical. Never speak of a picture being '*painted*;' say, rather, '*studied*' or '*handled*.'

The following terms are indispensable, and may be used pretty much at random: – '*Chiaroscuro*,' '*texture*,' '*pearly greys*,' '*foxy browns*,' '*cool greens*,' '*breadth*,' '*handling*,' '*medium*,' '*vehicle*.'

CHARACTERISTICS OF PARTICULAR STYLES

1. *To criticise a Picture by Turner.* – Begin by protesting against his extravagance; then go on with a 'notwithstanding.' Combine such phrases as '*bathed in sunlight*,' '*flooded with summer glories*,' '*mellow distance*,' with a reference to his earlier pictures; and wind up in a rapturous rhapsody on the philosophy of art.

2. *To criticise a Picture by Stanfield.* – Begin by unqualified praise; then commence detracting, first on the score of '*sharp, hard outline*;' then of '*leathery texture*;' then of '*scenic effect of the figures*;' and conclude by a wish he had never been a scene-painter.

3. *To criticise a Picture by Etty.* – Begin by delirious satisfaction with his '*delicious carnations*' and '*mellow flesh-tones*.' Remark on the skilful arrangement of colour and admirable composition; and finish with a regret that ETTY should content himself with merely painting from '*the nude Academy model*,' without troubling himself with that for which you had just before praised him. – N.B. Never mind the contradiction.

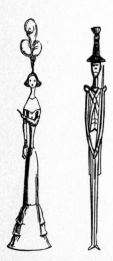

A Pair of Tongs

118

A Shovel   A Poker

4. *To criticise a Picture by E. Landseer.* – Here you are bound to unqualified commendation. If the subject be PRINCE ALBERT's Hat or the QUEEN's Macaw, some ingenious compliment to royal patrons is expected.

Punch will be happy to supply newspaper critics with similar directions for 'doing' all the principal painters in similar style.

He subjoins some masterly specimens of artistic criticism: –

The '*facilè princeps*' of daily critics of art (he of '*the Post*') has the following, in a criticism of HERBERT's *Gregory and Choristers*: –

'There is a want of *modulative melody* in its colours and mellowness in *its hand* (whose?), *pushed to an outré simplicity in the plainness and ungrammatical development of its general effect.* The handling is firm and simple, though in the drapery occasionally too square and inflexible.'

This is an admirable illustration of our fourth and sixth apothegms; and we defy the most ingenious reader, artist or no artist, to understand the meaning of the phrases in italics. This is something like criticism, which has no more business to be conveyed in ordinary English than acting has to imitate nature.

So the same great authority speaks of

'An ungainly group of sharp colour and clumsy forms, *excepted* by a few passages of natural grace.'

An entirely new use of the word '*excepted*.' Mark the following, and say whether it is praise or blame: –

'The light and shade is neither scientific nor unaffected, and pure in its want of breadth.'

The Critic of Art may dispense with ordinary rules of grammar. Thus, when the gentleman who does the exhibition for '*the Globe*' says of No. 570, *Settling for the Cargo*, H. P. PARKER,

'*One* must almost go on *their* knees to see this beautiful specimen of one of the most *characteristic* artists of the present day,'

We have no right to call him to account. It is critical, not vulgar English he is writing.

We feel sure that, when the criticism of Art has reached its present high position, Art itself cannot long lag behind at the immeasurable distance which now separates the artist from the judge.

A Hurried Peep into the Catalogue of the Etty Gallery

15. Bathing.
28. Women Bathing.
33. Nymphs Bathing.
39. Woman at the Bath.
44. Girls Bathing.
58. DIANA surprised at the Bath.
69. VENUS Rising from the Sea.
77. Naiads Bathing.
109. Bathing.
122. The Bathers.

An Ewer   A Coal-scuttle

THE DUKE THAT TRENCH BUILT

THIS is the Duke that TRENCH built.

This is the arch in Grosvenor Place, where they'll put up the Duke that TRENCH built.

This is MR BURTON, a very hard case, who designed the arch in Grosvenor Place, where they'll put up the Duke that TRENCH built.

This is the Committee grown black in the face, with swearing 'gainst BURTON, that very hard case, who designed the arch in Grosvenor Place, where they'll set up the Duke that TRENCH built.

This is autocrat TRENCH, who's contrived to debase the taste of the Committee grown black in the face, with swearing 'gainst BURTON, that very hard case, who designed the arch in Grosvenor Place, where they'll put up the Duke that TRENCH built.

This is his original Iron Grace, kootoo'd to by TRENCH, who's contrived to debase the taste of the Committee grown black in the face, with swearing 'gainst BURTON, that very hard case, who designed the arch in Grosvenor Place, where they'll put up the Duke that TRENCH built.

This is the public, who feel that the place don't suit his original Iron Grace, kootoo'd to by TRENCH, who's contrived to debase the taste of the Committee grown black in the face, with swearing 'gainst BURTON, that very hard case, who designed the arch in Grosvenor Place, where they'll set up the Duke that TRENCH built.

These are 'competent persons,' all sneer and grimace, in contempt of the public, who feel that the place won't suit his original Iron Grace, kootoo'd to by TRENCH, who's contrived to debase the taste of the Committee grown black in the face, with swearing 'gainst BURTON, that very hard case, who designed the arch in Grosvenor Place, where they'll set up the Duke that TRENCH built.

This is *Punch*, taste and art to support with his mace, 'gainst the 'competent persons' all sneer and grimace, in contempt of the public, who feel that the place won't suit his original Iron Grace, kootoo'd to by TRENCH, who's contrived to debase the taste of the Committee grown black in the face, with swearing 'gainst BURTON, that very hard case, who designed the arch in Grosvenor Place, where they'll put up the Duke that TRENCH built.

A Confrontation with the Architectural Experts

119

WRITING MADE EASY

PUNCH, having noticed the growing practice in Parliament of quoting from private letters, undertakes to supply members with letters upon any subject whatever at the following low rates: –

	s.	d.
A Letter from a young Lady, speaking highly of the peaceful state of Ireland, and eulogising its peasantry – or *vice versa*	5	0
A Letter from a liberal Scotch nobleman, animadverting on the iniquitous operation of the Income Tax	1	0
Ditto, from Ditto, in favour of Ditto	15	0
Letters from Farmers, describing the beneficial tendency of the Corn Laws, and exposing the infamous practices of the League, per dozen	1	6
Letters on the Toll system of Wales, (an additional charge if written in Welsh)	2	0
Letters from Magistrates, or the Masters of Workhouses, expatiating on the admirable working of the New Poor Law, per hundred	2	6

Letters procured from Canada, India, or any of the Colonies, at an hour's notice.

*** *A Complete Letter Writer always on the premises.*

CATALOGUE OF THE BRITISH MUSEUM

ALL the thing's a farce,
And all the time and labour merely wasted.
It has its entries and its indexes,
And one man with his time plays but the fool
In poring o'er the pages. First the Volume,
Bulky and ponderous in the porter's arms,
And then the heavy binding, with its edges
And greasy leather backs, letting it slide
Gradually to the ground. And then the titles,
Mixed up like hodge-podge – here a book of ballads
Publish'd by BEALE or BOOSEY. Then a quarto,
Full of strange types, and letter'd all in black,
Printed on vellum – ancient in type and paper,
Cramming the author's reputation
Right down the student's mouth. And then the
    law-book,
In pale brown calfskin, with gross humbug lined,
With rules severe, and forms of rigid cut,
Full of strange laws and musty precedents:
And so this forms a part. The volume shifts
Like change to clown or slipper'd pantaloon,
To subjects no one knows – from side to side
The eye may roll – the topics are too wide
To be embraced – and the loud public voice,
Turning again to childish treble, pipes
And whistles for its wants. Last scene of all,
That ends this strange mysterious catalogue,
Is perfect uselessness and mere oblivion,
Sans head – *sans* tail – in fact, *sans* everything.

THE NEW PATENT NOVEL WRITER

TO MR PUNCH

SIR,

I have to apologise for some delay in answering your obliging favour, in which you did me the honour of suggesting to me the manufacture of a Lawyer's Clerk. After much consideration, I regret that I have found it impossible to produce an article which should be satisfactory to myself, and to the profession. I have, however, been completely successful in the production of a New Patent Mechanical Novel Writer – adapted to all styles, and all subjects; pointed, pathetic, historic, silver-fork, and Minerva. I do not hesitate to lay before you a few of the flattering testimonials to its efficacy, which I have already received from those most competent to judge.

I am, sir, your obedient servant,

J BABBAGE.

Testimonial from G. P. R. JAMES, ESQ., *Author of 'Darnley,' and of* 300 *other equally celebrated works.*

SIR, – It is with much pleasure I bear testimony to the great usefulness of your New Patent Novel Writer. By its assistance, I am now enabled to complete a novel in 3 vols. 8vo., of the usual size, in the short space of 48 hours; whereas before, at least a fortnight's labour was requisite for that purpose. To give an idea of its application to persons who may be desirous of trying it, I may mention that some days since I placed my hero and heroine, peasants of Normandy, in the surprising-adventure-department of the engine; set the machinery in motion, and, on letting off the steam a few hours after, found the one a Duke, and the other a Sovereign Princess; they having become so by the most natural and interesting process in the world.

I am, Sir, your truly obliged servant,

J. BABBAGE, Esq.   G. P. R. JAMES.

Testimonial from SIR E. L. BULWER LYTTON, BART.

I AM much pleased with MR BABBAGE's Patent Novel-Writer, which produces capital situations, ornate descriptions, a good tone, sufficiently unexceptionable ties, and a fund of excellent, yet accommodating morality. I have suggested, and have therefore little doubt that MR BABBAGE will undertake what appears to me to be still more a desideratum, the manufacture of a Patent Poet on the same plan.

E. L. BULWER LYTTON.

PATRIOTISM BY THE YARD

Mr BRIGHT says we have no right to interfere with Russia, because 'the Seat of War is 3000 miles away from us!'

Mr PUNCH, in a conversation the other day with the worthy Member, delicately elicited that in anticipation of the probability of his one day being entrusted with the Seals of Office in a Manchester Ministry, he had prepared for his own private reference a 'graduated scale' of war policy, 'as per distance.' Having insinuated the delight our readers (especially those at St Petersburg) would experience from its perusal, he most obligingly favoured us with a copy, which we subjoin: –

WHEN BRITISH INTERESTS ARE THREATENED
OR ATTACKED AT A DISTANCE OF

3000 Miles – Let them alone. There will be sure to be a market for Manchester Goods under any circumstances.

2000 Miles – Ditto, ditto. Where's the good of interrupting commerce by quarrelling? Perhaps get embroiled in a nasty wicked war.

1000 Miles – If anything very important, a polite inquiry may be permitted.

500 Miles – A gentle remonstrance is allowable, but if assured by the other parties that they mean no harm, we are bound to believe them. The days of MACHIAVELLI are gone.

250 Miles – Within this distance we might assume a little more dignity, and inquire 'If they know what they are about?' &c.

100 Miles – Send word we shall be down upon them if they don't mind.

50 Miles – Get the *Morning Herald* to talk about the 'British Lion,' in order to frighten them.

20 Miles – Tell them they have no idea what a lot of ships and soldiers and sailors and cannons and balls, and other horrible things we've got at home.

10 Miles – We'll only give them this one more warning to keep off.

1 Mile – We might now fire some blank guns; and even if they WON'T go away, I don't see it will matter much. They're all Christian people no doubt, and won't hurt us if we let 'em have their own way.

The idea of a certain critic who 'looked only at the shop watch,' flitted across our mind as we left the distinguished free trader; and we thought it not improbable that if we had suddenly asked him 'Did you see the Bear trying to swallow the Turkey?' he would have answered, 'No, I looked only at the *Yard Measure*.'

ONE of the Horrors of War. – MR DAVID URQUHART lecturing upon it.

EXTRACTS FROM A PEACE DICTIONARY

ARISTOCRACY. The only true aristocracy are the Cotton Lords of Lancashire.

ARMY. A Military Police that is always haunting the Area of civilisation.

AUSTRIA. The experienced Captain of the Jesuit's Craft.

BALE. For keeping the Peace you can have no better Bail than the one Manchester would willingly give – a Bale of Cotton.

BALLS. Ugly customers to meet.

BILLS. See Balls.

BLOODSHED. The red ink in which warriors write their despatches.

CANNON. A vulgar mouther and fiery spouter that is always stopping the way of Progress.

COTTON. The material of which the Flag of Truth is composed.

COTTON TREE. The Tree of Knowledge.

CZAR. The poor Lamb that the English and French wolves wish to devour, because they declare he is disturbing the stream of events.

DRILL. A good thing for trowsers.

ENGINEER. The worst of breeches-makers.

GLADSTONE. One of the few men who are holding the Pale of Civilisation that France and England are trying all they can to upset.

GLORY. The Red Fire that lights up the Theatre of War.

HERO. A Fool who dies for his country, when he could stop at home perfectly safe.

HUMILIATION. What England deserves being brought to for going to War.

MAN OF PEACE. A moral tourniquet that puts the screw on to stop the effusion of blood.

MANCHESTER. The Cottonopolis of the Universe – the Capital of the World.

MILLENIUM. The period when the whole world will be covered with nothing but Cotton Mills.

NAVY. A floating speculation, in which sailors embark their lives either to sink or swim.

NEUTRAL. The only true neutral colour is Drab.

PEACE PARTY. In connection with the Quakers, it is MR COB-DEN's Thou-and-Theeology.

PLANT. Cotton is certainly the best plant now-a-days for making money.

POPE. The occupant of a French caserne.

PRUSSIA. The only throne of Sober Reason.

QUAKER. A Friend who doesn't fight but talk – one who, in the art of making inflammatory speeches, takes his hat off to no man.

REPUTATION. The bubble a fool seeks in the cannon's mouth.

RUSSIA. The place that England gets its hiding from.

SAILOR. The scum of the sea.

SOLDIER. The dirt of the land.

SHOT. What nations that go to war cannot always pay for.

SINEWS OF WAR. Money – without which an Army cannot advance the valuè of a penny, or the distance of an inch.

TRANSPORT. What a soldier goes out in, but seldom returns home with.

WOOL. What our wits are always gathering, when we say anything against the War; and what we stuff our ears with, when we hear anything said in favour of it.

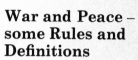

War and Peace – some Rules and Definitions

A Female Library

A BIBLIOMANIAC died on the 3rd ult., at Padua, who had collected 32,000 volumes, all written by female authors. We have seen the catalogue, and are able to give our readers the following details:—

Woman's Mission	12,090 vols.
What is the True Position of Woman?	1,780 ,,
The Rights of Woman	10,273 ,,
The Wrongs of Man	3,645 ,,
Woman the Regenerator	1,733 ,,
The Female Mind	1,063 ,,

The above seem to be the principal subjects upon which the female authors have exhausted their voluminous eloquence. Singular to say, the collection is rather weak in fashionable novels. We need not tell our readers that the works of MRS GORE, for instance, are not included in a library which consists only of 32,000 volumes.

STEAM-BOAT STATISTICS

WE find by statistical returns that there are about thirty steam-boats running between London Bridge and Richmond, all of which have at different times run against the tide, while twenty-five have had the benefit of the wind on some occasions. Sixteen have run aground, and twelve have run into fourteen, while the remaining six have dashed against the bridges. Out of thirty Captains, two have served in the Royal Navy as cabin-boys, sixteen have been in the Merchant Service as bargemen, and all have rowed wherries between London and Westminster. Of thirty bottles of ginger-beer taken on board by one steward, eight have been sold, fifteen have burst, and seven remain on hand at present. There have been ten boxes of cigars carried within the last twelve months in all the thirty vessels, out of which two of the boxes have been stolen, the contents of one have been sold, and the remainder still form part of the cargo.

MINISTERIAL MEASURES

MINISTERS have not brought forward many Measures this Session; and bringing forward nothing, it stands to reason they have not been able to carry much. In fact, the whole business of the present year may be found collected on the subjoined

TABLE OF MINISTERIAL MEASURES

40 Members make	One Full House.
1 Full House makes	One Defeat.
1 Defeat makes	One Large Minority.
20 Minorities make	One Whig Ministry.
1 Whig Ministry makes	One regret the death of SIR ROBERT PEEL!

ANALYSIS OF OUR COLLECTIVE WISDOM

A CAREFUL analysis of the Parliament of 1852, as it is at present oddly constituted in this its moribund year, gives the following results: —

Members, who drop their H's, and are periodically the victims of misplaced aspirations	49
Members, who wear white hats	7
Ditto, who part their hair down the middle	3
Fanatics, who cheer SPOONER	111
Enthusiasts, who believe in LORD JOHN	5
Ditto, who place confidence in DISRAELI	2
Lawyers, who have gone into Parliament in the hopes of political preferment	108
Commercial and Railway men, whose object is to puff their own schemes and support their own Companies	109
Red Tapists, and Members holding office, or connected with persons holding office under Government	100
Sanguine, speculative, or seedy Members, with the hope or promise of holding office under Government	79
Army and Navy Members, who have an interest in backing up, or currying favour with, the Admiralty or Horse Guards	32
Members under the influence of petticoat government, and voting precisely as their wives, or mothers-in-law, or any congenial-minded old women bid them	21
Men of letters, science, and proved ability	20
Vacant seats, and by no means the worst filled	7
High-minded patriots – (say, so as to be on the safe side)	3
Total seats	654

We only hope that the next general election will have the effect of presenting the nation with a more favourable analysis. If not, we shall move that an Analytical Commission, under the presidency of DR HASSALL, be formed to inquire into the corruptions and adulterations of Government.

Table Showing the Probable Duration of Life

(100 *Representing the chance of living longest.*)

	Years
Railway Traveller	$\frac{1}{4}$
Reader of the *Morning Herald*	1
Vegetarian	3
Member of the Peace Society	$4\frac{1}{2}$
Table-Mover, or Balloonatic	7
Parliamentary Reporter	$8\frac{1}{8}$
Husband of a Strong-minded Woman (*unless he runs away from her*)	9
Distressed Agriculturist	$99\frac{3}{4}$
A Constant Reader of *Punch*	100

THE PERPETUAL YOUTH OF THE WOMEN OF ENGLAND

IT appears from the Census, that the people of Great Britain are the youngest people in the world. We are not surprised at this result, and indeed we only wonder that there is any woman in England above the age of thirty, which we are convinced would have been impossible, had the ladies been left to make their own returns. We have had a striking proof of the numerical strength of the Young England party, to which it seems that nearly the whole of the fair sex belongs. There is such a tendency to youth in our female population that we find them ranging themselves under the different heads of 'children,' 'girls,' 'infants,' 'maidens,' and 'young women,' as if juvenility were a luxury to be enjoyed under as many different denominations as possible. We verily believe that if the women had their own way, they would never adopt the epithet 'old,' should they even live to be a hundred, and that they would class themselves in the category of 'second childhood' rather than admit their arrival at the stage of anility. Such is the female horror of the vale of years, that a woman would sooner declare herself to be in her dot-age, than to have reached that 'certain age' which any figure above thirty is supposed to indicate.

FILLING UP THE CENSUS PAPER

WIFE OF HIS BOSOM. 'Upon my word, Mr Peewitt! Is this the Way you Fill up your Census? So you call Yourself the "Head of the Family" – do you – and me a "Female?"'

Census and (female) Sensibility

THE CENSUS

HEAD OF THE FAMILY (*filling up the paper*). 'Well, Miss Primrose, as a Visitor, I must put your age in! What shall we say?'
MISS P. 'Oh, it's best to be Straightforward. The same as dear Flora. Twenty last Birthday!'

A WHOLESOME CONCLUSION

LADY CRINOLINE. 'Yes, Love – a very Pretty Church, but the Door is certainly very Narrow!'

'Gentle Subscriber! Did you ever see two strange Englishmen breakfasting at a Table d'hote abroad. Well! Isn't it a cheerful thing?'

V·LIGHTNESS OF HEART

HORRIBLE ATTEMPT

OUR criminal statistics cannot be considered complete until a new offence that has lately become exceedingly prevalent is added to the record which is published from time to time for the information of the public and the guidance of the legislature. The enormity to which we allude, though it has for years been recognised as on a par with larceny, has not yet occupied the attention of any but the mere moralist. We refer of course to the atrocious habit of making puns, which has become at last more dangerous than the practice of picking pockets; for a man may baffle the pilferer, but against the punster it is impossible to be upon one's guard at all times. A very sad case has lately happened to ourselves, from which we have not yet quite recovered. An individual respectably dressed, and having all the appearance of a tradesman in a good way of business, pounced out upon us from behind the $4\frac{1}{2}$ mile-stone on the Hammersmith Road, and placing a loaded conundrum to our brains, called upon us to 'stand and deliver' an answer to the question, 'When is a chicken like a policeman?' We of course had no alternative but to surrender at once all our self-respect, and to reply, 'When he's a cap(e)on.' Having accomplished his object, our assailant made off, apparently well satisfied with the result of his unjustifiable proceeding. Something should be immediately done to protect the public from these attacks, which are calculated to revive the terrors of the old days, when the highways were not safe; and for our own parts, we had as leave have a pistol presented to our heads as a pun, when we are not expecting it.

LESSONS IN PUNMANSHIP

WE have been favoured with the following announcement from Mr Hood, which we recommend to the earnest attention of our subscribers: –

MR T. HOOD, *Professor of Punmanship,*

Begs to acquaint the dull and witless, that he has established a class for the acquirement of an elegant and ready style of punning, on the pure Joe-millerian principle. The very worst hands are improved in six short and mirthful lessons. As a specimen of his capability, he begs to subjoin two conundrums by Colonel Sibthorpe.

COPY

'The following is a specimen of my punning *before* taking six lessons of Mr T. Hood: –

'Q. Why is a fresh-plucked carnation like a certain *cold* with which children are affected?

'A. Because it's *a new pink off* (an hooping-cough).

'This is a specimen of my punning *after* taking six lessons of Mr T. Hood: –

'Q. Why is the difference between pardoning and thinking no more of an injury the same as that between a selfish and a generous man?

'A. Because the one is *for-getting*, and the other *for-giving*.'

N.B. Gentlemen who live by their wits, and diners-out in particular, will find Mr T. Hood's system of incalculable service.

Mr H. has just completed a large assortment of jokes, which will be suitable for all occurrences of the table, whether dinner or tea. He has also a few second-hand *bon mots* which he can offer a bargain.

*** A GOOD LAUGHER WANTED.

A Con. by Tom Cooke

WHY is the common chord in music like a portion of the Mediterranean? – Because it's the E G & C (Aegean Sea).

A Pro and Con

WHEN is Peel not Peel? – When he's candi(e)d.

A Celestial Coin

WHY is wit like the Chinese lady's foot? – Because brevity is the *sole* of it.

The Poorest Platitudes

A MATHEMATICAL line is straight enough, but the lines in Geology are Strata.

Short and Straight

THE LEGAL FRATERNITY – Brothers-in-Law.

Judgement on a Contemporary

GENTEEL INTELLIGENCE. – The *Standard* is universally spoken of in the servants' halls, as the evening organ of the Harris – tocracy.

Back to the City

ANYTHING BUT AN ALDERMAN'S MOTTO. – 'Dinner forget.'

Latest from Italy

WHAT A CONGRESS OF THE GREAT POWERS IS LIKELIEST TO DO WITH THE ITALIAN BOOT. – Put their foot in it.

Still later

WHY is GARIBALDI like the CHEVALIER BAYARD and a cat in a bad humour?
Because he is *sans purr*.

Philanthropy

DONE IN A MELTING MOMENT

WHY is Ice in a thaw like Philanthropy? Because it *gives* in all directions.

The Two Great Movements

THE two great movements of the present day are the tremendous exertions of the Roman Catholics to extend their religion, and the strenuous endeavours of all good men to elevate the condition of the working classes. These two movements, so dissimilar, and somewhat contradictory in their tendency, nevertheless do agree in one important respect, for the object with each is decidedly a solemn desire to *celebrate the mass*.

The Value of *Punch*

A PUZZLER FOR EVEN SENIOR-WRANGLERS

GIVEN: A number of *Punch*.
TO FIND: Its equal.

The Value of Medicine

The anticipated eruption of Mount Vesuvius is said to have been prevented by throwing a box of Holloway's Ointment into the crater.

Inquest – not extraordinary

GREAT Bulwer's works fell on Miss Basbleu's head,
And, in a moment, lo! the maid was dead!
A jury sat, and found the verdict plain –
'She died of *milk* and *water on the brain*'.

Professions

A DESIGNING CHARACTER. – An Architect.
AN IMPOSING CHARACTER. – A Magistrate, when he fines you.

Farmers

A BRITISH FARMER'S PHILOSOPHY. – The philosophy of Bacon.

The Paper Duties

WHAT A FOOL HE MUST BE!

A SMALL punster of our acquaintance who seems to know more of French history than he does of English spelling, says the battle which has recently been fought upon the Paper Duties, in some degree, reminds him of the famous Siege of Reams.

Clearing the Strangers' Gallery

Punmanship

Going to Blazes?

Dropping his Acquaintance

Taking the Chair

A Friend to look up to

The Truck System

Prince Albert's Own Native Infantry

127

Preparation

Decoration

Realisation   THE EVENING PARTY   Termination

THE NATURAL HISTORY
OF COURTSHIP

PLAIN DIRECTIONS FOR COURTING THE UGLY

THERE is not throughout the whole range of the difficult science we are discussing a more arduous task than that of courting an ugly woman. The decided beauty attracts and exactingly demands our admiration and addresses as matters of course. The cut-and-dried compliments which were doubtless handed down to posterity by the inmates of Noah's Ark are frequently fished for and led up to by herself, and one pays them as currently as courtiers do homage to the throne – for etiquette sake. The 'plain' attach to themselves a suspicion of beauty which affords sufficient foundation for a superstructure of civil things, the truth and sincerity of which they may be made most implicitly to believe. But the ugly –

Yes, to the mere lover the ugly present a blank. He has no cue for his sighs and tears – no excuse for his preference. Upon what text can he discourse in his first love-letter? To what reasonable cause can he refer the lighting up of his flame? To the grace of her figure? – that is almost deformed. To the fire of her eyes? – they are small, grey, and lustreless. To the sweetness of her smile? – it wrinkles her face into the puckers of scorched parchment. Where there is nothing to admire, how is he to prove the integrity of his admiration?

Yet there *is* a cause for his preference; but, alas! that spring must ever remain a sealed fountain. Far from daring to hint, he must ingeniously conceal, the true origin of his tenderness. Blighted are his hopes should she once suspect he sighs for her fortune instead of herself! And, be it remarked, *en passant*, all ugly women *have* fortunes.

Those who have not are never courted: they are either entirely passed over, or, if the windfall of a sigh should happen to alight upon them, they never lose a chance; they accept and get married as soon as possible, before there is time for the operations of courtship even to commence.

Thus 'cribbed, cabined, and confined' in the range of *matériel* for sentiment, what is to be done? Hear our plain directions – they are infallible.

You must in every case begin by using all the dowager and *passé* arguments against beauty. 'Fleeting dowry! – evanescent as the summer cloud – worthless as the withered flower – often leading its unhappy possessor into the paths of temptation – abandoning her in the depths of destruction – leaving her at last to mourn over blighted hopes' – and all that. But, on the other hand, 'who can sufficiently estimate the lasting blessings of congenial sentiment – of hearts fondly beating in a blissful union? – the never-dying graces of the mind' – and so forth. But the most effectual topic of all – especially in a case where a few thousands a year are at stake – is the delights of content and love in a cottage. 'With such a mind as yours, even poverty would be endurable,' will always prove a clencher.

You will find that every woman who is remarkable for her ugliness is said to be also remarkable for some especial virtue, accomplishment, or specific perfection. Whenever you hear it remarked that 'she certainly is very plain,' there will always follow a 'but,' which introduces an addendum on the amiability of her disposition, the superiority of her talents, or the beauty of her foot.

When an ugly woman cannot, with any conscience, lay claim to talent or good temper, the redeeming personal advantage is boasted of in an exquisite foot or a delicate hand. My friend Lady Flabble weighs at least sixteen stone, and is ill-looking in proportion.

'But then,' say her toadies, 'did you ever see such a beautifully-shaped hand?'

Laws of Attraction

A DICTIONARY FOR THE LADIES

PUNCH

Solicitous to maintain and enhance that reputation for gallantry towards his fair readers which it has ever been his pride to have merited, has much pleasure, not unmixed with self-congratulation, in thus announcing to the loveliest portion of the creation the immediate appearance of

A DICTIONARY ENTIRELY AND EXCLUSIVELY FOR THEIR USE

in which the signification of every word will be given in a strictly feminine sense, and the orthography, as a point of which ladies like to be properly independent, will be studiously suppressed. The whole to be compiled and edited by

MADAME PUNCH

To which will be appended a little Manual addressed confidentially by PUNCH himself to the Ladies, and entitled

TEN MINUTES' ADVICE ON THE CARE AND USE OF A HUSBAND

or 'what to ask, and how to insist upon it, so that the obstreperous bridegroom may become a meek and humble husband.'

SPECIMEN OF THE WORK

Husband – A person who writes cheques, and dresses as his wife directs.
Duck, in ornithology – A trussed bridegroom, with his giblets under his arm.
Brute – A domestic endearment for a husband.
Marriage – The only habit to which women are constant.
Lover – Any young man but a brother-in-law.
Clergyman – One alternative of a lover.
Brother – The other alternative.
Honeymoon – A wife's opportunity.
Horrid; Hideous – Terms of admiration elicited by the sight of a lovely face anywhere but in the looking-glass.
Nice; Dear – Expressions of delight at anything, from a baby to a barrel-organ.
Appetite – A monstrous abortion, which is stifled in the kitchen, that it may not exist during dinner.
Wrinkle – The first thing one lady sees in another's face.
Time – What any lady remarks in a watch, but what none detect in the gross.

The Niceties of Love

THE CHEMIST TO HIS LOVE

I love thee, Mary, and thou lovest me.
Our mutual flame is like th'affinity
That doth exist between two simple bodies:
I am Potassium to thine Oxygen.
'Tis little that the holy marriage vow
Shall shortly make us one. That unity
Is, after all, but metaphysical.
O, would that I, my Mary, were an acid,
A living acid; thou an alkali
Endow'd with human sense, that, brought together,
We both might coalesce into one salt,
One homogeneous crystal. Oh! that thou
Wert Carbon, and myself were Hydrogen;
We would unite to form olefiant gas
Or common coal, or naphtha – Would to Heaven
That I were Phosphorus and thou wert Lime!
And we of Lime composed a Phosphuret.
I'd be content to be Sulphuric Acid,
So that thou mightst be Soda. In that case
We should be Glauber's salt. Wert thou Magnesia
Instead, we'd form the salt that's named from Epsom.
Could'st thou Potassa be, I Aqua-fortis,
Our happy union should that compound form,
Nitrate of Potash – otherwise Saltpetre.
And thus, our several natures sweetly blent,
We'd live and love together, until death
Should decompose the fleshy *tertium quid*,
Leaving our souls to all eternity
Amalgamated. Sweet, thy name is Briggs
And mine is Johnson. Wherefore should not we
Agree to form a Johnsonate of Briggs?
We will. The day, the happy day, is nigh,
When Johnson shall with beauteous Briggs combine.

THE FOX AND THE GRAPES

ELDERLY SPINSTER. 'So you're going to be married, dear, are you? Well, for my part, I think nine-hundred-and-ninety-nine marriages out of a thousand turn out miserably; but of course every one is the best judge of their own feelings.'

THE POETRY OF THE RAIL

LOVE ON THE OCEAN

Love in Motion

WE have already pointed out the alteration likely to be made in poetry and song-writing by the introduction of Railroads, and we this week give another specimen of the probable effect of the change. We shall hear no more now of the Lily of the Vale or the Village Rose, but the Pearl of the Refreshment-room and the Daisy of the Rail will supersede the once popular maidens alluded to. The following touching ballad is supposed to be addressed by one of the luggage superintendents to one of the female waiters at the same station, and may be called –

THE PORTER TO HIS MISTRESS

Oh maiden, but an instant stay,
  And let me breathe my vow;
I know the train is on its way,
  I hear its thund'ring row.

Another moment crowds will stand
  Where now to thee I kneel;
And hungry groups will soon demand
  The beef, the ham, the veal.

Turn not away thy brow so fair,
  'Tis that, alas! I dread;
For thou hast given me, I swear,
  One fatal turn a-head.

I've linger'd on the platform, love,
  My brow with luggage hot;
A voice has whisper'd from above,
  'Porter, take heed, love knot!'

O'er thee mine eye doth often range:
  I've mark'd thee take the pay
From those who, ere you bring their change,
  Rush to the train away.
    Turn not, &c. &c.

'"Oh! is there not something, dear AUGUSTUS, truly sublime in this warring of the elements?" But AUGUSTUS's heart was too full to speak.' – *MS. Novel, by Lady ***.*

THEY met, 'twas in a storm,
  On the deck of a steamer;
She spoke in language warm,
  Like a sentimental dreamer
He spoke – at least he tried;
  His position he altered;
Then turn'd his face aside,
  And his deep-ton'd voice falter'd.

She gazed upon the wave,
  Sublime she declared it;
But no reply he gave –
  He could not have dared it.
A breeze came from the south,
  Across the billows sweeping;
His heart was in his mouth,
  And out he thought 'twas leaping.

'O, then, Steward,' he cried,
  With the deepest emotion;
Then totter'd to the side,
  And leant o'er the ocean.
The world may think him cold,
  But they'll pardon him with quickness,
When the fact they shall be told,
  That he suffer'd from sea-sickness.

Love at Home

YOUTH AT THE PROW, AND
PLEASURE AT THE HELM

The Happy Pair then started for the Continent,
via Folkestone, to spend the Honeymoon

EDWIN. 'Now, upon my life, Angelina, this is too
bad – no buttons again.'
ANGELINA. 'Well, my dear, it's of no use fidgetting
me about it. You must speak to Ann. You can't
expect me to do everything.'

DOMESTIC BLISS
Time, half-past 3; Thermometer 30 deg.

WILLIAM. 'What a violent ringing there is at the
street-door Bell!'
MARIA. 'Oh! I know what it is, dear. It's the
Sweeps; and I dare say the girls don't hear. Just
run up, and knock at their room door.'

A PERFECT WRETCH

WIFE. 'Oh, don't Smoke in the Drawing-Room,
Charles! – You never used to do such a thing!'
PERFECT WRETCH. 'No, my dear – but then the
Furniture was quite new!'

MORE HINTS TO MAKE HOME HAPPY – TO WIVES

YOUR first consideration before marriage was, how to please your lover. Consider any such endeavour, after marriage, to be unnecessary and ridiculous; and, by way of amends for your former labour, let your sole object be, to please yourself.

Be at no pains to look well of a morning. A long toilet is tiresome; particularly when it is cold. 'Taking the hair out' occupies nearly ten minutes: come down to breakfast, therefore, in curl papers; also in a flannel dressing-gown; and, unless you expect callers, remain in *déshabille* all day. Husbands are nobodies, and comfort is to be studied before appearance.

But are you to neglect your attire altogether? By no means. Indulge your taste in dress to the utmost. Be always buying something new; never mind the expense of it. Payments belong to husbands. If you see a shawl or bonnet in a window, order it. Should a silk or a muslin attract your eye, desire it to be sent home. Does a feather, a ribbon, a jewel, strike your fancy? purchase it instantly. If your husband is astonished at the bill, pout; if he remonstrates, cry. But do not spoil your finery by domestic wear. Reserve it for promenades and parties. It is the admiration of society that you should seek for, not your husband's. . . .

Practise, however, a reasonable economy. Take every opportunity of making a cheap purchase; and when asked of what use it is? reply, that it is 'a bargain.'

Enjoy ill health. Be very nervous: and, in particular, subject to fits; which you are to fly into as often as your husband is unkind, that is, whenever he reasons with you. Make the most of every little ache or pain; and insist upon having a fashionable physician. There is something very elegant in illness; a prettiness in a delicate constitution – affect this attraction if you have it not – men admire it exceedingly.

Put yourself under no restraint in your husband's presence. Sit, loll, or lie, in just what way you like, looking only to the ease of the posture, not to its grace. Leave niceties of conversation and sentiment to the single; never mind how you express yourself; why should wives be particular? When your husband wishes to read or be quiet, keep chattering to him; the more frivolous and uninteresting the subject, the better. If he is disposed for conversation, be dull and silent: and whenever you see that he is interested in what he is talking about, especially if he wishes you to attend to him, keep yawning. . . .

If your husband has to go out to a business-dinner, or to the play, never let him have the latch-key; and should he, on any occasion, stay out late, send the servant to bed, sit up for him yourself, and make a merit of the sacrifice to 'the wretch.'

Have a female confidant, who will instruct you in all the ill qualities of husbands generally, and will supply any deficiencies in the above hints. In conclusion, bear these grand principles in mind – that men must be crossed and thwarted continually, or they are sure to be tyrants; that a woman, to have her rights, must stand up for them; and that the behaviour which won a man's affections, is by no means necessary to preserve them.

Matrimonial Weather Report – Feb. 7th.

DAYS OF THE WEEK	WEATHER	OBSERVATIONS
Monday	Rather cloudy	Washing Day.
Tuesday	Rain	Wife cried, because I wouldn't take her out shopping.
Wednesday	Unsettled	Housekeeping book for last week examined.
Thursday	Slight breeze	Dined at the Club.
Friday	Fine	New velvet dress given to Wife.
Saturday	Stormy	Cold meat for dinner.
Sunday	Sunshine	Took a walk with wife and children in the Park.

NOTE. – These reports are always written down as I smoke my last pipe upon going to bed.

(SIGNED) JOHN SMITH,
Clerk of the Matrimonial Weather.

With the Servants: Above the Stairs . . .

FLUNKEYIANA – A FACT

FLUNKEY (*out of place*). 'There's just one question I should like to ask your Ladyship – Ham I engaged for Work, or ham I engaged for Ornament?'

LADY. 'Resign your Situation! Why, what's wrong now, Thomas? Have they been wanting you to eat Salt Butter again?'
GENTEEL FOOTMAN. 'Oh no, thank you, Ma'am – but the fact is, Ma'am – that I have heard that Master were seen last week on the top of a Homnibus, and I couldn't after that remain any longer in the family!'

THE KNEE-PLUSH ULTRA

In the *Times* of May 14 may be read the original of the subjoined advertisement: –

FOOTMAN – a good-looking young fellow, tall and handsome, looks well behind a carriage, age 21, height 5 feet 11½ inches, broad shoulders and *extensive calves*. Two years' good character. Family with town house preferred, and *a preference for Belgravia or the north-side of Hyde Park*. Address to A. M. D., Post Office, Grenville Street, Brunswick Square.

Now, is A. M. D. chargeable with conceit of height, with vanity of shoulders? By no means; he merely addresses himself to the prejudices of the plush-market; and when he speaks of his 'extensive calves,' he merely proves that he perfectly well knows the asses he appeals to.

BUTLER (*to personal Friend*). 'There, my boy! I wonder what My Lord would give, if he could get such a glass of Madeira as that!'

SERVANT MAID. 'If you please, Mem, could I go out for half-an-hour to buy a bit of Ribbin, Mem?'

The Delights of the Table: Anticipation . . .

ANGELINA. 'Will my darling Edwin grant his Angelina a boon?'
EDWIN. 'Is there anything on earth her Edwin would not do for his pet? – Name the boon, oh, dearest – name it!'
ANGELINA. 'Then, love, as we dine by ourselves to-morrow, let us, oh! let us have roast pork, with plenty of sage and onions!'

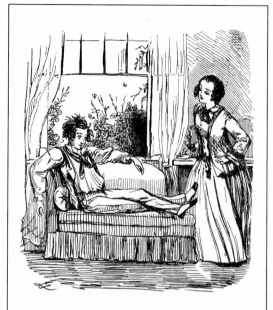

VERY PROPER DIET FOR THIS HOT WEATHER

MRS TURTLEDOVE. 'Dearest Alfred! Will you Decide now what we shall have for Dinner?'
MR TURTLEDOVE. 'Let me see, Poppet. We had a Wafer Yesterday – Suppose we have a Roast Butterfly To-day.'

Experiment . . .

QUITE A NOVELTY

AMIABLE EXPERIMENTALIST. 'Makes a delicious Side Dish, doesn't it? But it is not the common Mushroom; it's a large Fungus, called the Agaricus Procerus. It grows solitary in hedge rows, is called Colubrinus, from the snake-like markings on its stem. The Pileus is covered with scales, which are formed by the breaking-up of the mud-coloured Epidermis, and –
[*General panic takes place*].

OLD PARTY (*very naturally excited*). 'Why, confound you! You are Wiping my Plate with your Handkerchief!'
WAITER (*blandly*). 'It's of no consequence, Sir – It's only a Dirty One!'

BACHELOR HOUSEKEEPING

MR BROWN. 'Pray, Jane, what on earth is the reason I am kept Waiting for my Breakfast in this way?'
JANE. 'Please, Sir, the Rolls isn't come, and there's no Bread in the house!'
MR BROWN. 'Now, upon my word! How can you annoy me with such Trifles? No *Bread*, then bring me some *Toast*.'
[*Exit* JANE *in dismay*.]

Arrival . . .

Departure

A RISE IN BREAD-STUFFS! – EFFECTS OF EATING AERATED BREAD

Poor Cocker having been Recommended to try the 'Aerated Bread,' does so, and is Discovered, along with his Family, Floating about the Ceiling of his Parlour, in an utterly Helpless Condition.

**The Rising
Generation**

HOSTESS. 'Now, my dear – Will you come and dance a Quadrille?'
JUVENILE. 'Tha-a-nk you – It's so many years ago since I danced, that I would rather be excused, if you please. In fact, I – aw, haven't danced since I was quite a boy.'

SOUND ADVICE

MASTER TOM. 'Have a Weed, Gran'pa?'
GRAN'PA. 'A what! Sir?'
MASTER TOM. 'A Weed! – A Cigar, you know.'
GRAN'PA. 'Certainly not, Sir. I never smoked in my Life.'
MASTER TOM. 'Ah! then I wouldn't advise you to begin.'

OLD GENTLEMAN. 'Well, Walter, I suppose you have got into Latin and Greek at School by this time, eh?'
JUVENILE. 'Oh, yes, Sir; I have just finished Xenophon and Thucydides, and am now in Euripides. By the way, Sir, how would you render the passage beginning κακῶς πέπρακταί πανταχῆ?'
OLD GENTLEMAN. 'Ahem! Hey? – what? – ahem! Here, Ruggles! bring another bottle of Claret, and – eh? – what? Walter, I think you had better join the Ladies.'

NOTHING LIKE PRUDENCE

MARIA *loq.* 'My dear Charles, before we think of Marrying, I must ask you, what you have?'
CHARLES. 'My dear Maria. I will tell you frankly that all I have in the world is a Drum and a Cricket-Bat; but Papa has promised me a Bow and Arrows, and a Pony, if I am a good Boy.'
MARIA. 'Oh! my dear Charles, we could never live and keep House upon that!'

COMPARATIVE LOVE

PAPA. 'So, Charley, you really are in Love with the little Black-eyed Girl you met last night?'
CHARLEY. 'Yes, Papa, I love her dearly!'
PAPA. 'How much do you Love her, Charley? Do you Love her as much as Pudding?'
CHARLEY. 'O yes, Papa! and a great deal better than Pudding. But – (*Pausing to reflect*) – I do not Love her – so much as – Jelly!'

A WORD TO THE WISE

DISCERNING CHILD (*who has heard some remarks made by Papa*). 'Are you our new Nurse?'
NURSE. 'Yes, dear!'
CHILD. 'Well then, I'm one of those boys who can only be managed with Kindness – so you had better get some Sponge Cakes and Oranges at once!'

BON-BONS FOR JUVENILE PARTIES

ALFRED. 'I say, Frank, aren't you going to have some Supper?'
FRANK. 'A – not at present. I shall wait till the Women leave the Room.'

THE BEST SEWING-MACHINE

THE very best Sewing-Machine a man can have is a Wife. It is one that requires but a kind word to set it in motion, rarely gets out of repair, makes but little noise, is seldom the cause of a dust, and, once in motion, will go on uninterruptedly for hours, without the slightest trimming, or the smallest personal supervision being necessary. It will make shirts, darn stockings, sew on buttons, mark pocket handkerchiefs, cut out pinafores, and manufacture children's frocks out of any old thing you may give it; and this it will do behind your back just as well as before your face. In fact, you may leave the house for days, and it will go on working just the same. If it does get out of order a little, from being overworked, it mends itself by being left alone for a short time, after which it returns to its sewing with greater vigour than ever. Of course, sewing machines vary a great deal. Some are much quicker than others. It depends in a vast measure upon the particular pattern you select. If you are fortunate in picking out the choicest pattern of a Wife – one, for instance, that sings whilst working, and seems to be never so happy as when the husband's linen is in hand – the Sewing Machine may be pronounced perfect of its kind; so much so, that there is no make-shift in the world that can possibly replace it, either for love or money. In short, no gentleman's establishment is complete without one of these Sewing Machines in the house!

HOW TO 'FINISH' A DAUGHTER

1. BE always telling her how pretty she is.
2. Instill into her mind a proper love of dress.
3. Accustom her to so much pleasure that she is never happy at home.
4. Allow her to read nothing but novels.
5. Teach her all the accomplishments, but none of the utilities, of life.
6. Keep her in the darkest ignorance of the mysteries of house-keeping.
7. Initiate her into the principle that it is vulgar to do anything for herself.
8. To strengthen the latter belief, let her have a ladies' maid.
9. And lastly, having given her such an education, marry her to a clerk in the Treasury upon £75 a year, or to an ensign that is going out to India.

If, with the above careful training, your daughter is not finished, you may be sure it is no fault of yours, and you must look upon her escape as nothing short of a miracle.

YOUNG LADY (*whose birthday it is*). 'Oh, yes! I have had a great number of nice presents: but I wonder who sent me this beautiful Bouquet?'
HANDSOME PARTY (*with moustaches, presence of mind, and great expression of eye*). 'And can't you guess?' (*Sighs deeply.*)
[N.B. Poor BINKS, who was at all the trouble and expense of getting the said bouquet from Covent Garden, is supposed to be watching the effect of his gift with some anxiety.]

CONSOLATION

YOUNG SNOBLEY. 'Ah, Jim! Noble Birth must be a great Advantage to a Cove!'
JIM (*one of Nature's nobility*). 'H'm! P'raps! – but egad! Personal Beauty ain't a bad Substitute!'

A DELICATE CREATURE

YOUTHFUL SWELL. 'Now Charley – you're just in time for Breakfast – have a Cup of Coffee?'
LANGUID SWELL (*probably in a Government Office*). 'Thanks! No! I assure yah – my de-ah fellah! if I was to take a Cup of Coffee in the Morning, it would keep me awake all Day!'

A Gent at Cost Price

THE VALUE OF A GENTLEMAN

A GENTLEMAN lately exhibited himself at a ball, which took place in one of the most brilliant *salons* of St Mary Axe, in a full dress evening suit.

The gentleman was apparelled as follows: – He wore a superior blue dress coat, with figured gilt buttons, and lined with white satin; an ultra-marine-coloured silk waistcoat, embroidered with orange and crimson flowers; best black kerseymere trousers; the Corazza shirt; the new Sutherland stock; and the Albert pumps.

Each article of the above was decorated with an ornamental figure. This was neither more nor less than the 'figure' at which they were manufactured for the slop-seller. It was worked in fancy silk, and very showily variegated. On the facings of the coat, on each side, was marked 2s 9d; on each half of the waistcoat, 7d; on the knees of the trousers, 7d; in the centre of the stock was embroidered 2s 6d; on the bosom of the shirt, 2½d; and 2s below either instep. The fashionable novelty exhibited in this *tout-ensemble* excited universal admiration, and the wearer of the suit was declared on all hands to be 'quite the gentleman.' Nine tailors are commonly allowed for the making of a mere man, but in this instance two made the gentleman. . . .

POLITE
CONVERSATIONS

The Art of Conversation

MR BROWN. Good morning, Mrs Smith. I hope I have the pleasure of seeing you quite . . .?
MRS SMITH. Quite, thank you.
MR B. And Mr Smith, I hope he is quite . . .?
MRS S. Quite, thank you.
MR B. And all the . . .?
MRS S. Quite, thank you.
MR B. Has your eldest boy quite recovered from the . . .?
MRS S. Quite, thank you.
MR B. The weather is exceedingly . . .
MRS S. It is, indeed.
MR B. Have you been riding to-day in the . . .?
MRS S. No; the day was so very . . .
MR B. Ah – yes – exactly.
                    (*A pause.*)
MR B. A – a – a – a – a –
MRS S. I beg your pardon?
MR B. I didn't say . . .
MRS S. Oh, I thought you were saying . . .
MR B. No.
MRS S. Indeed?
MR B. Well, I mustn't detain you from your . . .
MRS S. Good mor' . . .
                    (*Exeunt severally.*)

'Pardon me, Madam – you remember me, Mr Smith?'
YOUNG LADY (*innocently*). 'Smith – Smith! I really, Sir, can't say that I recollect your face; but I think I remember having heard the name before.'

VERY INTERESTING, IF ONE DID
BUT KNOW A LITTLE MORE

'And so Missus says, Mary, she says, tell me all about it, she says – and so I says, me, Marm? I says – and with that, that's how it was, yer see.' – 'Lor!'

PUNCH'S GUIDE TO PARTIES

To those who are just emerging from the verdancy of youth, and to those 'young men in the city' who wish to 'wriggle' themselves into good society, PUNCH affectionately addresses the following advice, – commiserating the pitiable mortifications inflicted on young gentlemen whom he has seen defiling drawing-rooms (consecrated to evening parties and full-dress) with railway-pattern trousers and Blucher boots. – Keenly pitying the situation of others who have found themselves in the very midst of the uncivilised orgies of a bachelor's feed, adorned with satin waistcoats and full-dress stocks, – he benevolently publishes an infallible scale of evening dress, marked and arranged from the various terms in which invitations are usually conveyed, that the inexperienced aspirant to elegant society may no longer be at a loss.

When the invitation is in the following form: –

	You may wear	
'Come up old fellow to my rooms, and take a chop.'	*You may wear*	Anything you please, from a Velveteen shooting-jacket upwards.
A note asking you to join 'A few friends to dinner next Thursday.'	,,	A black coat; but you need not change your Tweed nethers for black ones, if you have not time.
An MS. request for 'Your company to dinner on Thursday week.'	,,	Dress-coat and trousers, fancy waistcoat, and Wellington boots.
An engraved ditto	,,	Dress ditto ditto, for a 'dinner-*party* on Thursday fortnight.'
'A few friends to tea.'	,,	white waistcoat, long satin stock, brilliant breast-pin, and dress boots.
		You need not be particular. Surtouts and coloured continuations won't be objected to.
'An evening party – cards.'	,,	Same as a week's notice 'to dinner' with the addition of a pound's worth of silver in a card-purse.
An engraved invitation on enamelled paper in a fancy envelope, soliciting 'the pleasure of your company to an evening party at half-past nine o'clock on that day five weeks' – with the addendum in one corner of 'quadrilles.'	,,	Blue coat with gilt buttons, black trousers, patent leather dancing boots, satin waistcoat with gold sprigs, white neckerchief, frilled shirt, and two pairs of light kid gloves for fear one should get soiled.

As the greatest Reformer of the age, PUNCH desires that every member of 'Young England' – from the clerk to the Count – from the SMITHS of the East, to the SMYTHES of the West End – will get the above directions printed in large letters, framed, glazed and hung up over their washing stands.

The Laws of Etiquette

ETIQUETTE OF BURGLARY

CALL when the family is out of town.

Choose a dark night for your visit.

Make as little noise as possible.

Walk on tiptoe, as you keep moving from room to room, for fear of disturbing any one who might be asleep.

Remove all articles of value that come in your way.

Don't slam the doors.

Before leaving, drink your host's health in his best Sherry.

Shut the street-door carefully as you go out.

As you are not expected to show your faces on such occasions, you may as well protect them from the cold by wearing pieces of black crape over them.

You needn't leave your Card, much less your Ticket-of-Leave, behind you, because if your host troubles himself in the least by attempting to return your call, you would only be putting him to a great deal of inconvenience, and besides you would not be able to treat him with the same hospitality. Moreover, such visits, paid, as they are, with such little ceremony, are never expected to be returned.

Should you, by any accident, meet with a policeman, do not behave meanly or discourteously to him, but invite him by all means to join your little festive party, unless he should prefer to keep watch for you by remaining outside.

**The wrong Size:
More
Incongruities**

'Your bath is quite ready, Ma'am.'
'Well, but my good girl, I can't get into such a
bit of a thing as that!'

COMFORTABLE LODGINGS

'This is Your Bed, Sir.'

A PUZZLING ORDER

'I'll trouble you to measure me for a New Pair
of Boots.'

FANCY DRESS BALL

'Sir! – Please Mr! – Sir! You've forgot the
Door-Key!'

DIRECTIONS TO
LADIES FOR SHOPPING

thing suggests another; as bonnets – ribands for trimming, or flowers; and handkerchiefs – perfumery. In considering what more you want, try and recollect what your acquaintances have got that you have not; or what you have seen worn by strangers in going along. See if there is anything before you superior in any respect to a similar thing which you have already; if so, get it instantly, not reflecting whether your own will do well enough. You had better finish your streets before you take your bazaars and arcades; for there the shopping, which one might otherwise call cover-shopping, though excellent sport, refers mostly to articles of no manner of use; and it may be as well to reserve toys and superfluities to the last. Married ladies, when they have laid in all they want for themselves, are recommended to show their thoughtfulness by purchasing some little trifle for their husbands, who, of course, will have to pay for it in the end.

SHOPPING is the amusement of spending money at shops. It is to a lady what sporting is to a gentleman; somewhat productive, and very chargeable. Sport, however, involves the payment of one's own shot; shopping may be managed by getting it paid for. Ride all the way till you come to the shopping-ground in a coach, if you can; in an omnibus, if you must; lest you should be tired when you get there. If you are a lady of fashion, do not get out of your carriage; and when you stop before your milliner's, particularly if it is a cold, wet day, make one of the young women come out to you, and without a bonnet, in her thin shoes, stand on the kerb-stone in the damp and mud. The best places for shopping are fashionable streets, bazaars, and the like. Street-shopping principally relates to hosiery, drapery, and jewellery of the richer sort. Bazaar and Arcade-shopping, to fancy articles, nick-nacks, and perfumery. In street-shopping walk leisurely along, keeping a sharp look-out on the windows. In bazaar-shopping, beat each stall separately. Many patterns, colours, novelties, conveniences, and other articles will thus strike your eye, which you would otherwise have never wanted or dreamt of. When you have marked down some dress, or riband, for instance, that you would like, go and inquire the price of it; haggle, demur, examine, and, lastly, buy. You will then be asked 'whether there is any other article to-day?' Whether there is or not, let the shopman show you what wares he pleases; you will very likely desire one or more of them. Whatever you think very cheap, that buy, without reference to your need of it; it is a bargain. You will find, too, as you go on, that one

TASTE

SHOP-GIRL (*who has been expected to possess* TENNYSON'S '*Miller's Daughter*'). 'No, Miss! We've not got the Miller's – but here's the Rat-catcher's Daughter, just Published!!'

THE MERRY COMMONERS

HEY for the Merry Commoners! the jocular M.Ps
How very little wit it takes their little minds to please;
How rampant is their laughter at each attempt at fun;
And gramercy! what loud guffaws at every little pun!

Hey for the Merry Commoners! who says debates are
  slow,
When at each sentence out there drops a beautiful *bon
  mot?*
So from the newspaper reports the fact at least appears,
For after every paragraph there comes 'a laugh' or
  'cheers.'

Hey for the merry Commoners! how jovial their life,
With oceans of facetiousness to season party-strife!
Two hundred jolly Momuses upon the benches sit,
The country to illuminate with ever-sparking wit.

Hey for the merry Commoners! how nobly they adhere
To what's been handed down to us from distant year to
  year!
Attachment to antiquity through all their labours runs;
The spirit of the past pervades their quips, their jokes,
  their puns.

Hey for the Merry Commoners! how pleasant 'tis to
  know
That all that's novel in their jokes to *Punch* alone
  they owe!
From the debates, each morning, we might select a
  bunch
Of gems, that prove the Commoners both read and
  mind their *Punch.*

**The lighter side
of Politics**

Portrait of Colonel Sibthorp on hearing that he
had signed the Chartist Petition. (By an Eye-
witness)

146

DOMESTIC HYDROPATHY

HYDROPATHY is making its way, and the continual dropping of water on to the mind of the public is at last producing some impression. Water is in fact taking a very high position, but its elevation will not be of long continuance, for it is in the very nature of water to find sooner or later its level. At the present moment, hydropathy is being received as a science of the first water, and it has been allowed to find its way into several domestic establishments. The turncock is in fact the family physician, the cistern is the medicine chest; the New River is a sort of Apothecaries' Hall, and the doctor's bill come in, in the shape of the water rate. This is all very agreeable if it is kept within bounds, and we believe that not only are water and soap the best soporific, but that the ordinary suds form a sudorific of as salubrious a kind as any that can be furnished by pharmacy. It is not the use of water, but its abuse we protest against, and we therefore object to the substitution of the bath itself for the Bath chair, as well as to the watering of the patient with the watering-pot while lying in his bed, as if he were a geranium, or any other occupant of an ordinary flower-bed. Such is the out-door treatment under the Domestic Hydropathic system, which occasionally places the patient under the pump, until it is doubtful whether he is not as great a pump as the machine by which he allows himself to be played upon.

Fun in a Fossil

THE world of scientific gastronomy will learn with interest that Professors Owen and Forbes, with a party of other gentlemen, numbering altogether 21, had an exceedingly good dinner, the other day, in the interior of the Iguanodon modelled at the Crystal Palace at Sydenham. We congratulate the company on the era in which they live; for if it had been an early geological period, they might perhaps have occupied the Iguanodon's inside without having any dinner there.

Progress of Science

A SCIENTIFIC young lady of considerable personal attractions has a mole on her face. She read, the other day, a learned Professor's Lecture, delivered at the British Association, Section B., 'On the Organic Elements.' Ever since that, she has called her mole a molecule.

The lighter side of Science

THE HAT-MOVING EXPERIMENT

It is necessary to get a Hat. Two or more Persons place their hands on the rim thereof, the little fingers of each person being in contact. In about twenty minutes or half-an-hour, or perhaps more, the Hat will begin to jump, and revolve rapidly. (*N.B. The Party above, with the Moustaches, thinks that in the pursuit of Science he could perform the Experiment over and over again.*)

The lighter side of Art

IGNORANCE *WAS* BLISS

WAITER. 'Yes, Sir. We had a Gentleman here, only last week, as took a sketch of that very 'ill, Sir.'

ARTIST (*abstractedly*). 'Oh, indeed! Was he an Artist?'

WAITER (*indignantly*). 'Oh, no! Sir, – a perfect Gentleman.'

This is Young Dawdlemore, the artist. Not that he is idle, O dear, no, 'but he is obliged to think a great deal before he begins to work.'

N.B. It is 6 PM, and he has been thinking ever since he got up at 11 AM, and now thinks he should dress for dinner.

ENTHUSIASTIC ARTIST. 'My dear Sir, keep that Expression for one moment! You've got such a splendid Head for my Picture of the "Canting Hypocrite!"'

Advice to Pre-Raffaelites

THE Pre-Raffaelite Brethren are right as to their prefix, but we object to the rest of the name by which they call themselves. It should not be Pre-Raffaelite, but Pre-posterous. As these gentlemen depict *rachitis, struma*, and other diseased conditions of system so admirably, why do they not give up oils, and paint in distemper?

HOUSEMAID. – 'I tell you what it is, Parker, I shall be very glad when Missus has got tired of this Pusey-usm. It may be the Fashion; but, what with her comin' home late from Parties, and getting up for early Service, and then goin' to Bed again, we poor Sarvints has double work A'most.'

ALL IS VANITY

FREDERICK. 'There, now, how very provoking! I've left the Prayer-Books at Home!'
MARIA. 'Well, dear, never mind; but do tell me, *is my bonnet straight?*'

GRANDMAMA. 'Why, what's the matter with my Pet?'
CHILD. 'Why, Grandma, after giving the subject every consideration, I have come to the Conclusion that – the World is Hollow, and my Doll is stuffed with Sawdust, so – I – should – like – if you please, to be a Nun?'

A MORAL LESSON FROM THE NURSERY

ARTHUR. 'Do you know, Freddy, that we are only made of Dust!'
FREDDY. 'Are we? Then I'm sure we ought to be very careful how we pitch into each other so, for fear we might crumble each other all to pieces!'

LIBERAL EDUCATION

The lighter side of Learning

Now that the 'little dears' of domestic life are home for the holidays, the cheap school-masters are baiting their hooks, and throwing out their lines, in the form of advertisements calculated to catch the eyes of poor parents or grasping guardians. We have now almost daily an entire column of the *Times* devoted to the announcements of 'Homes for Little Boys,' 'Colleges for Young Ladies,' 'Inclusive Terms,' 'Parental Treatment,' and other advantages, at prices ranging from sixteen to sixty guineas per annum. As some of our readers may be looking out for a 'good school,' and as there may be a few who think no school so good for a child as the 'school of adversity,' we place before the public a selection, from which a choice may be made by those who are anxious to get a young idea taught how to shoot, without any serious expenditure in shot or powder. To those who are anxious to bring up a child cheaply, or rather to cut him down to the very lowest figure, we think we may safely recommend the following: –

EDUCATION. – For £18 per annum, YOUNG GENTLEMEN are BOARDED, Clothed, and Educated. The situation healthy, in the country. This advertisement is worthy the attention of persons in want of a good school. Unexceptional references given.

As we presume the board will be ample, we may be justified in estimating its very lowest cost at 1s per day, which, for a year of forty weeks (allowing twelve for vacations) will amount to £14; and taking the education at 2d per week (the price of mere manners at the cheapest seminary with which we are acquainted), and the same sum for washing, we have a residue of £3 6s 8d a-year for clothing each young gentleman. There must be something rather diminutive in the wardrobe to be had for this primaeval price, and we should say the costume would not be quite as modest as the outlay.

The next advertisement is a curiosity, even among scholastic announcements: –

EDUCATION. – A young lady, having a good voice and taste for music (whether cultivated or not) might be EDUCATED, for half the terms, in a first-class school. Genteel parentage indispensable.

This seems to offer an eligible opportunity to a family having among its members a 'regular screamer' of the female sex, and anxious to get rid of the nuisance. Why a young lady with a voice, 'cultivated or not,' should be accepted at half-price in a first-class school is a marvel to us: nor do we see how 'genteel parentage' can mitigate the horrible effect of having a female Stentor in one's family. Aristocracy of birth seems a strange kind of compensation for plebeian lungs, and as far as our own taste is concerned, we should not consider patrician parentage a counterpoise to the voice of a coalheaver.

There is something bold and original in the following, which to that numerous class of pupils who look on books as a bore, and who indeed had rather not look at them at all, will prove a boon of no ordinary nature: –

EDUCATION, chiefly without Books. – A gentleman, whose experience has convinced him that the usual routine pursued in schools is very objectionable to the pupil, guarantees to parents to advance their sons on a system sound and expeditious, at the same time most pleasing and easy. The situation is very healthy.

This idea seems to be taken from the practice of the late – but not by any means lamented – SQUEERS, who repudiated the book system, and proceeded on the sound, expeditious, pleasing, and easy system of setting a boy to spell horse in the best way he could, and sending him to form an acquaintance with his subject by rubbing the animal down; so that a lesson was obtained at the same time in orthography and natural history.

We have not space for other specimens of scholastic advantages at ridiculous rates, but we can assure our readers that the educational columns in the *Times* at this season of the year will well repay perusal. We must not omit to do justice to the simple-mindedness of a certain 'principal' of a two-and-twenty guinea concern, who announces that 'floricultural grounds are fitted up for the recreation of the pupils.' Considering the effect which the 'recreation' of exuberant boyhood would probably produce on a 'floricultural' arrangement, we cannot help comparing the fitting up of a flower-garden as a playground for boys to the preparation of a china shop for the antics of a mad bull, or the careful collection of a brood of chickens for the express gratification of the Terpsichorean propensities of a dancing donkey.

The Things to Teach at Cambridge

To Mr Punch

'SIR, I perceive that the new Cambridge Curriculum includes the science of Political Economy. Now, Sir, I have a son at that seat of learning, and I speak feelingly. It may be all very well to instruct undergraduates in Political Economy; but I wish the University authorities would also contrive to teach these young gentlemen a little personal frugality.

I am, Sir, greatly indebted
'To various Wine-merchants, Bootmakers,
'Liverystable-keepers, and Tailors,
'Your most unfortunate humble servant,

'PATERFAMILIAS.'

Something for the Next Cambridge Examination Paper

'WHAT is a Don?' asked a little child, who had heard the word mentioned several times in an account of the Installation. 'Why, my dear,' answered the puzzled father, 'I don't know, but from this account of what they did at Cambridge, I should say that a Don is half a Donkey.'

TOO FASTIDIOUS
SCENE. – *A Tavern*

WAITER. "Am, Sir? Yessir? Don't take anything with your 'Am, do you, Sir?'
GENTLEMAN. 'Yes, I do; I take the letter H!'
[*Waiter faints.*]

FASHIONABLE
TRANSLATIONS

Out (mostly) means In.
Any day (decidedly) means No day.
A general invitation means No invitation.
Pot luck means Cold meat, or hashed mutton.
A little music means Songs all the evening.
A few friends means About a hundred people or so.
Engaged three deep means Rather not dance with you.
'Will you have any more wine?' means It's time to go upstairs.
'We do not visit now' means A decided cut.
Residing on the Continent for the benefit of your health means Extreme economy, or evading your creditors.
Breaking up one's establishment means Outrunning the constable.
'A little misfortune' means Insolvency, or a slight bankruptcy, or an elopement, or a marriage with a tradesman, or a bit of shoplifting, or any other fashionable casualty.
Threw herself away means Married for love.
Comfortably settled means Married for money.
Past the meridian of life means Any year between 50 and 100.
Not dying so well as was expected means Dying poor.
Universally respected means Dying rich.

The lighter side of Language

FRANK. 'Oh, I say, Emily! Ain't the Sea-Side Jolly?'
EMILY (*who is reading The Corsair to Kate*). 'I do not know, Frank, what you mean by Jolly. – It is very Beautiful! – It is very Lovely!'
FRANK. 'Hah! and don't it make you always ready for your Grub, neither?'
[*Exit Young Ladies, very properly disgusted.*]

DREAMS FOR THE MILLION

PUNCH'S DICTIONARY OF DREAMS

The Stuff of Dreams

Acquaintance – To dream that you fall out with an – implies danger in gigs, railways, &c. &c.

Altar – To see an – betokens henpeckedness, or the workhouse, – in fact, some great affliction.

Ants – To dream of – betokens good: a rich legacy generally follows.

Angels. To speak to an angel in your dream forebodes evil. It implies a quarrel with your wife, and the cold shoulder for dinner.

Ass – To hear the braying of an – proves that you are talking in your sleep.

Attorneys. To dream of an attorney is an infallible sign of nightmare.

Beheading. To dream you have lost your head implies an acceptance to a bill, or an offer of marriage.

Bells. If of a muffin-bell, it forebodes indigestion; of a postman's bell, a tailor's bill; and of a dustman's bell, a loss of silver forks and spoons.

Buried alive. Denotes an ushership in a Yorkshire school.

Buying goods. To a poor man, this dream foretells some extraordinary novelty.

Cerberus. An illiberal governor.

Chain. A small salary.

Cheese. If it is the Stilton, egregious vanity or excessive perfection.

Children – To dream of – portends a serious diminution in your income.

Comedies and Farces. To see a comedy or a farce, indicates great pain or nausea.

Crocodiles. Portend lawyers, Sheriffs' officers, tax-collectors, &c.

Darkness. Being in – is a proof you do not subscribe to PUNCH.

Deer. (When hunting) implies a courtship.

Devil. To see him, implies a visit to your lawyer.

Drinking. If it is British Brandy, a great imposition.

Ears. Long *ears* denote a long life.

Feet. A small foot foretells tight boots and bunions; a large foot, constant laughter and derision from your friends.

Fingers. If they are burnt, implies an action for libel; if they itch, a Scotch sequestration.

Fire. To see the house on fire indicates that it is too hot to hold you.

Fire-brands. Latch keys & mothers-in-law.

Flattery. Indicates sickly appetite and want of taste.

Fleas – To catch – is to overcome your enemies.

Fly. – A wish to – implies you are involved in debt.

Fruits. To an author, this means robbery and starvation; to a publisher, an equipage and estate.

Goose. – To dream of a – implies sitting for your portrait.

Gibbet. Some one hanging on you.

Globes. – If three – a loan of money.

Gold. – Heaps of – indicate misery and avarice; a few pieces, honesty and industry.

Hat. If a four-and-nine, ridicule and contempt.

Head. To a person waiting for a situation; if he sees his head, he may be sure of a vacancy.

Hornets. Denote annoyance from your creditors.

Hot water. – To be in – denotes cognovits.

Household utensils. The candle denotes the purse; the extinguisher the wife; the hearth the home; the bellows the friends; the flue the Queen's Bench.

Hungry. – To dream of being – is nothing very extraordinary.

Husbandry. If prosperous, implies widowerhood.

Idiot. Being an idiot. (This is a thing a person never dreams of.)

Infernal things. The Income-Tax papers.

King or Queen. To see a king or queen denotes a strong disappointment.

Kite. If flying, loss of money and reputation.

Knave. – That you are one yourself, implies an old acquaintance.

Lamb. – To eat – imports a love of abstract good.

Letter. Reading a long letter, great hardship; answering one, great charity.

Lions. To see, denotes a love for the Drama.

Looking-glass. – To look into a, (after 30,) denotes great courage.

Lord – To speak to a – implies the great want of a companion.

Lost. Wedding-ring – denotes freedom and happiness; senses – having trusted a woman with a secret.

Monomania. Denotes a provision for life.

Man – To dream of a man you know, denotes a Sheriff's officer.

Milk – If sour, denotes the milk of human kindness.

Monsters – Dreaming of – is generally caused by French romances of pork chops.

Music. If Jullien's, great discord.

Nails – Long nails to a woman, denote quarrelsomeness; short nails, to an author, indicate slowness of thought.

Night-birds. Denote vigilance and portend danger. Of this class are burglars and policemen.

Nightmare. Is caused by reading the *Morning Post*.

Noises. Denote a habit of snoring.

Olives. A fondness of the bottle.

Onions. Portend domestic jars.

Palm – An itching in the – indicates an election.

Plague. A literary wife.

Queen – To see the – in an English theatre, denotes an extraordinary novelty.

Rat. Denotes a politician; frequently the Premier.

Raven. Confinement, if it's *a raven mad*. (*Vide* Sibthorpe *passim*.)

Reading. Romances and novels, indicates loss of time; the MORNING POST, extreme drowsiness; the SPECTATOR, the cold water cure.

Ride. In an omnibus, implies an insult; on a railway, an accident.

Sleep – To dream of – denotes ingenuity and invention.

Slaughter. To a reviewer, success.

Snares. Promises of marriage.

Sold into Slavery. To a milliner's girl, this forebodes an apprenticeship.

Spinning – To dream of – means you will become a member of Parliament.

Stars. The ruin of the Drama.

Statues. Exposure to the wind and rain.

Swallow. Signifies a good appetite.

Tavern. That you will soon make a start to the Station house.

Teeth. Represent the visitors in your house.

Tempests. Signify matrimonial endearments, and Parliamentary debates.

Theft – To dream of having committed – implies the translation of a French farce.

Thorns. In your side, are poor relations.

Tigers – To see – implies the same as Lions.

Top of the poll, signifies, to a member, bribery and corruption.

Travelling. On the continent, that you will be taken in.

War. Portends to a military man, selling his commission.

Weasel. To catch him asleep, signifies great cleverness.

WEDNESBURY STATION

FIRST COLLIER. 'Trains leave for Birmingham, 10.23 A.M., 6.23 P.M.'
SECOND COLLIER. 'What's P.M.?'
FIRST DO. 'A Penny a Mile, to be sure.'
SECOND DO. 'Then, what's A.M.?'
FIRST DO. 'Why, that must be a A'penny a Mile.'

RAILWAY PORTER. 'Any Luggage, Sir?'
TRAVELLER. 'Yas – Carpet Bag and Cigar Case.'

Problems of Travel by Rail: Luggage and Timetables

THE BEARD AND MOUSTACHE MOVEMENT

RAILWAY GUARD. 'Now, Ma'am, is this your Luggage?'
OLD LADY (*who concludes she is attacked by Brigands*). 'Oh yes! Gentlemen, it's mine. Take it – take all I have; but spare, oh spare our lives!!'

153

LIFE IN LONDON!

ISABELLA. 'Well, Aunt, and how did you like London? I suppose you were very gay!'
AUNT (*who inclines to embonpoint*). 'Oh yes, Love, Gay enough! We went to the Top o' the Monument o' Monday – and to the Top o' St Paul's o' Tuesday – and to the Top o' the Dook o' Yoork's Column o' Wednesday – but I think altogether I like the quiet of the Country.'

2 A.M.

DOMESTIC. 'Please, Sir, the guide says you told him to take you up Snowdon to see the sun rise.'
ENTHUSIASTIC TOURIST. 'Oh! Ah! ye-es! You will tell the guide that I have been thinking the Sun-*set* will be much better worth seeing; so I shall not want him just yet.'

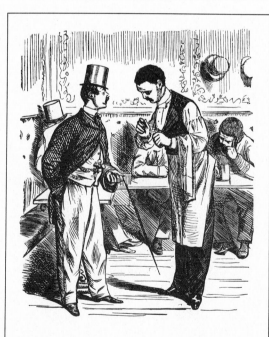

MR 'ARRY BELVILLE, ON
THE CONTINENT GENERALLY

'ARRY BELVILLE. 'Yes! I like it extremely. I like the *Lazy ally* sort of feeling. I like sitting at the door of a *Caffy* to smoke my Cigar; and above all (*enter noo*) it's a great comfort to wear one's beard without bein' larfed at!'

SNOB. 'Garsong! Haver-vous les hoeufs?'
GARÇON. 'Hein!'
SNOB. 'Hein! Can't the Fellar speak his own Language?'

WHY ENGLISHMEN ARE SO BELOVED UPON THE CONTINENT

BECAUSE they never foster the delusion that, by letting their moustache grow, they may succeed in passing themselves off as natives of the Continent, and never fly into a passion and a use of English expletives, when their bad accent has betrayed their insular extraction.

Because, whatever quantities of luggage they may take with them, they always are so careful to leave their pride at home.

Because, when honouring an hotel, they never act as though they were the only people in it, and never get put out because the best apartments happen to be full, or because they cannot have the dinner-hour altered about every other day to suit their sole convenience.

Because they are at all times so simple in their tastes, and so considerate in making due allowance for any cause that may prevent their being properly supplied; for instance, never ordering stewed eels or pickled salmon at Chamouni, or blowing up the hospitable monks of Great St Bernard for not having scolloped oysters and draught London stout for supper.

Because they never bluster about 'writing to ze *Times*,' nor profess themselves astounded at the ignorance of foreigners who seem quite undismayed by the terrors of the threat.

Because they never strut about and slap their breeches' pocket, and show by all the pantomime they anyhow can muster, that Englishmen are all completely CROESUSES in wealth, and could buy up everything and body that they meet with.

Because, when they are looking at the sea-fights in the Louvre, they never make allusion to COLLINGWOOD or NELSON; nor, in talking of the battles fought on canvas by French artists, do they lug in the word 'Waterloo' more than twice per minute.

Because, if by some exceedingly improbable fortuity they happen to be forced to fall out with a foreigner, they never have recourse to their stock of British Billingsgate, nor tell him to 'come on,' and have his 'head punched' at *la Boxe*, nor imagine that the strength of their national anathemas is appreciable by those even who do not comprehend them.

Because when they are 'doing' a cathedral during service, they always are so careful not to interrupt those persons whom they find at their devotions; and never stalk and stare about, as though the congregation were a part of the exhibition. . . .

Because whatever grievance they may fancy they've sustained, they never more than twenty times per diem swear LORD PALMERSTON shall hear of it. . . .

WHAT AN ENGLISHMAN LIKES

AN Englishman likes a variety of things. For instance, nothing is more to his liking than:

To talk largely about Art, and to have the worst statues and monuments that ever disgraced a metropolis!

To inveigh against the grinding tyrannies practised upon poor needle-women and slop-tailors, and yet to patronise the shops where cheap shirts and clothes are sold!

To purchase a bargain, no matter whether he is in want of it or not!

To reward native talent, with which view he supports Italian operas, French plays, German singers, and in fact gives gold to the foreigners in exchange for the brass they bring him!

To talk sneeringly against tuft-hunting and all tuft-hunters, and yet next to running after a Lord, nothing delights him more than to be seen in the company of one!

To rave about his public spirit and independence, and with the greatest submission, to endure perpetually a tax that was only put on for three years!

To boast of his cleanliness, and to leave uncovered (as in the Thames) the biggest sewer in the world!

To pretend to like music, and to tolerate the Italian organs and the discordant musicians that infest his streets!

To inveigh against bad legislation, and to refrain in many instances from exercising the franchise he pays so dearly for!

To admit the utility of education, and yet to exclude from its benefits every one who is not of the same creed as himself!

To plunge into raptures about SHAKSPEARE and the national Drama, and to leave them any night to run after DUMAS, SCRIBE, a dancing dog, a jumping elephant, or a gentleman who walks like a fly with his legs on the ceiling!

To swagger about his tremendous love of comfort, and to ride in the most uncomfortable omnibuses, the dirtiest cabs, and the shabbiest railways of any civilised state in Europe, – besides encouraging a system of hotels, where every species of discomfort is vended at the very highest possible prices!

And lastly, an Englishman dearly likes:

To grumble, no matter whether he is right or wrong, crying or laughing, working or playing, gaining a victory or smarting under a national humiliation, paying or being paid – still he must grumble, and in fact he is never so happy as when he is grumbling; and, supposing everything was to his satisfaction (though it says a great deal for our power of assumption to assume any such absurd impossibilities), still he would grumble at the fact of there being nothing for him to grumble about!

Always the Englishman

The Seaside, or the Art of making pleasant Discoveries

A SKETCH AT RAMSGATE

ELLEN (*who loves a joke at* AUNT FIDGET'*s expense*). 'Good gracious, Aunt! There are two Officers!'
AUNT FIDGET (*a short-sighted lady*). 'Bless me, so there are! Well; they may be Officers, but they are not *Gentlemen*, I'm sure, or they wouldn't stand looking at us in that Impudent Manner.'

Common Objects at the Sea-side – generally found upon the Rocks at Low Water.

A PHOTOGRAPHIC POSITIVE

LADY MOTHER (*loquitur*). 'I shall feel obliged to you, MR SQUILLS, if you would remove these stains from my daughter's face. I cannot persuade her to be sufficiently careful with her Photographic Chemicals, and she has had a misfortune with her Nitrate of Silver. Unless you can do something for her, she will not be fit to be seen at LADY MAYFAIR's to-night.'
[MR SQUILLS *administers relief to the fair sufferer, in the shape of Cyanide of Potassium.*]

A PHOTOGRAPHIC PICTURE

OLD LADY (*who is not used to these new-fangled notions*). 'Oh, Sir! Please, Sir! don't, Sir! Don't for goodness' sake Fire, Sir!'

ART-PROGRESS

ARTIST (!) 'Now, Mum! Take orf yer 'ead for Sixpence, or yer 'ole body for a Shillin'!'

CATCHING PEOPLE'S EYES

COMPASSIONATING the exceeding difficulty to which advertisers seem to be reduced, at this period of the year (when, as there are, of course, no Christmas bills coming in, one's wives and children ought to be reminded to make onslaughts upon the marital and paternal purse), *Mr Punch* has kindly prepared, and hereby places at the disposal of the mercantile interest, a variety of advertisement headings calculated to attract the eye. Any person using any of them will enclose samples of his wares (carriage free, or porterage paid), to No. 85, Fleet Street.

A THING OF BEAUTY IS A JOY FOR EVER, an exquisite remark which would have derived additional force from the fact, if it had ever happened, that the Poet KEATS, on the day he penned it had tasted the delicious Dairyfed Pork, sold by &c.

WILL MR DISRAELI TAKE OFFICE? is a question asked by many, and answered by many others, according to their political views. But there would be no question at all, whether, if the article were placed before him, MR DISRAELI, whose taste is unrivalled, would take our Potted Bloaters, price One Shilling, and to be had only, &c.

THE RUSSIAN FLEET HAS SUNK in the estimation of Europe since ADMIRAL BOTCHAMOFF refused to victual it with our pressed Beef. Surely this will raise the Beef in the regard of all true Britons, who have only to apply to No. &c.

LORD JOHN RUSSELL HAS HAD A FIT. – To be sure he has, and you may have a fit too, if you will have the good sense to clothe yourself, as his Lordship does, at the establishment of SMOUCH Brothers, Tailors, &c. &c.

HUSBANDS! BEAT YOUR WIVES, that is, if you can, in the struggle to make home happy. You will have the best chance of succeeding, by presenting them with scrubbing brushes, tooth brushes, hair brushes, bottle brushes, blacking brushes, bonnet brushes, paint brushes, and other domestic comforts, from BRISTLES AND CO., at &c.

THE CHURCH IS IN DANGER! – No, not while her Ministers do their duty. But those who go to church, this weather, are in great danger of catching severe colds unless they wear Furs, and these can be best obtained at &c.

MURDER! – This very objectionable practice will never be persevered in by any person who will peruse the new and startling Novel of the 'Tinderbox and the Tombstone,' now publishing in TRASH's Weekly Miscellany, price One Penny.

YOU DID IT! I SAW YOU. – And seeing you made me do it, and I will never again omit to do it every Saturday night of my life, Ma'am. 'Do it – do what?' Can you ask? Buy Tallow Candles at DIPPS's, Tottenham Court Road, &c.

THE LOVELY YOUNG LAVINIA ONCE HAD FRIENDS, and would have preserved them to this day, if, when she had them to dinner she had abstained from giving them deleterious compounds, which made them drop her acquaintance, and had caused them to drink the Sparkling Pale Ale, sold by &c.

THE TIMES NEWSPAPER HAS STOPPED – Yes, and we hope it will continue to stop the mouth of many an impudent pretender, especially any one, should he arise, who should pretend that BUGGINS's Patent Warming Pans are not one-third cheaper, two-thirds handier, three-thirds neater, and four-thirds lighter than any other. To be had at &c.

YOUR WIFE HAS BOLTED. – She has indeed bolted the front door, thinking that you are not coming home to-night. But you will return, and the poor thing will be roused from her first sleep, and have to come down in the cold to let you in, for as for waking that EMMA, you might as well try to arouse LORD ABERDEEN to a sense of the honour of England. Why, then, not save your wife's health by furnishing your door with one of TUMBLER AND CO.'s Latch Locks? To be seen in action at &c.

GREAT FIRE IN THE PALACE. – 'And a very good one too,' as HER MAJESTY was graciously pleased to remark, desiring H. R. H. the PRINCE OF WALES to let the poker alone, as with Coals at two pounds a ton, he must not be extravagant. Matrons of England, learn a lesson of economy from the first Lady of the Land, and show that you have done so by ordering your Coals at SLATES AND COMPANY, Whiteash Wharf.

NEVER GO TO A THEATRE, at least not without one of WINDUM's Air Cushions, which afford so luxurious a seat that you will be able to enjoy most performances, and almost to endure the deathless Clown without much annoyance.

MR HARRISON AINSWORTH IS QUITE WELL. – This circumstance will gratify that gentleman's myriad admirers, and their satisfaction will be complete when they are informed that, not only MR AINSWORTH's masterly works, but those of all other writers of celebrity, are bound by VELLUM AND TOOLEY, corner of Bobchurch Lane, upon the most reasonable terms, and with the greatest expedition.

A NEW PLAY BY SHAKSPERE, if now produced, would probably be called 'slow' by one writer, 'ill-constructed,' by a second, and as 'not in accordance with the time,' by a third. More reverent judges would say that it contained the true Gold, that there were real Gems in it, and the Springs of action were seen in perfect working. Any one who should apply the above unfavourable opinion to BUNK's Watches (warranted) would libel those masterpieces, but the terms of approbation, which we have said would be used towards SHAKSPERE, exactly characterise the Watches sold by BUNK at &c.

PALMERSTON HAS TAKEN POISON out of the London Atmosphere, so far as his admirable Smoke Prevention Act enables his Lordship to do. Eager to second his Lordship in promoting the purity of the metropolis, MESSRS. BORAX AND CO. respectfully recommend their White Curdy Soft Windsor Antigrimeopolis Soap, in packets of One and Sixpence, to be procured, &c.

FISHING OFF BRIGHTON

'O yes! It's very easy to say "Catch hold of him!"'

The Deer are Driven for MR BRIGGS. He has an Excellent Place, but what with Waiting by Himself so long, the Murmur of the Stream, the Beauty of the Scene, and the Novelty of the Situation, he Falls Asleep, and while he takes his Forty Winks, the Deer Pass!

New Cricketing Dresses, to protect all England against the present swift bowling

NOTICE TO CORRESPONDENTS

Oh dear No! Old Br – ggs is *not* Dead – He has taken to
Yachting for the Benefit of his Health.

THE MUSIC OF NATURE

WHEN we are out upon the hills,
　'Tis sweet to list to rural sounds;
A mingled noise of purling rills,
　Of lowing kine, and baying hounds,
And many a small bird's mingled song
　Arises from the vale below;
Unless perchance the wind is wrong,
　And from our ears the sound should blow.

We note the crowing of the cock,
　We mark the steed's far distant neigh,
We hear the bleating of the flock,
　And donkey after donkey bray,
All these are common notes 'tis true,
　Which humble instruments produce,
Yet are they sweet to listen to;
　And there's the cackle of the goose:

The duck, too, lends her tuneful quack,
　To swell the music of the vale,
The mill supplies its ceaseless clack:
　Add songs that smack of too much ale,
All these are sounds remembered well,
　And o'er the memory oft they ring;
On such the Poet loves to dwell,
　When he invokes the Muse to sing.

But oh! there is one simple sound,
　Amid the rustic symphony,
That never yet hath poet found,
　Most sweet, most striking though it be.
It is a pleasing cry of pain,
　First loud and strong, then soft and weak,
Which language to describe in vain –
　The dying pig's perpetual squeak.

Country Life

Delight of the Grouse at the Prospect of a Late Session

ASTOUNDING ANNOUNCEMENT FROM THE SMALL COUNTRY BUTCHER
(Who does not often kill his own meat).

MAID. 'Please, Ma'am, Mr Skewer says he's a-Going to Kill *Hisself* this Week, and will you have a Joint?'

UTILITY COMBINED WITH ELEGANCE

VI·PUNCH'S IMAGES

'Pretty Image! Beautiful Image!'

As Young Aurora, with her 'blaze' of light,
Into the shade throws all the pride of night,
And pales presumptuous stars, which vainly think
That every eye is on them as they blink:

So *Punch*, the light and glory of the time,
– His wit and wisdom brilliant as sublime,
Scares into shade Cant's hypocritic throng –
Abashes Folly, and exposes Wrong.

THE MORAL OF PUNCH

As we hope, gentle public, to pass many happy hours in your society, we think it right that you should know something of our character and intentions. Our title, at a first glance, may have misled you into a belief that we have no other intention than the amusement of a thoughtless crowd, and the collection of pence. We have a higher object. Few of the admirers of our prototype, merry Master PUNCH, have looked upon his vagaries but as the practical outpourings of a rude and boisterous mirth. We have considered him as a teacher of no mean pretensions, and have, therefore, adopted him as the sponsor for our weekly sheet of pleasant instruction. When we have seen him parading in the glories of his motley, flourishing his baton (like our friend Jullien at Drury-lane) in time with his own un-rivalled discord, by which he seeks to win the attention and admiration of the crowd, what visions of graver puppetry have passed before our eyes! Golden circlets, with their adornments of coloured and lustrous gems, have bound the brow of infamy as well as that of honour – a mockery to both; as though virtue required a reward beyond the fulfilment of its own high pur-poses, or that infamy could be cheated into the forgetfulness of its vileness by the weight around its temples! Gilded coaches have glided before us, in which sat men who thought the buzz and shouts of crowds a guerdon for the toils, the anxieties, and, too often, the peculations of a life. Our ears have rung with the noisy frothiness of those who have bought their fellowmen as beasts in the market-place, and found their reward in the sycophancy of a degraded constituency, or the patronage of a venal ministry – no matter of what creed, for party *must* destroy patriotism.

The noble in his robes and coronet – the beadle in his gaudy livery of scarlet, and purple, and gold – the dignitary in the fulness of his pomp – the demagogue in the triumph of his hollowness – these and other visual and oral cheats by which mankind are cajoled, have passed in review before us, conjured up by the magic wand of PUNCH....

We now come to the last great lesson of our motley teacher – the gallows! that accursed tree which has its *root* in injuries. How clearly PUNCH exposes the fallacy of that dreadful law which authorises the destruction of life! PUNCH some-times destroys the hangman: and why not? Where is the divine injunction against the shedder of man's blood to rest? None *can* answer! To us there is but ONE disposer of life. At other times PUNCH hangs the devil: this is as it should be. Destroy the principle of evil by increasing the means of cultivating the good, and the gallows will then become as much a wonder as it is now a jest.

We shall always play PUNCH, for we consider it best to be merry and wise –

'And laugh at all things, for we wish to know,
What, after all, are all things but a show!' – *Byron*.

As on the stage of PUNCH's theatre, many characters appear to fill up the interstices of the more important story, so our pages will be interspersed with trifles that have no other object than the moment's approbation – an end which will never be sought for at the expense of others, beyond the evanescent smile of a harmless satire.

The First Image Projected (Vol. I, 1841, p.1)

Punch the Regent: Crowned King (and Queen)

KING PUNCH
'The end doth crown the work,' 'tis said.
Then I am very much afraid,
No crown on *Punch* can e'er descend,
Because his work will never end.

QUEEN JUDY
Five princes fair, my children are,
　And many more I hope will be;
For, strange to add, John Bull is glad,
　To see my growing family.

PUNCH'S REGENCY

INTRODUCTION

THE only man of any mark
　In all the town remaining,
I sauntered in St James's Park,
　And watched the daylight waning.
'The SPEAKER's lips,' I said, 'are sealed,
　They've shut up both the Houses;
SIR ROBERT's gone to Turnabout field,
　SIR JAMES to shoot the grouses.
The QUEEN and all the Court are out
　In Germany and Flanders,
And, happy midst his native *kraut*,
　My princely ALBERT wanders.
No more the dumpy Palace arch
　The Royal Standard graces;
Alone, upon his lonely march,
　The yawning sentry paces.'
Beneath an elm-tree, on a bank,
　I mused, (for tired my hunch was,)
And there in slumber soft I sank,
　And this the dream of *Punch* was.

THE DREAM

I dreamed it was a chair of gold,
　The grassy bank I sat on;
I dreamed SAINT EDWARD's sceptre old
　I wielded for a baton.
Men crowded to my throne, the elm,
　In reverend allegiance;
And *Punch* was publish'd through the realm,
　The jolliest of Regents.

Back came the ministerial rout
　From touring and carousing;
Back came SIR BOB from Turnabout,
　And back SIR JAMES from grousing.
I turn'd upon a scornful heel,
　When GRAHAM ask'd my favour;
I sternly banish'd BOBBY PEEL
　To Turnabout for ever....

O then! all other reigns which shine
　Upon our page domestic,
Were mean and dim compared to mine,
　That Regency majestic.
And ages hence the English realm
　Shall tell the wondrous legend
Of *Punch*, when at the nation's helm,
　HER MAJESTY's High Regent.

166

A VACANCY IN THE PUBLIC AMUSEMENTS

IT has long been a matter of surprise with us, that a celebrated character has not been included amongst the *illustrissimi* of Baker Street. He has for years been a public favourite – has won more battles than the luckiest general – has corrected more abuses than the greatest reformer – has put down more quackeries, nuisances, and delusions, than the mighty SIR PETER – and has made more people laugh than SIBTHORP or GRIMALDI.

We flatter ourselves we know this honourable individual – and a better and a truer creature never existed. Who so welcome at every one's fireside? Who mixes more with every grade of society, from the palace to the skittle-ground, and is more generally liked? Who is there that possesses the same chance of turning his enemies – if in any odd corner of the globe there now lurks one – into bosom friends? He is the Poor Man's Friend, and the Rich Man's Best Companion. We say all this confidently; for we know this honest fellow almost as well as we know ourselves; and can say from our hearts, that the more we know him, the better we love him. It is, therefore, with this profound conviction of his merits, that we are astonished he has not yet been allowed the very foremost rank at MADAME TUSSAUD's popular Walhalla of waxen heroes. We hope this accidental omission, however, will soon be repaired, and that we shall shortly read on the placards of the Metropolis, the following announcement, now long due: –

Punch's Images in Stone and at the Wax-works

PUNCH'S STATUE

WE understand a memorial, innumerably signed, has been presented to the Commissioners of Woods and Forests, calling for a statue of *ourself*, our *Suffolk Punch*, and our dog *Toby*, to be erected on one of the pedestals in Trafalgar Square. As national benefactors, we feel that we are liable to be placed in this very awkward position; but there is a consolation in knowing that we cannot be made more ridiculous than some of our fellow-statues in the same neighbourhood. We stipulate for nothing but the right of furnishing our own design, which we here subjoin; and we beg to announce that sealed tenders for the execution of the work in conformity with the annexed plan, may be sent in to the *Punch* Office.

'Just added, Mr Punch'

The Only Thing to Save France

SOCIETY in France is in a very bad state – none worse. The only thing to regenerate it is to throw open all the ports, and admit *Punch*.

**Punch expelled
from France
(1843) . . .**

PUNCH TURNED OUT OF FRANCE!

'I have this moment, in a half-tempest, arrived from Boulogne – thrust from the port by the point of the sword. Yes; it is true – *Punch* is no longer to be admitted into France.'

Punch was banned from France in 1843 for his denunciations of Louis Philippe.

PUNCH'S TOUR IN THE MANUFACTURING DISTRICTS

but welcomed in the Provinces

PUNCH is suddenly smitten with the spirit of utility; he therefore purposes to throw open his pages – wide as his heart – to *fac-simile* engravings of all that is new and beautiful in household decoration; and requests that pembroke-tables – scroll fenders – ottomans – lounging-chairs – reading-desks – with every description of new crockery and pottery, may be immediately forwarded to him. He promises to review them; and he also promises to keep them. For, shall not the reviewer be paid for his ink?

In this brief preface, however, *Punch* can only hint his intentions. It is his purpose to make a tour in the manufacturing districts, that he may, in his pages, display to astonished Englishmen the wealth and ingenuity of England. *Punch* purposes to begin with the eatables. Hence he will make a pilgrimage to Richmond, to report upon and give cuts of the melting maids-of-honour. He will next visit Chelsea, for the purpose of making known the virtues of the humble bun. He will then proceed to Epping, to inspect the large sausage manufactory, taking with him his artist to faithfully represent the scene. He will next make a descent upon the town of Banbury, distinguished for its cakes; and, heedless of time, labour, and expense, will go through the whole of Hampshire, giving splendid cuts of its bacon. Cambridge butter will find a place in his pages, which will also be open to Canterbury brawn.

It being the wish of *Punch* to furnish his larder with the greatest possible despatch, and the least possible expense, dealers in the above commodities are requested to furnish early copies for *Punch's* artist.

Further particulars in *Punch's* next.

'The Start'

The Winner

Punch the Pope
(1847)

ROMAN PUNCH

A rare pro-papal cartoon by Doyle. By 1850 the 'Papal Aggression' agitation had broken out and *Punch* was in the vanguard of the attack on what he believed to be sinister Roman Catholic influence in England.

PUNCH TONANS

Punch with Weapons

THOUGH *Punch* unites, on ordinary occasions, the noble daring of the lion with the gentlemanly bearing of the lamb, he can, when roused to a pitch of indignation, combine the ferocity of the wolf, the tearing tendencies of the tiger, and the *brusquerie* of the bear. It is only, however, when the object is one of real provocation that his fierceness can be excited, and his tremendous vengeance put forth. Circumstances may occasionally arise to ruffle his placidity; and an incident has occurred within the last few days, which has excited in him a degree of irritation by which his equable bosom is, happily, seldom disturbed.

The rage of *Punch* is not very easily aroused, for he does not find it worth while to get up the steam of his indignation on every paltry occasion; but he candidly confesses that his blood, at last, is fairly on the boil. JUPITER TONANS is mildness itself in comparison with *Punch Tonans;* for if the Eagle of the former has an aversion to taking flies, the Dog of the latter is quite as aristocratic, and never sullies his mouth by snapping at foul things. But *Punch* can remain patient no longer under a provocation that has just been offered him. He is roused at last; and what does the world imagine can have ruffled the smooth coat of the faithful *Toby*, or made the *bâton* of *Punch* tremble in his indignantly agitated hand? The fact then must come out: *Punch* is furious at not having been invited to the dinner of the new LORD MAYOR. What can be the meaning of the slight that has been thus put upon him? RUSSELL was there; and though RUSSELL deserves honour as the Premier of the Government, is not *Punch* the People's Premier, and as such entitled to be present at the civic feast? We may be told that our wooden nature precludes us from the enjoyment of such luxuries as a Lord Mayor's dinner; but this can be no excuse, for GOG and MAGOG, who are made of the same tough materials as *Punch* himself, were there. Besides, is it not the true *lignum vitae* of which we are composed? We shall not easily pardon the insult passed upon us by the new LORD MAYOR, who never asked us to partake of the luxuries that formed his inaugural repast.

Our heart has been leaping about our bosom like an egg in a saucepan full of boiling water, ever since our eye rested upon the civic bill of fare. To think of 80 roast turkeys and 250 jam tarts, 13 sirloins or beef jumbled temptingly together with 250 ice creams, and, worst of all, 400 penny cheesecakes, followed up by 600 custards – for which our weakness is known! *Punch* is not generally vindictive, but it will take him at least a week to get over the insult passed upon him by the new LORD MAYOR.

FIRST OF SEPTEMBER – PUNCH SHOOTING FOLLY AS IT FLIES

Punch and his Rivals

To Senior Wranglers

WANTED, a person competent to explain the meaning and grammatical analysis of the Leaders in the *Morning Post*. Salary 5,000*l.* a year, if the candidate be successful.

HOW TO KEEP A THING A PROFOUND SECRET – Advertise it in the *Morning Post*.

Utopia Discovered

THE papers have been telling us that 'the village of Merthyrwahr, in Wales, has no lawyer, no tax-gatherer, no doctor, no Dissenting chapel, no paupers,' and, to complete the Paradise, 'no MORNING POST!'

MRS GAMP AFTER HER 'EPIGRAMS'

DOCTOR PUNCH. 'So you feel weak and languid, and then irritable, and all-overish like, do you? The fact is, my good woman, there is something very wrong about your circulation; but I think I know of something that will touch you up a little.'

MRS GAMP. 'Ah! Doctor Punch, I wish I had your health and spirits.'

Mrs Gamp, getting a little beside herself, sends for a poet to annihilate Punch

THE NEW BOY

HEAD MASTER. 'Here's a New Boy, Johnny
Russell. Now you see that nobody bullies him.'

MINISTERIAL 'ADVICE GRATIS'

PUNCH. 'You are very shaky, D—by. You'll
injure your Constitution if you don't "GO TO
THE COUNTRY".'

**Punch
admonishes the
New Boys,
advises a Patient,
and addresses the
House of
Commons**

PUNCH TELLING THE MEMBERS TO GO ABOUT THEIR BUSINESS

SPECIMENS FROM MR PUNCH'S INDUSTRIAL EXHIBITION OF 1850
(To be improved in 1851)

A PLEASANT HOLIDAY TASK
MR PUNCH. 'Now, Boys and Girls! You must Find out the Use of these Globes before you go back
to School!'

P—NCE ALB—RT. 'Save me, dear *Punch*, from these most Ridiculous Friends.'

A PICTURE FOR THE INTEMPERATE

PHOTOGRAPHER. 'Now, Sir, step in and have your Likeness taken. It might be useful to your Family!'

TO ALL WHOM IT MAY CONCERN

MR PUNCH takes the liberty of requesting all candidates who may be returned as Members of the House of Commons for the next Parliament, to avail themselves of the earliest opportunity of sitting for their photographs, and to forward them, whether as positives or negatives, to *Mr P.* In the event of any gentleman distinguishing himself in Parliament, either by folly, conceit, proficiency in bunkum, penny-wisdom, bigotry, or humbug, – or in the much less probable case of any Member becoming conspicuous by intelligence, eloquence, sound sense, toleration, and genuine patriotism, – it may become the duty of *Mr Punch* to hand down the Honourable Member's likeness to the execration or regard of posterity, as the case may be.

Honourable Members are hereby warned, that if they neglect this precaution it will be the worse for them, as *Mr Punch* will not be answerable for the consequences of any misrepresentation to which he may be reduced by the want of a reliable portrait. It is for Honourable Members to decide whether they will go down to future ages under *Mr Punch's* version of their features, or Phoebus Apollo's. If, like the national beverage, they prefer being drawn in their own mugs, they will attend to this recommendation; if not, they must take the consequences, which may be of the most frightful description. . . .

**Punch's Dream
of Peace, despite
which he is the
best Shot in
England**

PUNCH'S DREAM OF PEACE

THE VOLUNTEER MOVEMENT – CHAIRING THE BEST SHOT IN ENGLAND

MR PUNCH AND THE VICTORIA CROSS

PERHAPS; no, we scorn a qualified expression, and begin again with – Decidedly the most imposing ceremonial which has ever taken place in a free or any other country, was exhibited to the eyes of the million, on Friday, the 26th of June, 1857, in Hyde Park, when and where HER MOST GRACIOUS MAJESTY was pleased to confer upon *Mr Punch* the Victoria Cross, or Order of Merit, in acknowledgment of many years of gallant, daring, and faithful service to the Throne, the Altar, and the Nation. . . .

That immortal man was decorated (*inter alia*)

For having in the most gallant manner, and single-handed, stormed the fortress of Protection, and opened the gates to COMMANDER R. COBDEN and the League.

For having protected the country when it was threatened by the Chartists, and for having completely put down Chartism.

For having attacked the Post Office when in the hands of the Brigand GRAHAM, and for having delivered the correspondence of the nation from that plunderer.

For having a second time attacked the Post Office, and handed it over to ROWLAND HILL, whereby the tremendous letter-tax was put down in favour of the present system.

For having completely put down Repeal, and driven all Repealers out of Ireland.

For having destroyed the Welsh Toll Gates, and for being ready, and what is more determined, to do the same by those of England.

For having charged into Capel Court, and routed out its nest of pirates, and for having afterwards shot down all the wild stags that were so dangerous to society.

For having utterly defeated the Papal Aggressionists.

For having made War upon Russia, and for having finally humiliated her, and compelled her to sign a Treaty.

For having smashed the ALBERT hat.

For having repulsed intended invasions by France and America.

For having overthrown the timid Ministry of LORD JOHN RUSSELL.

For having overthrown the foolish Ministry of LORD DERBY.

For having overthrown the un-English Ministry of LORD ABERDEEN.

For having made LORD PALMERSTON, Minister of England, and pledged him to Reform.

For having put down the Sabbatarians, and for having secured rational liberty to the millions in respect to Sunday observance.

For having created the Great Exhibition of 1851.

For having built and christened the Crystal Palace.

For having compelled the Government to reduce the Income-Tax.

For having suggested every reform and improvement which have been effected in the world since July 1841, and for intending to pursue the same course as long as the world requires any amendment whatever.

[*The list to be continued through many numbers.*]

Punch, V.C.

MR PUNCH RECEIVING THE VICTORIA CROSS

Punch Presenting his Fourteenth Volume to the Genius of his Country

Punch praises himself as an immortal Institution in a Year of Revolution . . .

PUNCH'S BIRTHDAY ODE TO HIMSELF

I

AMID the crash of toppling crowns,
    The crack of dynasties,
And thunder of bombarded towns,
    Far booming o'er the seas,
While Europe with an earthquake-shock
    Is reeling to and fro,
JOHN BULL sits calmly on his rock,
    Begirt with Ocean's flow,
Watching the storm with quiet survey,
    He being safe ashore;
And whilst abroad all thing are topsy-turvy,
He sees his QUEEN upon her throne,
His Lords and Commons holding still their own,
    And some of them, perhaps, a little more.

II

Oh, pride! our Institutions –
    The old, the wise, the free –
In a world of revolutions
    Still flourishing to see!
To view our own majestic native Oak,
Whilst other trees of Liberty decay,
Still whole and sound from stem to spray,
Not in the least inclined to droop;
    Indeed, without a joke,
This sight should make each Briton cock-a-hoop!

III

But of our Constitution
    There's one peculiar boast,
Its finest Institution –
    That is to say, almost –
With warmest exultation,
    And self-congratulation,
With admiration utterly unbounded,
    Should every mother's son
Regard THAT Institution, founded
    In Eighteen Forty-one!
Yes, *Punch*, for ever vernal,
    By strife and storms unshaken,
Thy celebrated Journal
    The proudest feelings must awaken
In every patriotic breast
    That throbs beneath a British vest.

IV

Lo, *Punch*, whose Fifteenth Volume now appears,
Begins the eighth of his immortal years;
    Exhaustless his outpourings as the sea,
        And also quite as shiny,
With laughs innumerable, as the 'briny.'
        Thus AESCHYLUS, you know,
        Describes the Ocean's glow,
    When its countless ripples glitter
    In a universal titter,
A tremendous Ha, ha, he!
        Ho, ho, ho!

V

This is the happy day of *Punch*'s birth,
    And that is why he crows,
    And his own trumpet blows
        In plenitude of mirth.
    He makes his fresh appearance,
    Intent, with perseverance,
To follow out the good HORATIAN rule
    With which he first began:
That is, in season still to play the fool,
        Which to do well,
And wear with decent grace the cap and bell,
        Takes a wise man.
Thus, being now septennial,
Punch trusts to be perennial;
To him Oblivion's trunk and dusty shelf
        Suggest no fears.
He only hopes his readers – like himself –
        May live a thousand years.

178

This is the first instalment of the famous 'Caudle Lectures' by Jerrold, which did more than anything to establish Punch's popularity.

Punch the
Priest-baiter

'HIS EMINENCE' FIGHTING WITH PUNCH

PUNCH has often had occasion to complain – though a proper pride has always prevented him from complaining – of the want of attention which he has experienced from public personages. LORD JOHN RUSSELL has never had the politeness to acknowledge his obligations for renown and celebrity to *Mr Punch*. LORD STANLEY, and the DUKE OF RICHMOND, and MR DISRAELI have behaved equally ill. Even LORD BROUGHAM has, with the grossest discourtesy, hitherto neglected to take any notice whatever of the frequency with which his name has been mentioned, and the handsome manner in which his portrait has so often been drawn, by *Mr Punch*. One distinguished individual has, however, at last shown his sense of what is due to a gentleman of *Mr Punch's* consequence. *Mr Punch* has been honoured with the animadversions of a person no less eminent than his EMINENCE CARDINAL WISEMAN – so, at least, it is understood – in the *Dublin Review*. It is true that the Cardinal calls *Punch* 'old and drivelling.' But then he says that '*Punch* was once the playful companion of everybody's railway journey.' Well, well! *Punch* is used to be thus vilified. 'That once facetious, but now malignant, periodical' was – long before CARDINAL WISEMAN was ever thought of by *Mr Punch* – an established formula for traducing this paper. Those whose corns *Mr Punch* has trodden upon have always said that; but the proprietors of the corns were 'humble, very humble,' like URIAH HEEP, and did not wear red stockings. But our Cardinal is also humble, to condescend to a bout with *Punch;* crosier against cudgel. And 'Mother' – Mother Church – 'she's humble too,' to have reared so exalted a son in so much humility. To think of his Eminence volunteering to be a combatant on *Punch's* stage; taking off his *pallium* and setting to work to give us a drubbing! And here are a few of the knocks with which we have been honoured by the Cardinal. *Punch*, he says, besides having 'become old and drivelling,'

'Had taken to preach and be a saint, had lost all his good-humour, had turned sulky, and then pugnacious and ill-tempered; and, not content with this, had come down to his old street-occupation of playing the hangman. *Punch* was before MCNEILE in wishing Catholic Bishops to be sentenced to death, and then mercifully transported as felons.'

Nay, but this is rather too condescending, good Cardinal; it is stooping so low as to the assertion of that which is inexact. MCNEILE has already pointed out your mistake in his behalf. As to *Mr Punch*, you are equally mistaken in representing him as usurping the functions of MR CALCRAFT.

Nor would he, as you imaginatively insinuate, have Catholic bishops transported – any more than other people – except for stealing. With respect to your territorial titles, my Prince of the Church, the cry of *Mr Punch* is not so much 'No Popery!' as 'No Robbery!'

As to his good-humour, *Punch* flatters himself that he had preserved that hitherto. But he really fears that he is a little nettled by one thing CARDINAL WISEMAN has said about him. *Mr Punch* is not aware that he 'had taken to preach and be a saint.' But suppose he had. Surely the cap of *Mr Punch* denotes his right to preach equally with the Cardinal's Hat, nay, with the Tiara itself, – having, equally with them, been derived from the primitive ages. And as certainly *Mr Punch* has a right to be a saint if he pleases. Is he not the very image of one, and any that ever winked? Look at the stained mediaeval windows, and observe the attitudes of the saints therein depicted. See how their heads are set on their necks, and mark the manner in which they hold their crooks; and then look at *Punch*, and say whether he is not a saint of the original pattern all over.

But, come; *Mr Punch* must not wax too warm, even in defence of his sanctity. *He* is not seeking to impose upon Englishmen the spiritual domination of a priesthood, by a pretence to absolute holiness; the refutation of which pretence – as by proved complicity in false miracles and cruel persecution – would be fatal to his scheme.

MASTER PUNCH. 'Please, Mr Bishop, which is Popery, and which is Puseyism?
BISHOP. 'Whichever you like, my little dear.'

MANAGER PAM (*looking through the Curtain*). 'How they are squabbling for seats! – Really, a Capital House!'
MR PUNCH. 'Well, you've a good chance of success, but it depends entirely upon what you produce!'

YOUNG 1860

MR PUNCH (*to the New Year*). 'There's the work before you, my boy.'

Triumphant Re-Election of Mr Punch as Member for Everywhere

'STRIKE, BUT HEAR ME!'

STRIKE, but hear me, my good fellow,
  If you will reflect, you can.
Be not as the brutes which bellow;
  List to reason, like a man.
Wages fair for fair day's labour
  If you like, you may refuse;
Whereupon your foreign neighbour
  Work will get which you will lose.

Your employers will not lack you;
  Spurn their proffer if you like.
And the Public then will back you,
  Do you fancy, in your strike?
You, that in these times of trouble,
  Do your best to make them worse,
When all food is costing double
  What it did, to every purse? . . .

Don't believe a word they utter
  Who are making you their tool.
Quarrel with your bread and butter!
  How can you be such a fool?
Come, return to your vocation,
  Trowel, plumb, and square resume,
Or go seek a situation
  At a crossing, with a broom.

**Punch the
Capitalist
(1861)**

'STRIKE, BUT HEAR ME.' – DON'T QUARREL WITH YOUR
BREAD AND BUTTER

A Footnote: Punch examines his own Image

CAUSE AND EFFECT

1ST FAST MAN. ' "Punch" is very dummy and
slow this week, I think.'
2ND FAST MAN. 'So do I. It's their own fault, too,
for I sent 'em some deuced funny articles,
which the humbugs sent back.'
1ST FAST MAN. 'That's just the way they served
me – the great fools!'

PORTRAIT OF A GENTLEMAN

BEFORE AND AFTER

Taking a Six Months' Course of *Punch*

Fifty Thousand Cures

OF drowsiness, dejection, dolour, dulness, depression, ennui, ill-humour, indigestion (mental) from
political or other reading, loss of temper, low
spirits, melancholy, moroseness, mental anxiety
(as, for instance, on a railway journey), sulks,
stupefaction (by a debate in Common Council),
sleepiness, spleen, general used-upishness, and
many other complaints, have already been effected
by the use of *Punch's Almanack*, which is Sold by
Everybody, and bought by the rest. The infant
may take it as well as the adult, as it is warranted
free from all impurity, and contains nothing hurt-
ful to the weakest mental stomach.

VII · RETROSPECT AND PROSPECT

RETROSPECT AND PROSPECT; OR, 1851 AND 1852

BETWEEN the year on which the night is sinking
  And that on which riseth the light of day,
I stand and mark the Hours, that, all unwinking,
  From year to year their service shift alway.

Attendant Hours, lift me up on my bed,
  That I may speak the things I have to say,
Before I am borne hence, with muffled head,
  To the great grave of the years pass'd away.

Before me lies my life; 'midst wrong and terror,
  And force and fraud, out of it shines a light,
Held by the balmy hand of Peace, from error
  A beacon to guide nations to the right.

And in the luminous orbit of that splendour
  Britain sits, throned by Peace, serenely strong;
While all the nations unforced homage render,
  And to the twain with ample offerings throng.

And all the sky is jubilant with voices
  Of brotherhood and hope without alloy;
Science is quickened, Industry rejoices,
  And Art's sweet eyes are radiant with joy.

This hush of calm 'mid the world's din of battle,
  This space of sunshine on Earth's twilight stage,
This choral song, heard through Life's wail and
    brattle,
  Fell in my life. Time writes it on my page.

THE RECONCILIATION

BELIEVE us, it is not true that wealth must be only another name for wickedness. It is not true that virtue must inevitably be found with rags. . . .

There are faults on both sides; otherwise, what a lop-sided world this would be!

Wealth and Poverty call one another hard names; and then reward themselves with an abundance of self-complacency. The rich man is an ogre, living upon the hearts of the poor; grinding them under his golden heel, like worms; penning them up like unthoughtful cattle in unions; for game and poor-law offences, locking them in jails; harrying them here and there; in any and every manner grinding their bones to make his fine white bread. And Wealth, with this report of wickedness upon it, is a monster – a new Dragon of Wantley – a hydra with a hundred heads, some bare, some coronetted. And so is Wealth abused, and pelted with hard names. To be sure, the missiles break like bubbles against its golden plates. Words are but air, – and Wealth, rattling its ingots, may laugh at the vocabulary of Want, be it ever so uncleanly.

And then Wealth has its say, too. Poverty is an ungrateful dog; a mere animal – an engine made for the express use of him who can purchase it. An ungracious, foul-tongued, coarse, disorderly wretch; a creature in no way tuned with the same moral harmony, ennobled by the same impulses, that animate the man with the pocket. Down with Poverty! Crush it! Imprison it – brand it! The offal and the weed of the earth; the blight of the world, and the nuisance of the rich.

And after this fashion do Wealth and Poverty traduce one·another. After this fashion do they – in the very hastiness of ignorance – commit a mutual wrong. After this fashion set up a false standard of mutual excellence.

'What!' says Wealth, 'do I not fulfil my ordained purpose? Do I not profess myself Christian? Do I not go to church, and enact all the "inevitable decencies" of life? Do I not pay the poor rates – Easter dues – and all that? I envy no man his worldly goods. I am content with my own. I fairly, nay honourably fulfil the station awarded me, and what care I – what should I care – for the rest? I know my duties, and I do them.'

And Poverty, in its sense of suffering, hugs itself that in the next world it will go hard with DIVES, and lays up for itself, in its own complacency, the reward of LAZARUS; confounding in its wretchedness, its wants for excellences.

Surely there will come a time when the Rich and the Poor will fairly meet, and have a great human talk upon the matter; will hold a parliament of the heart, and pass acts that no after selfishness and wrong – on either side – shall repeal! The Rich will come – not with cricket-balls or quoits in their hands – to make brotherhood with the Poor; but touched with the deep conviction that in this world the lowest created man has a solemn part to play, directed to solemn ends; that he is to be considered and cared for, in his condition, with tenderness, with fraternal benevolence; that there is something more than alms due from the high to the low; that human sympathy can speak otherwise than by the voice of money; and that, too, in at once a loftier and a sweeter tone of hope and comforting.

The time will come when Poverty will be relieved from its serfdom. We have emancipated the slave to the colour of his skin. We have next to emancipate the slave of Poverty: to take from him the stain and blot, the blight and the disgrace of pauperism; to cure him of the leprosy he takes from want alone; to divest him of the collar and the chain, which human pride and prejudice have, for centuries past, beheld about the neck of the Poor. When Poverty shall be declared no longer infamous – no, not declared; *that*, with pharisee-lip, we declare now – but thought, believed, made a creed of, then may Poverty expect its higher rights. At present, Poverty has an ignominious, a felonious character; and honest, yet withal worldly men, give good steerage-room to the foul disgrace.

Then will it be pleasant to see – whoever shall see it – the reconciliation of the Rich and the Poor. When all old selfishness, old prejudices, old feuds – on both sides – shall be buried and forgotten; when the Rich shall have cast away the arrogance of wealth, their pride, their wicked and irreligious sense of exclusiveness – and the Poor shall have quenched all heart-burnings, all thoughts of revengeful wrong, – then will it be a glorious sight (no bravery like it) to see man reconciled to man; and knowing that, whilst human life endures, there must still be human inequalities, – still to know there shall be a wise, a sympathising, and an enduring reconciliation.

Q.

A Prophecy

CHAPTER THE FIRST

FIRST CAUSES OF THE LIBERTY OF THE ENGLISH NATION

1066 and All That

WE should very properly expect to be rebuked for our impertinence, by the very youngest of our readers, and our conscience would certainly pinch us for our stale news, if we were to announce as a new fact, that Great Britain was abandoned by the Romans, when they found it necessary to look at home, and desist – as SPELMAN, the great sacrificer of spelling, says – from 'Romeing abroad.'

It is, however, undoubtedly true that the origin of our becoming our own masters, was our not being worth the trouble of keeping; and our first freedom came to us in the shape of a kick, which sent us about our business, to get on as we could by ourselves. No sooner were we abandoned by the Romans as mere leavings, than there came from the shores of the Baltic small picnic parties, to avail themselves of the nice pickings we might still present; and, having destroyed the ancient inhabitants or earliest pot-wallopers, these gentlemen began wallopping each other, because it was the only occupation – except the occupation of the place itself – which the island seemed to afford. After a good deal of Baltic sound and fury, signifying nothing, and after the establishment of a set of small sovereignties, which, under the name of the Heptarchy, kept the place in a state

A PROSPECT OF Ye Heptarchye

of sevens – if not of sixes also – for many years, the whole southern part of the island was united under that illustrious seven in one, the renowned EGBERT. He accepted the allegiance of those most acute of all angles, the East Angles, who knew their own interest too well to resist. He reduced Mercia without mercy; deputed his son to ravage Kent, whose people were soon led a pretty dance among their native hops; while the same bold youth was despatched to Essex, whose inhabitants were pillaged of their herds until they had not a leg to stand upon, and were deprived even of their exceedingly popular calves. Northumberland, in the midst of a civil commotion, very civilly offered EGBERT the somewhat shaky throne, which no other upholsterer, whether royal or otherwise, seemed so likely as himself to be able to uphold. Making short work of further opposition, and in no quarter doing anything by halves, he managed to achieve the extraordinary feat of sitting, not

simply upon two, but upon no less than seven stools, without falling to the ground. Our Constitution had not advanced very far in its formation at this early period; and as to our liberties, we had little to boast of under that head, unless they could have been beaten into us by the series of drubbings we received. The grand principle of Government appears to have consisted in the right of some powerful personage to do what he liked with our ancestors' own, until the Anglo-Saxon princes licked us a little into shape, after the various unprofitable lickings we had endured. ALFRED THE GREAT, who was less happy at cooking a cake than concocting a code, was the most illustrious of this line, and EDWARD THE CONFESSOR, who seldom kept himself out of a hobble, was exactly what nature fitted him to be – the last of his race. He had, however, in violation of the strict principles of copyright, compiled a body of laws out of those framed by his predecessors, and he dishonestly put his own name on the title-page of the piratical work. Little is known of our Constitution under this successional crop of early Royals, until that Pink of invaders, known familiarly as Sweet WILLIAM THE CONQUEROR, shot up on our soil.

There had previously been a King and a Nobility; but SIR WILLIAM TEMPLE, who gives us this information, might fairly take for his motto –

'I tell thee all, I can no more –
Though poor the offering be;'

for poor, indeed, is this contribution of SIR WILLIAM's to our early Constitutional history.

It is from the Conquest we are told to date the real commencement of our freedom; and it is a remarkable illustration of the wisdom of the maxim, 'Spare the rod, spoil the child,' that the more we have been thrashed, the stronger our liberties have grown, as if, like an old carpet, we wanted a good beating to show us in our true colours. WILLIAM OF NORMANDY turned his sword at once into a carving-knife, with which he sliced up our native land, and divided the bits among his followers. He treated Old England like its own immortal roast beef, and finding it in capital cut, he, without making any bones about it, proceeded to serve it out, by distributing large helpings of it among his hungry retinue. In his large interpretation of the word *meum*, he altogether lost sight of its ordinary companion *tuum*, and he appropriated the land so extensively that he left no other possession but self-possession to its former owners. He handed over the soil to his creatures, who held it subject to WILLIAM's will, and thus what is termed the Feudal,* System was established in England.

* We do not mean to go into the depths of philology as to the derivation of the word feudal from feud, *feudum, fides*, fief, or fife; for, as SPELMAN says, 'that fife has been already too much played upon.'

PUNCH'S HANDBOOKS TO THE CRYSTAL PALACE

THE MEDIAEVAL COURT

MEDIAEVAL, a word signifying middle-aged, has given rise to much discussion, and indeed the middle age of art seems to be almost as much wrapped in obscurity as the middle age in nature, which is, especially among the female sex, a subject of much mystery. There is much dispute as to the point at which mediaeval art commenced; but we most of us know it when we see it, just as we can tell a middle-aged woman when we see her, however she may try to baffle us by an argument as to the point at which the middle age begins. The Pointed style has been termed the key-note to the mediaeval in art, and perhaps the Pointed style, as indicated by the sharpness of the nose, and other features, that have lost the roundness of youth, may be considered characteristic of the middle age in nature. A mediaeval window has the smoothness of its arch interrupted by a point, and the middle-aged eyebrow is drawn up into what is termed a peaked shape, which takes from the eye its arch look. There is a further analogy between the mediaeval in art and in nature, both of which resort in middle age to an amount of ornament, which is equally· unknown to the early period of the one and the youth of the other. With advancing age ornament becomes more profuse and elaborate till the original object is almost lost sight of in the gaudy adornments with which it is overlaid.

Much learning has been bestowed on the origin of the Pointed style, but we prefer that our own style would be found anything but pointed, if we were to dwell any longer on this rather profitless argument. MR RUSKIN, throwing overboard all fanciful theories, attributes the Pointed style to the necessity for throwing off the snow and the rain, and thus, by reference to the wet, he manages to get rid of a dry discussion.

Instead of entering any further into the dispute, we will enter into the Court itself, which, coming from the railway, is on the right hand, or eastern side of the building. . . .

As we go in at the centre we pass under a doorway from Tintern Abbey, adorned with statues from Wells and Westminster, and find ourselves in a cloister from Gainsborough, in Lincolnshire, a combination which, though pleasing to the eye of taste, is rather embarrassing to the mind of the geographer. Opposite to us as we enter is the Great Door from Rochester Cathedral, with all its original colouring and gilding, which were once very elaborate, but they have been swept by the fingers of Time, who has robbed it of its richness, and on whose hands all the gilt remains. On the left of the inside of the Cloister is the door of PRINCE ARTHUR's chapel from Worcester, having at the sides two crowned kings, whose heads, the Official Guidebooks tell us, are 'exceedingly well executed;' but the heads must have been exceedingly well restored, if the execution was really performed. There are numerous other objects of interest, but our Handbook would become a mere Catalogue if we were to note down separately the lots of attractive articles with which the Mediaeval Court abounds. . . .

We cannot quit the Mediaeval Court without expressing our admiration of its beauties, though we cannot go with MR RUSKIN in his proposed expedition 'through the streets of London, pulling down those brackets and friezes and large names' over the shops of the tradesmen, in order to supply 'each with a plain shop casement with small frames in it, that people would not think of breaking in order to be sent to prison.' Our love for the Gothic would be tempered by our fear of the police, and we should in smashing the largest windows, put ourselves literally to the greatest panes, with no other attainable end than the station house. We cannot go the length of those who object to all decoration except the Gothic, and who insist on the nonconcealment of 'hinges, bolts, and nails,' as if something besides the door is supposed to hang on the hinge, and as if the only way to hit the right nail on the head is to leave the head visible.

Punch's Guide to the Mediaeval Court of the Crystal Palace

A CONTRAST

BETWEEN THE MEMBER FOR BUCKS AS WAS, AND THE MEMBER AS IS TO BE

PUNCH'S ADDRESS TO THE ELECTORS

An historical Contrast, and an historic Parallel

LOOK here upon this picture, and on this;
The counterfeit presentment of two members:
See what a grace was seated on his brow,
Devoid of curls – 'the front* of Jove himself!'
An eye like PEEL, to puzzle and command,
A station like the one at Euston Square,
New lighted with a million extra lamps;
A combination, and a form indeed,
Where every virtue seemed to set its mark,
To give the world assurance of a man –
This *was* your Member. Look you now what
    follows: –
There *is* your Candidate. O, have you eyes?
Could you the mem'ry of JOHN HAMPDEN leave,
And put up with this DIS.!

* We should have thought it was only JUNO who wore a front, but we have SHAKSPEARE's authority for the fact that JOVE himself patronised this early and curly substitute for the 'Gentleman's real head of hair.'

Look on this Picture!   and (then have the goodness to)   look on this!

AN HISTORICAL PARALLEL;

Elizabeth – 1580

OR, COURT PASTIMES

Victoria – 1845

190

THE GEORGES

As the statues of these beloved Monarchs are to be put up in the Parliament palace – we have been favoured by a young lady (connected with the Court) with copies of the inscriptions which are to be engraven under the images of those Stars of Brunswick.

GEORGE THE FIRST – STAR OF BRUNSWICK
He preferred Hanover to England,
He preferred two hideous Mistresses
To a beautiful and innocent Wife.
He hated Arts and despised Literature;
But He liked train-oil in his salads,
And gave an enlightened patronage to bad oysters.
And he had WALPOLE as a Minister:
Consistent in his Preference for every kind of
Corruption.

GEORGE II
In most things I did as my father had done,
I was false to my wife and I hated my son:

My spending was small and my avarice much,
My kingdom was English, my heart was High Dutch:

At Dettingen fight I was known not to blench,
I butchered the Scotch, and I bearded the French:

I neither had morals, nor manners, nor wit;
I wasn't much missed when I died in a fit.

Here set up my statue, and make it complete –
With PITT on his knees at my dirty old feet.

GEORGE III
Give me a royal niche – it is my due,
The virtuousest King the realm e'er knew.

I, through a decent reputable life,
Was constant to plain food and a plain wife.

Ireland I risked, and lost America;
But dined on legs of mutton every day.

My brain, perhaps, might be a feeble part;
But yet I think I had an English heart.

When all the Kings were prostrate, I alone
Stood face to face against NAPOLEON;

Nor ever could the ruthless Frenchman forge
A fetter for OLD ENGLAND and OLD GEORGE:

I let loose flaming NELSON on his fleets;
I met his troops with WELLESLEY's bayonets.

Triumphant waved my flag on land and sea:
Where was the King in Europe like to me?

Monarchs exiled found shelter on my shores;
My bounty rescued Kings and Emperors.

But what boots victory by land or sea?
What boots that Kings found refuge at my knee?

I was a conqueror, but yet not proud;
And careless, even though NAPOLEON bow'd.

The rescued Kings came kiss my garments' hem:
The rescued Kings I never heeded them.

My guns roar'd triumph, but I never heard;
All England thrilled with joy, I never stirred.

What care had I of pomp, or fame, or power, –
A crazy old blind man in Windsor Tower?

GEORGIUS ULTIMUS
He left an example for age and for youth
To avoid.
He never acted well by Man or Woman,
And was as false to his Mistress as to his Wife.
He deserted his Friends and his Principles.
He was so Ignorant that he could scarcely Spell;
But he had some Skill in Cutting out Coats,
And an undeniable Taste for Cookery.
He built the Palaces of Brighton and of Buckingham,
And for these Qualities and Proofs of Genius,
An admiring Aristocracy
Christened him the 'First Gentleman in Europe.'
Friends, respect the KING whose Statue is here,
And the generous Aristocracy who admired him.

BEAU BRUMMELL'S STATUE, TRAFALGAR SQUARE

PUNCH has received exclusive intelligence of a subscription which is now quietly growing at WHITE'S, at BROOKES'S, at the CARLTON, and other Clubs, for the purpose of erecting a statue to the memory of GEORGE BRYAN BRUMMELL, the man who invented starched neckcloths, and gave its newest gloss to blacking. The sculptor, whose name we are not at present permitted to reveal, has sent in a drawing of the contemplated statue, which, carved in wood, we here present to the world at large. BRUMMELL's neckcloths, the trophies of his life, are, it will be seen, chastely grouped behind him.

Trafalgar Square has very properly been selected as the place for the erection. There again will dwell in kindly neighbourhood GEORGE THE BEAU and GEORGE THE FOURTH. Their lives were lovely, and their joint memories will be appropriately eternized in congenial bronze. The grandson of the pastrycook and the descendant of the Guelphs will be reconciled by the good offices of posterity, and the peculiar virtues that each possessed be brought out in stronger relief by the association. Looking at BRUMMELL, we shall remember with glowing admiration, the man 'who never failed in his tye.' Beholding GEORGE THE FOURTH, we shall not readily forget the man to whom all ties were equally indifferent. . . .

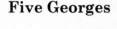

191

Young France mewling and puking in the nurse's arms

The ouvrier creeping like snail unwillingly to school

THE SEVEN AGES OF THE REPUBLIC

– FRANCE is a stage,
And all her heroes little more than players.
Her Kings their exits have, and entrances;
And the Republic runs its round of parts,
Its acts being seven ages. First, Young France,
Emeuting and plotting, e'en in the nurse's arms;
Then *ouvrier* out of work, casquette on head,
And frowning hairy face, going, in faith,
To LOUIS BLANC to school. Then LAMARTINE,
Spouting away, writing a score of sonnets
Unto Dame Liberty's eyebrow; then *Mobile*,
Clapped in strange clothes, and bearding barricades,
Zealous against old friends in sudden quarrel,
Taking a sight at death and devastation
E'en in the cannon's mouth; then CAVAIGNAC,
In power despotic and a state of siege,
With frown severe, and beard of Algiers cut,
O'er-riding Law with a soldier's insolence –
And so he plays his part. The sixth age shows
Poor Liberty, with Constitution weak,
Halting 'twixt Anarchy and Despotism,
Her youthful *bonnet rouge* a world too wide
For her shrunk brains, and the big boastful voice,
Turning again to the old treble, pipes
LOUIS NAPOLEON in. Last scene of all,
That ends this strange, eventful history,
Is second childishness, and mere oblivion,
Sans trade, sans tin, sans press, sans everything.

Lamartine inditing a sonnet to Liberty's eyebrow

The Garde Mobile seeking the bubble reputation in the cannon's mouth

The Justice, with eyes severe and beard of formal cut

The lean and slippered Pantaloon, with spectacles on nose

The last scene of all in this eventful history.

THREE EPOCHS OF HALF-A-CENTURY

1804

I WONDER what his thoughts were – that sallow,
    silent man –
As athwart the lines of bayonets the dancing sunlight
    ran,
Steeping in golden glory the white tents on the down,
And the old gray Roman watch-tower that looms o'er
    Boulogne town.

Did he think of all that he had done – or of what was
    yet to do? –
Of nations he had conquer'd, or of *one* still to subdue?
Was he prouder that he stood there, acknowledged
    Europe's lord,
Or angrier one small island should yet defy his sword?

For from that tower by daylight, if seaward turn'd his
    gaze,
NELSON's blockading squadron show'd its white sails
    through the haze;
If after dark he paced the cliff – on the verge, but full
    in sight,
There were England's beacons blazing, like red eyes,
    through the night.

And he knew those ships were waiting, if his dared put
    to sea;
And he knew those fires were lighted by men who still
    were free.
And though his soldiers, ships, and guns were as
    twenty unto one,
He knew what Englishmen could do – what Englishmen
    had done.

Like an unquiet tiger, that chafes, and champs, and
    cries
Before a couchant lion, that stirs not where he lies,
So chafed fierce France upon the cliff which looks on
    Boulogne town –
So still – so stern – lay England, upon the Kentish
    down.

1840

I wonder what his thoughts were – that shabby, silent
    man –
As thirty-six years later to shore a pinnace ran,
Bearing a homeless penniless adventurer, with his
    train,
A draggled pinioned Eagle, and some cases of
    champagne.

Was it trusting to the magic of his great uncle's name,
That on a desperate venture thus recklessly he came?
Or deemed he, like that uncle, he was following a star,
That beckoned him still forwards, on a road no force
    could bar?

Had he well read the people, when thus he came unto
Their sympathy with hardihood, their love of *l'imprévu;*
Deem'd he the attendant eagle would guarantee the
    JOVE?
Or was't trust in five-franc pieces – like to his with
    whom he strove?

Did he foresee the downfall of that throne that
    seemed so sure?
Deem'd he that desperate evils would hail a desperate
    cure?
Was it Debt, or was it Destiny that drove him on his
    way
To the maddest act that madmen did ever yet essay?

How lured he on the scanty band that made his cause
    their own?
Saw he or they the shadow of Revolution thrown
From the dim Future forwards? – saw he the prison-
    cell
Opening upon the palace? His thoughts – what man
    can tell?

Enough that to this shore he came – landed and fought
    and failed:
Nor in that madman's enterprise – nor ever after –
    quailed:
A pleader for his forfeit life – a prisoner – but still
Silent and stern and saturnine, and of an iron will.

We cite the first NAPOLEON, when a banned and
    banished man,
With his handful of old grenadiers he sprang to shore
    at Cannes,
As one who threw a desperate throw, and thereby won
    a throne –
What was he unto his nephew – in *that* landing at
    Boulogne?

1854

I wonder what his thoughts were – that sad-eyed,
    silent man,
As alongside Boulogne's jetty England's royal steamer
    ran;
While with a King beside him, that adventurer was
    seen
Greeting, as Emperor of France, the Consort of our
    QUEEN?

The ships around are gay with flags, the streets are
    green with boughs;
The people press about him, with cheers and prayers
    and vows;
The court, the camp, the church, its best, its bravest,
    holiest brings;
There stands the madman of Boulogne – a Kaiser
    among kings!

What memories are sweeping through that impassive
    brain?
Thinks he of that first landing – of his out-at-elbows
    train?
Of the oath – or of the ballot – or of June's red
    barricades?
Or thinks he of December's yet bloodier fusillades?

Why question thus? Heaven sends the scourge; but in
    that guiding hand,
What chastens still to blessing turns. So doth this
    man's command.
Own we in him an instrument, through sin, and pain,
    and blood,
That worketh still, as all things work together, unto
    good.

'Tis due to him that France's flag floats side by side
    with ours,
'Tis due to him that France's hosts are leagued with
    England's powers;
Thankful for this, 'twere out of place too curiously to
    scan,
Through the good deeds of the monarch, the ill deeds
    of the man.

Changing Times: the Course of Modern British History

AMERICA *VERSUS* ENGLAND

THERE is no hope for poor old England; for America seems to be running fairly ahead of us. She beats us on the seas, as far as speed is concerned; and now we are to have a race-horse from America who is to win the next year's Derby, as a matter of the merest (Epsom) course. An American comes over and picks our locks; and we dare say every reward that is ever offered, henceforth, for anything in England will be carried off by our big brother JONATHAN. We really must look about us a little, if we do not wish to be utterly eclipsed by the stars and flogged by the stripes of America. We are afraid JOHN BULL is a little self-sufficient at times, and a wholesome rub on that very tender point – his vanity – will have a very beneficial effect. We are not, however, quite disposed to allow the Yankees, yet, all the superiority they claim; and we are not much disturbed in our mind by anticipations of the result of the Derby Day; for we fully believe that the American horse which is to beat the field resides in some mare's nest or other which will never be found.

THE GOOD OLD DAYS OF JOSEPH HUME

I SING, I sing, of good times over,
When we lived in peace, if not in clover,
Were free from alarm as to what the French meant,
And the popular cry was for Retrenchment;
When, instead of paying for new defences,
We tried to cut down all such expenses,
And, in the estimates' construction,
Economists compelled Reduction.
    Sing hey, sing ho, in sorrow and gloom,
    For the good old days of JOSEPH HUME!

When France was not than England stronger,
And we thought that war would be no longer;
When the Millennium we expected,
And our Army and Navy alike neglected;
Talked of swords into ploughshares turning,
And gunpowder only for pastime burning,
In fireworks, or on stubble or heather,
And lions and lambs lying down together.
    Sing hey, sing ho! &c.

When young men thought they acted wise in
Cultivating Arts, and Arms despising;
When – ah, how much folks were mistaken! –
Martial studies were forsaken.
But swords and bayonets in these days are
Furbished, sharp as needle and razor,
Soldiers and sailors all hard drilling
For practice in the art of killing,
    Sing hey, sing ho! &c.

When old Brown Bess her purpose suited,
The Queen of Weapons then reputed,
The Rifles were a mere Brigade then,
Because we thought of little but trade then;
But now each man has his Enfield Rifle,
And that, alone, doesn't cost a trifle;
Then Armstrong guns, and shells, and mortars
We must provide to guard all quarters.
    Sing hey, sing ho! &c.

When men would have been accounted dreamers
Who talked of a fleet of war screw-steamers,
When we, by wooden walls defended,
Against attack, on wood depended.
But now we find we must environ
Our isle with vessels cased in iron,
With iron walls must be surrounded,
That iron costing tin unbounded.
    Sing hey, sing ho! &c.

When self-protection asked but flannel;
But now that steam has bridged the Channel,
Each freeborn Briton has occasion
To hold his own against invasion;
So Volunteers have formed, are forming,
Like bees – with stings about them – swarming:
That is the cheapest way to do it;
But times are changed, and how we rue it!
    Sing hey, sing ho! &c.

PERSECUTION AND PUNCH IN 1851

(A Page from Posterity's *Decline and Fall, &c.*)

SHOULD England, in the course of centuries, yielding to the encroachments of Popery, sink in the scale of nations, and ultimately disappear from among the Powers of the Earth, the future historian of the *Decline and Fall of the British Empire*, writing in Australia, may perhaps, with reference to the existing controversy, compose a few paragraphs of this sort: –

'The first attempt of the See of Rome to reduce the haughty and obstinate English to subjection beneath the papal yoke, provoked a furious and sanguinary resistance. The pious zeal of ecclesiastical writers has destroyed the partial, and perhaps untrustworthy, records of heretical adversaries; but, for the conjectural inferences of historical criticism, we may substitute the unimpeachable testimony of infallible churchmanship. If any credit is due to the declarations of the most eminent prelates, a persecution, unparalleled in extent and cruelty since the atrocities of DIOCLETIAN, was set on foot against the Archbishop and Bishops of the restored hierarchy. Popes, Cardinals, and Monks, after being paraded with ignominy through the streets of London during the day, were burnt, at night, amid the acclamations of the multitude; and the flames, which excited the sufferings of the martyrs, illuminated the revels of a frantic populace. The addresses of the Irish Clergy to ST NICHOLAS WISEMAN, coupled with the language of the Saint himself, by their frequent allusions to the fires of persecution, attest the nature of the torments which he had endured for the faith. Yet, after having suffered barbarities more savage than any that could have revealed the weakness or tested the fortitude of the victim of the North American Indian, we find this holy confessor in so short a space of time performing the duties of his pastoral office, that the supposition of a miracle is absolutely necessary to reconcile a fact of church history with possibility in the nature of things.

'Foremost among the persecutors of ST NICHOLAS and his holy associates, was a tyrant, whom the popular will and favour had invested with almost absolute power. The name of this merciless and inhuman despot was *Punch*. This monster, in character and disposition, appears to have been a combination of RICHARD THE THIRD with the eighth HENRY; and a physical resemblance corresponded to the mental similitude; for to the corpulence of the latter of these tyrants was added, in his person, the deformity of the former. From his magnificent residence, which desecrated the holy precincts of St Bride's Court, he was accustomed to sally forth periodically, armed with privileged impunity, and a huge cudgel with which he belaboured his victims, who were for the most part dignitaries of the only orthodox Church. The ingenuity of malice seems to have been exhausted by the variety of the tortures which he not only devised, but inflicted. Ecclesiastics most venerable for their station, if not for their virtues, were unsparingly lashed, and caustic, applied to the most sensitive places, added poignancy to anguish. Some of the martyrs were slowly roasted by a process which lasted in several instances for months; others were exposed on the gibbet, or in the pillory; and many slaughtered by being completely cut to pieces; yet shortly afterwards resuming both their integrity and their avocations, afforded at once examples of extraordinary cruelty, and supernatural interposition. Retribution, however, at length overtook the persecutor. Having incautiously penetrated into a remote part of Ireland, he was seized upon by the indignant faithful; and having been solemnly condemned by the Synod of Castlebar, expiated, if the expression can be allowed, his accumulated atrocities in the avenging flames.'

Such is the account which unerring Tradition has handed down to us, of the renownéd *Punch*; yet the perversity of scepticism has not failed to insinuate that the whole history is a hyperbolical allegory; that the deformity of the tyrant was only the grotesqueness of a puppet, and that his cruelties were but the sarcasms of a biting humourist.

ST NICHOLAS.

His sufferings.

And miraculous cure.

The tyrant *Punch*.

The Present as History

His personal appearance.

Persecutes the new hierarchy.

His barbarities.

And punishment.

Historic doubts concerning him.

HISTORICAL CHARACTER FOR CARDINAL WISEMAN. – The Great Plague of London.

MORE ARCHAEOLOGY

The Taste for Antiquity: Punch identifies some cultural Fads – Archaeological, Antediluvian and Architectural

THE Archaeologists are at it again, and have been riding their hobbies, rolling about their barrows, tumbling over their tumuli, and rubbing up their monumental brasses, with more than their usual energy. We last heard of them at Lincoln, where they mounted a dead wall, and, sticking to it like bricks, declared it to be the relic of the 'Old Mint of Lincoln.' It is usually a sign of weakness to fly to the wall; but the Archaeologists were in great force, and E. HAWKINS, ESQ., 'read a paper upon the wall;' his brother members sitting, of course, upon the wall to support and encourage him. He went into the wall brick by brick; dwelt forcibly on the buttress; revelled among the mortar; and hanging upon the coping with affectionate tenacity.

He followed the cement from the lime-kiln to the hod; he handled cleverly the clay that gave the material for the foundations; and then, taking a rapid glance at walls in general, he touched lightly on the Great Wall of China; passed gracefully over the walls of the Colosseum, and came playfully down upon Blackwall with a pun that shook the old wall of the Mint of Lincoln with the laughter of his audience. He then proceeded to a digression on wall-fruit, and went cleverly into the peach, which he laid open with such effect, that in his mouth the peach seemed to be a different thing from what it appeared before he

set his tongue and his jaw in motion, to show what might be done with it.

After the paper on the wall was concluded – a paper by which, if walls have ears, the subject of the discourse must have been greatly edified – an energetic Archaeologian insisted on reading a paper about 'The family of the DYMOCKS,' which might have been very interesting if MR and MRS DYMOCK, or any of the little DYMOCKS, had been there to hear it; but as this was not the case, the audience stole away by degrees, and the *savant* was for some time holding forth alone on 'The family of the DYMOCKS,' until a rustic voice, exclaiming, 'Halloa! you chap; come down off that there wall,' induced him to look around, and led to his discovery of his loneliness. By way of gratifying the Archaeologian, who had inquired if there was any barrow in the neighbourhood, he was wheeled home in what was supposed to be his favourite vehicle; and, his remonstrances being set down to the score of modesty, were of course wholly disregarded.

The Effects of a Hearty Dinner after visiting the Antediluvian Department at the Crystal Palace

A GOOD GOTH WANTED

That very young Architect, Fadly (who believes in nothing of later date than the Thirteenth Century), invents a Gothic Hat!

WHAT queer people there are in life! This is not a new reflection; but, plaguing although it be, when one takes the *Times* up, one can hardly avoid making it. Who are the odd people who advertise their wants, and who the odder people are by whom those wants are ministered, are questions we despair of ever seeing answered, and which therefore it is clearly a waste of space to put. As a sample of what strange requirements are announced, and what curious people are invited to supply them, we take the following at random from a lot of curiosities with which our advertising literature has been recently replete: –

WANTED, a First-rate GOTHIC ASSISTANT and DESIGNER, temporarily. If suitable, a portion of his time would be engaged for. – Apply to X. D., Deacon's News Rooms, 154, Leadenhall Street.

We thought we had heard long since of the Last of the Goths, but it seems we were mistaken. There are some of them still extant. Whether this advertisement will bring them from their hiding-places, and what tests will be tried to prove they are 'first-rate,' are points on which our readers, if they please, may speculate; but we, who never speculate, cannot lend them any help. We only hope that the 'designs' for which a Goth's aid is required are not designs on JOHN BULL's pocket for some temporary trumpery, which, like the Monster Statue, is sure to become permanent. We are inclined to frame this hope from the knowledge of what Goths our public architects have been, and the fear lest some new pepper-box calamity befall us.

THE MIDDLE-AGE MANIA

THE system of decoration is, just now, all of the character of the Middle Age, and our rooms are crowded with Elizabethan ornaments. We may reasonably expect, therefore, that the next age will adopt for its adornments the style which is prevalent at the present period. What the armed knight of our ancestors is to us, the policeman in uniform will be to our posterity. Already the watchman of olden times is almost eligible to the honours of statueship, and the stage-coachman of our boyish days will soon be entitled, on the score of antiquity, to take his place among our effigies.

We can fancy the effect of a room a hundred years hence, decorated with figures clothed in the fantastic garb of the present century. Of course it is only antiquity that gives value to many of those objects which figure in the catalogues of the present period, and are clutched up as bits of *vertu* by the connoisseurs of our own era. In the course of a century the cape of a policeman will have acquired to the dignity of the cuirass of the past, and the official highlow of the present day will have obtained, from the ripeness of age, the same curious interest that now belongs to the steel clogs or sabatynes of our ancestors. We can imagine what a catalogue might be made by the EDMUND ROBINS of the twentieth century, who might be intrusted with the sale of some collection of curiosities.

LOT 1. – A Staff, supposed to have belonged to the Beadle of Burlington. The brass nob is rendered doubly interesting by an indenture which has been traced immediately up to the skull of a boy of the period.

LOT 2. – Is a Staff of peculiar construction, supposed to have been used by the celebrated Solitary of the Exeter Change Arcade. This staff has a legend attached to it, of peculiar interest. It is said that the staff was so long the only companion of its master, that he at length became incapable of enjoying any other society. There is an affecting anecdote also related in connection with the staff, which, it is said, was ultimately seized as an heir-loom of an ancient family, which broke the heart of the beadle.

LOT 3. – The Truncheon carried by MR COMMISSIONER MAYNE, when in attendance at the opening of Parliament. This valuable relic is supposed to have dispersed four hundred mobs by the mode in which its celebrated owner stretched it forth in moments of tumult.

LOT 4. – A Policeman's Cape; supposed to have been worn in four hundred different kitchens during the celebrated crusade against the larders, by which the middle of the nineteenth century was distinguished.

Such will probably be a few of the lots in the catalogue, destined to comprise the numerous objects that will become interesting by the course of time, which alone appears to give value to the most worthless articles.

A hundred years hence. – A room in the style of the nineteenth century.

LONDON IN A.D. 2346

'But the great feature of this meeting of the Archaeological Institute, was the Secretary's report on the interesting discoveries made on the site of Old London, with the discussion it gave rise to.' – *Times, of April 1st.*, A.D. 2346.

THE Secretary begs to lay before the members of the New London Archaeological Institute the following report of the very curious discoveries made in the course of the excavations now going on for the Universal Railway Terminus, to which the officers of the Society have had access by the gracious permission of His Majesty, HUDSON XIV.

The site of Old London had long been known to the Society, but the immense expense of laying bare its remains, owing to the great mass of scoriae and the solid coating of lava, which overwhelmed that great and once famous city, in the fearful eruption of Mount Vesuvius, which rises in the district still known as the Surrey Zoological Gardens, they had hitherto despaired of making those discoveries, which the liberality of His Majesty has enabled them to effect.

In the total absence of all documentary evidence, the officers of the Society have been compelled to assign conjectural characters and destinations to the several buildings and works discovered. Our imperfect knowledge of the habits of a bygone and barbarous race may impair the value of these theories: but they seem to the authors of the report to be the only interpretations at all consistent with probability. The part of the old city first laid bare, was peculiarly rich in objects calculated to excite interest and stimulate, while they baffle, curiosity. It was a large area, in form an irregular square, into which debouched three streets, which, for the period they belong to, may be called wide. From the unique copy of that inestimable work, *Mogg's Guide to London*, in the Society's library, we believe we may confidently state, that this area is what was known as Trafalgar Square.

The north side of this irregular area, we found occupied by a low and singularly unsightly range of building, apparently uniting the purposes of a stone-mason's or sculptor's shed, and a store-room for pictures. The former conclusion is drawn from the numerous casts and copies of statues found in the lower part of the building. From the dark, damp, and unventilated state of the rooms, they obviously could not have been intended for exhibition or study. They were probably warerooms for depositing unsold or condemned works. The mean appearance of the exterior of the building forbids the notion that this can be the 'National Gallery,' often spoken of as standing in Trafalgar Square, in the precious single volume of the 'Annual Register for 1842,' now in the possession of the Society. It is true that the building is there unfavourably criticised. But this building is below all criticism. The pictures, many of them of great value, were found crowded together in low close rooms. This fact strikingly illustrates the ignorance of art, which we know, from other sources, prevailed in this island five hundred years ago. Here are artistic treasures, (now deposited with solemnity and reverence in our Grand World Museum,) evidently treated as things of no value whatever, stowed away like rubbish. It is clear that no one could have seen the merits of the pictures in these apartments; so that this may be confidently pronounced to have been a lumber-room, in which the pictures were considered as the lumber. The opinion of one of the Society, that this must have been the 'National Picture Gallery' alluded to by the old chronicler, GRANT, in his imbecile but curious volume, 'The Great Metropolis,' we have not thought worth combating. . . .

A melancholy ruin in A.D. 2346

WHAT MAY BE DONE IN FIFTY YEARS

AN American paper is eloquent upon the many inventions and discoveries for which the world is indebted to the first half of the nineteenth century. Amongst others, may be enumerated the following: – *Punch*, Steamers, railways, the electric telegraph, gas, photography, and chloroform.

The second half of the nineteenth century scarcely promises to be so rich. Its claims to originality do not, at present, extend much beyond – Crinoline, all-round collars, peg-top trousers, perambulators, penny ices, halfpenny steam-boats, and penny papers. The list is not a lively one.

However, there is plenty of time between this and the commencement of the twentieth century. The next forty years may witness the birth of some tremendous genius, who may hit upon the means of setting the Thames on fire; or, for aught we know, abolishing the National Debt. All things are, we believe, possible to the genius of Man, even down to the completion of Trafalgar Square!

Three Dreams of the nearer Future

PALMERSTON AT THE ANTIPODES

WE were rather startled a few days ago by reading in capital letters in a column of the *Times* the somewhat striking words, 'LORD PALMERSTON AT MELBOURNE.' We knew that Australia was in a condition to need the aid of statesmanship; but we also felt, that whatever might be the necessities of Victoria in the Colonies, there is a VICTORIA at home with a paramount claim on the services of the PREMIER. We were next disposed to think, that the affair was a joke, and that by way of showing how completely the PRIME MINISTER had been 'transported' by the news of the fall of Sebastopol, he had caused himself to be announced as 'LORD PALMERSTON at Melbourne.' Again, we fancied we might be indulging in a dream of the future, and that we might be living in the year 1875, when it is probable that a minister may be running over from Downing Street to Melbourne as rapidly as he now passes from London to Paris. All these hypotheses were, however, put to flight by the sudden recollection that there is a place called Melbourne in England as well as in Australia, and that the former locality rejoices in the ownership of LORD PALMERSTON, who can go to Melbourne when duty does not call him to VICTORIA.

A Dream of the Future. – The Centenary of Punch

GRAND INVENTION!

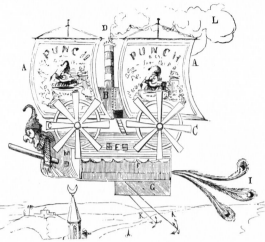

It is this week a task of the deepest and most gratifying pride to lay before our readers the present representation and account of our extraordinary invention. Time and space are now annihilated – an era has arrived in which all ordinary methods of locomotion are for ever subverted – and Punch's Aerial Courier – The Gull – will henceforth be the sole means of communication from one country to another, however distant.

The annexed engraving represents the vessel as she will appear, cleaving her way through the air with the velocity of a shooting star, and carrying upwards of an hundred passengers. The suspensory and propelling power is obtained by the union of Steam with Punch; and the following account of the manner in which these gigantic forces are brought to act, will assist the reader in comprehending the construction. The letters have reference to the illustration.

A. The main suspenders, of a peculiarly light nature, being entirely formed of numbers of PUNCH, coupling power with volatility, and acting as shown above.

B. The engine-room, in which are contained the principal steam-works, by the action of which are turned

C. The propellers, or fantail revolvers, making 10,000 revolutions per minute, and fashioned like the sails of the windmill in common use.

D. The chimney, for making a current of air in the fire-place, and carrying away the smoke.

E. The saloon, provided with every comfort and luxury, from piano-fortes to bottled porter, fitted up to represent a castle in the air, with gossamer couches and cobweb tapestries.

F. The promenade in fine weather, filled with company, and enlivened by a band of instrumental performers, who will, on the day of starting, perform the *Scarus Quadrilles*, composed expressly for the occasion by Jullien.

G. The ballast-box and wine-cellar. Arrangements have been made with the Society for the Diffusion of Useful Knowledge to buy all their heavy back stock, for ballast.

H. The figure-head, being a colossal likeness of MR PUNCH, with apartments in the head for select passengers.

I. Three gigantic peacock's feathers of sheet brass, to act as a rudder, with immense power, and realize the '*sturdy steer*' of Spenser.

K. Two grapnels, for the double purpose of assisting the descent of the courier, (should such auxiliaries be found necessary, which some doubt), and also to clutch hold of anything on the journey worth taking. It is calculated a few statues, ships, and objects of art and value may be grabbed every voyage by these means, sufficient to pay for the fuel, which will be entirely formed of former inhabitants of Memphis, who burn beautifully.

L. The smoke.

M. Barracks for troops, and stores for the ammunition, removed to this part for the accommodation of those who dislike the smell of powder.

The fares will be regulated by the weight, and not by the age of the passengers. The line of road has been already determined upon, from London to Bombay, nearly as the crow flies; and the Courier will stop at intermediate stations for passengers. The whole voyage will be performed in two hours, including stoppages. For the use of commercial gentlemen we have added the following

TIME TABLE	HOUR OF ARRIVAL
NAME OF STATION	A.M.
LONDON TERMINUS. – Top of Nelson Column	10 0
PARIS. – Column of Place Vendôme	10 15
SUMMIT of MONT BLANC	10 30
VENICE. – Campanile of St Mark	10 45
CONSTANTINOPLE. – Minarets of St Sophia	11 7
BAGDAD. – Summit of Mosque	11 30
BOMBAY. – Wherever they can	12 0
GRAND JUNCTION BRANCH TO CHINA	P.M.
BOMBAY	1 0
HIMALAYA MOUNTAINS	1 10
NANKIN. – Porcelain Tower	2 0

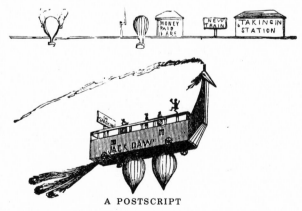

A POSTSCRIPT

Why is PUNCH like the aerial ship? – Because he has not made a *trip* yet, and never will.

ELECTRIC TELEGRAPHS FOR FAMILIES

IT has been suggested that the Electric Telegraph is too good a thing to be confined to public use, and that it may be introduced with considerable effect into the domestic circle. It sometimes happens that a husband and wife are, for a time, not upon 'speaking terms,' though communication between them may be requisite. This desirable result might be easily accomplished by means of the Electric Telegraph, which should be fitted up in the apartments of every married lady or gentleman. In fact reconciliations would often be much more easily effected by the plan we propose, for there is often something exceedingly provoking in the tone of a voice, while in the sound of the Electric Telegraph there is nothing whatever to irritate. There should be a station opposite the usual seats of the master and mistress of the house, and short signs could be used, expressive of 'When do you mean to get out of your ill-humour?' 'I'm ready to make it up, if you are,' and other amiable approaches to reconciliation, which could not be so well conveyed by word of mouth as by the mute eloquence of the wire. The annexed sketch furnishes some idea of how the plan could be made to operate, and by which the difficulty of saying 'the first word' towards reconciliation may be remedied.

A VISION VERY LIKE REALITY

SINCE justice took to tracking crime by the aid of the Electric Telegraph, she can no longer be described in the words of HORACE as 'Pede poena claudo.' No wonder the murderer is nervous, when he is, literally, very often 'hung upon wires.'

MUSIC BY ELECTRIC TELEGRAPH

IT appears that songs and pieces of music are now sent from Boston to New York by Electric Telegraph. Our American brethren have among them such remarkable musical instruments, and in fact such astounding lyres, that nothing coming from the other side of the Atlantic can take us by surprise; and we are, therefore, not altogether dumbfounded by the announcement of music having been carried from one portion of the States to another on the wires of the Electric Telegraph.

It must be delightful for a party at Boston to be enabled to call upon a gentleman in New York for a song.

The grand point of the invention, however, seems to be, that, if songs can be carried along the lines, our popular vocalists may treble or quintuple their present salaries, by singing in four or five places at once. Our own JENNY LIND, for example, who seems to be wanted everywhere at the same time, will have an opportunity of gratifying the subscribers to HER MAJESTY's Theatre, and a couple of audiences many hundred miles off at the same moment. The telegraph, being found applicable for singing, may also be used by the shareholders who are beginning to sing out pretty loudly for their dividends, as well as for the directors, who have been obliged to sing rather small during the last twelvemonth.

LETTER-WRITING BY TELEGRAPH

SINCE the Electric Telegraph is being extended everywhere, we think it might be laid down, like the water and the assessed taxes, to every house. By these means a merchant would be able to correspond with his factors at sea-towns – a lawyer would communicate with his agents in the country – and a doctor would be able to consult with his patients without leaving his fireside.

If this plan of Electric Telegraphs for the million should be carried out, the Post Office will become a sinecure, as all letter-writing would be henceforth nothing more than a dead letter. In that case it might be turned into a central terminus for all the wires, and any one found bagging a letter by means of false wires should be taken up for poaching.

The Electric Telegraph: Punch views the Implications – social, technological . . .

202

THE HOUSE TELEGRAPH

A TELEGRAPH all over London? The wires brought within 100 yards of every man's door? A company established to carry it out?

Well – I don't know. There's a good deal to be said on both sides.

It certainly would be pleasant to be within five minutes of such a message as 'Dine at the Club with me at seven;' or 'SQUATTLEBOROUGH JUNCTIONS' at six premium – I've sold your hundred, and paid in the cash to your account;' or 'Little stranger arrived safe this morning at twelve, mamma and baby doing well;' and one might occasionally be grateful for such a warning as 'KITE and POUNCE took out a writ against you this morning – Look alive;' or 'JAWKINS coming to call on you; make yourself scarce.'

But think, on the other hand, of being within five minutes of every noodle who wants to ask you a question, of every dun with a 'little account;' of every acquaintance who has a favour to beg, or a disagreeable thing to communicate. With the post one secures at least the three or four hours betwixt writing the letter and its delivery. When I leave my suburban retreat at Brompton, at nine AM for the City, I am insured against MRS P.'s anxieties, and tribulations, and consultings, on the subject of our little family, or our little bills, the servants' shortcomings, or the tradesmen's delinquencies, at least till my return to dinner. But with a House-Telegraph, it would be a perpetual *tête-à-tête*. We should all be always in company, as it were, with all our acquaintance. Solitude would become impossible. The bliss of ignorance would be at an end. We should come near that most miserable of all conceivable conditions, of being able to oversee and overhear all that is being done or said concerning us all over London! Every bore's finger would be always on one's button; every intruder's hand on one's knocker; every good-natured friend's lips at one's ear!

No – all things considered, I don't think society is quite ripe for the House-Telegraph yet. If it *is* established I shall put up a plate on my door with 'No House-Telegrams need apply.'

THE LONDON DISTRICT TELEGRAPH COMPANY

WE are promised a Telegraph Company that is to bind our housetops together, which will give the chimney-pots the appearance as though they were playing at scratch-cradle. We will not stop to ask whether the London sky will look any the better for being ruled like a copybook, but will simply proceed to observe, that such a company could not be inaugurated at a more promising period than the present, when the ruler who is in the ascendency in the City happens to be WIRE.

THE UNIVERSALITY OF ELECTRICITY

OUR daily reading proves that Electricity is now fairly taking the circuit of the entire globe. No barrister goes so extensive a circuit, or talks so much with so little noise. The beauty of electricity is, that it talks without being heard, an accomplishment which ladies have not yet acquired.

Amongst the recent marvels of electricity, we have to record two, viz.: – piano-forte-playing, and tooth-drawing. We need not say that both performances are at times equally shocking. There are occasions when we would sooner have a tooth drawn, we think, than listen to an excruciating extraction of agonising sounds from the piano. . . . We do not see what there is to prevent a pianist, who holds this electric accomplishment at his finger's-ends, from performing in every capital of Europe at precisely the same time. . . .

The question is, what will not electricity do next? We do not despair of the good time coming (and it has been a long time on the road), when we shall be able to sit quietly in our arm-chair and electricity will do everything for us. It will cook our dinner, sew on our buttons, write our letters, make our clothes, whip our children, black our boots, shave our stubbly chins, and even help us to a pinch of snuff, if we only wish it. We almost believe it will in time so far reach mortal perfection as to carry us up to bed, undress us, tuck us up, and blow out the candle, when we are too tired, or indifferent, to do it ourselves. But there is one thing, we are afraid, that it never will do, and that is, help us to pay our Income-Tax.

Alas! there is a limit even to electricity!

THE ELECTRIC STORY-TELLER

WHAT horrid fibs by that electric wire
    Are flashed about! what falsehoods are its shocks!
So that, in fact, it is a shocking liar,
    And why? That rogues may gamble in the stocks.

We thought that it was going to diffuse
    Truth o'er the world; instead of which, behold,
It is employed by speculative Jews,
    That speculative Christians may be sold.

Nations, we fancied, 'twas about to knit,
    Linking in peace, those placed asunder far,
Whereas those nations are immensely bit
    By its untrue reports about the war.

Oh! let us rather have the fact that creeps,
    Comparatively, by the Post so slow,
Than the quick fudge which like the lightning leaps,
    And makes us credit that which is not so.

aesthetic, moral

203

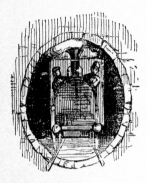

More Travel Prophecies: Subterranean, astronautical

THE LAST NEW RAILWAY SCHEME

OUR modern projectors having exhausted the old world of railways above ground, have invented a new world of a subterranean kind, in which they propose to construct lines 'under the present wide, leading streets of London.' This is a magnificent notion for relieving the over-crowded thoroughfares, and at the same time relieving any over-crowded pocket from its oppressive burden. The prospectus states that the thing 'can be accomplished without any serious engineering difficulties.' The difficulties, instead of being serious, will, we suppose, be merely laughable. If any great dilemma should arise, it will of course be overcome by a little jocularity.

We understand that a survey has already been made, and that many of the inhabitants along the line have expressed their readiness to place their coal-cellars at the disposal of the company. It is believed that much expense may be saved by taking advantage of areas, kitchens, and coal-holes already made, through which the trains may run without much inconvenience to the owners, by making a judicious arrangement of the time-table. It will certainly be awkward if a family should be waiting for a scuttle of coals, and should not be able to get it until after the train had gone by; but a little domestic foresight, seconded by railway punctuality, will obviate all annoyances of this kind.

As the contemplated railway must in several places be carried through the sides and centre of a street, it will be necessary to arrange with the gas and water companies, so that they may all co-operate in this great national work. If the atmospheric principle should be adopted, arrangements could perhaps be entered into to obtain the use of the principal main belonging to the water-works as a continuous valve; for if we are to judge by the arrangements on the Croydon line, this continuous valve is a tremendous pipe, which merely lies in the middle of the line without being used.

The Sewers, by the way, would, with a little enlargement, answer all the purposes of the projectors of this scheme. It is true they are half full of water; but this would not prevent the carriages from being propelled, and the wheels might be sufficiently high to keep the bodies of the carriages and the feet of the passengers out of the wet.

Considering the frequent stoppages of the existing thoroughfares, the scheme really seems to deserve encouragement. 'Nothing is wanted,' says the prospectus, 'for this grand undertaking, but public support.' If the people will only come down with their money, we should not wonder at seeing the company get as far as half-a-dozen advertisements in the daily papers, and a brass plate in the City. Those who are disposed to sink a little capital cannot do better than bury it under the Metropolis in the manner proposed.

We perceive that no amount of deposit is named, and nothing is said of the number or nominal value of the shares. The Secretary is announced to be in attendance to receive deposits from eleven to two; though, whether he gets any is, in our opinion, ten to one.

MARS

ASTRONOMICAL INFORMATION

From Punch's Almanack for 1945

MARS was first reached by the EARL OF MARCH and his stellar explorative expedition in 1916, and a very noble colony was added to the British Monarchical Republic. The planet is inhabited by a fine race of Anthropophagi, most of them eleven feet high, and extremely affable. The Earl, on landing, presented them with a few Irish, which he had taken for the purpose, and which were at once eaten, and the Marsites fired off sixteen-hundred wind-bags, which they use as bells, in honour of their visitors. The planet is at first awkward for strangers, owing to the ground being composed of red-hot iron, but with acclimatisation and clogs this is got over, and the boiling springs furnish an agreeable drink. The people have no particular religion, except that on the First of March they beat their wives severely, and their industry is limited to snoring and scratching their heads. They have no government, and get on very well without one.

THE MOON

ASTRONOMICAL INFORMATION

From Punch's Almanack for 1960

THIS locality is hardly entitled to the dignity of a planet, since the Lunar Caustic Railway was laid to it from Hanwell, and the Moon was laid out as an Evening Park for the People under the Act 1 Edw. VII., 1899. The discovery that our forefathers were right in supposing the Moon to be made of green cheese has been a severe shock to the Sciolists, and vast quantities of that article are now imported from the Moon to London. Some interest was excited when the railway was made, by the claim of the aged ALDERMAN MOON to be the sovereign of Lunaria; but his ridiculous pretensions were finally quashed by the appearance of the rightful Man in the Moon, who was dug out of a hole by the navvies, instructed by BISHOP SPURGEON, and appointed curator of the district. The established religion of the country is Leap-frog, but Spillikins are tolerated.

PHOTOGRAPHY FOR CRIMINALS

GOVERNOR has seriously proposed to establish a Portrait Gallery of Criminals in every prison in England, by subjecting every convicted offender to the photographic process. The idea may have some value, but we must confess that we never saw any photographic portrait yet, which did not give us the idea of a criminal; and if a man were to be hung on account of his look, there is hardly an individual that has been photographed, who might not have been fairly hanged instead of his own portrait. There is a *dictum* of the poet in favour of showing 'Vice its own image,' and arguments may be brought forward in support of the new scheme; but we do not see by what law the authorities will be justified in compelling a prisoner to sit to have his likeness taken. Should a collection be formed, there will be a certain amount of interest attached to it; and though not of the same kind as that which belongs to the Court Beauties of CHARLES THE SECOND, a gallery of Criminal Court Beauties would, in the eyes of some, be regarded as a very interesting series.

We fear it is just possible that the plan might serve as an inducement to the commission of petty offences, for the having one's portrait preserved in a public institution would form a sort of celebrity that some persons would think cheaply purchased at the price of a week's imprisonment.

Two more Predictions with social Consequences

ADVERTISING INGENUITY

THERE seems to be no end to the new advertising projects which are daily springing up in all directions. We have advertisements in omnibuses, placed in such a position, that unless you can turn your eyes upside-down, or sit upon your own head, there is no possibility of reading them.

As to the advertising-carts, they are now on so gigantic a scale, that no ordinary vision can take in more than half a letter at a time – and thus the perambulating van must fall into the rear by the excess to which the system has been carried. There is, however, still one method of advertising left untried, and we wonder no one makes the experiment. Our umbrellas are still left blank, and bear no announcement of some new pill, new paletot, or new periodical. We are quite sure that the *parapluie* is destined to become a tremendous vehicle for information. An umbrella-maker might try the experiment by placing a puffing broadside on all the articles of his own manufacture. Or perhaps it would be a better plan – as some persons might object to carry an advertising umbrella – that on wet days there should be stations, with placards ready printed, to be pasted on – for a consideration – to the umbrellas of any who might be willing to combine profit with convenience.

SPORTING FOR LADIES

WE are told by the *Aylesbury News* that the DUCHESS OF MARLBOROUGH recently 'brought down eight head of game with her own gun.' We have every hope that this love of sporting will increase in the bosom of the high and titled fair; and that gunpowder (if they do not use their own cotton) will be far more reviving to them than *sal volatile*. . . .

When, too, we think of the influence of high example, we do not despair to see maids-of-all-work learning pistol-practice at the shooting galleries, that they may bring down spiders with small-shot instead of besoms.

THE PARLIAMENTARY FEMALE

FATHER OF THE FAMILY. 'Come, dear; we so seldom go out together now – Can't you take us all to the Play to-night?'

MISTRESS OF THE HOUSE, AND M.P. 'How you talk, Charles! Don't you see that I am too Busy. I have a Committee to-morrow morning, and I have my Speech on the Great Crochet Question to prepare for the evening.'

WOMAN'S EMANCIPATION

(Being a Letter addressed to Mr Punch, with a Drawing, by a strong-minded American Woman)

It is quite easy to realise the considerable difficulty that the natives of this old country are like to have in estimating the rapid progress of ideas on all subjects among us, the Anglo-Saxons of the Western World. Mind travels with us on a rail-car, or a high-pressure river-boat. The snags and sawyers of prejudice . . . are dashed aside or run down in the headlong career of the United States mind. . . .

Our babies are preternaturally sharp, and highly independent from the cradle. The high-souled American boy will not submit to be whipped at school. That punishment is confined to negroes and the lower animals.

But it is among *our* sex – among women – (for I am a woman, and my name is THEODOSIA EUDOXIA BANG, of Boston, U.S., Principal of the Homoeopathic and Collegiate Thomsonian Institute for developing the female mind in that intellectual city) – that the stranger may realise in the most convincing manner the progressional influences of the democratic institutions it is our privilege to live under.

An American female – for I do not like the term Lady, which suggests the outworn distinctions of feudalism – can travel alone from one end of the States to the other – from the majestic waters of Niagara to the mystic banks of the Yellowstone, or the rolling prairies of Texas. The American female delivers lectures – edits newspapers, and similar organs of opinion, which exert so mighty a leverage on the national mind of our great people – is privileged to become a martyr to her principles, and to utter her soul from the platform, by the side of the gifted POE or the immortal PEABODY. All this in these old countries is the peculiar privilege of man, as opposed to woman. The female is consigned to the slavish duties of the house. In America the degrading cares of the household are comparatively unknown to our sex. The American wife resides in a boarding-house, and, consigning the petty cares of daily life to the helps of the establishment, enjoys leisure for higher pursuits, and can follow her vast aspirations upwards, or in any other direction.

We are emancipating ourselves, among other badges of the slavery of feudalism, from the inconvenient dress of the European female. With man's functions, we have asserted our right to his garb, and especially to that part of it which invests the lower extremities. With this great symbol, we have adopted others – the hat, the cigar, the paletot or round jacket. And it is generally calculated that the dress of the Emancipated American female is quite pretty, – as becoming in all points as it is manly and independent. I enclose a drawing made by my gifted fellow-citizen, INCREASEN TARBOX, of Boston, U.S., for the *Free Woman's Banner*, a periodical under my conduct, aided by several gifted women of acknowledged progressive opinions.

I appeal to my sisters of the Old World, with confidence, for their sympathy and their countenance in the struggle in which *we* are engaged, and which will soon be found among them also. For I feel that I have a mission across the broad Atlantic, and the steamers are now running at reduced fares. I hope to rear the standard of Female Emancipation on the roof of the Crystal Palace in London Hyde Park. Empty wit may sneer at its form, which is bifurcate. And why not? MAHOMET warred under the Petticoat of his wife KADIGA. The American female Emancipist marches on her holy war under the distinguishing garment of her husband. . . .

THEODOSIA E. BANG, M.A.,
M.C.P., Φ . △K., K.L.M., &c., &c., (of Boston, U.S.).

ENLARGED AND (NOT) BEAUTIFIED

WE furnish by anticipation a view of the new front of Buckingham Palace, with an additional suggestion of our own. The artist has been inspired apparently by a patriotic desire to assimilate the Palace of the Sovereign to the new shops of her subjects in the continuation of Oxford Street. It is a pity that this resemblance should be confined to the building. As the new front can hardly, by the wildest stretch of imagination, be deemed ornamental, why should it not be made useful? An agreeable addition to the Civil List might be obtained by letting out the ground-floor in shops, while HER MAJESTY and the Royal Family would be accommodated in the first floors, and the domestics in the attic story.

The Royal Children might be allowed to acquire a practical familiarity with the retail commerce of the country, by taking a round of attendance in the shops successively, which would infallibly draw immense crowds to the establishments so favoured, and might be considered in the rents. A rush would certainly follow such an announcement as 'Selling off. – The PRINCE OF WALES will serve out Groceries from 2 till 4;' or, 'Try our Wellington Surtouts! Customers measured by PRINCE ALFRED, for this day only;' or, 'The PRINCESS ROYAL and an immense lot of soiled Ribands.' We cannot conceive any measure more likely to promote affability in the Royal children, and loyalty among the subjects of our gracious Sovereign.

COMPLETION OF THE NELSON COLUMN

(A Paragraph extracted by Clairvoyance from the Times, March 2, 1901)

OUR readers will be gratified to learn that the work of completing this monument will shortly be resumed, and indeed we think we may with confidence predict that within another year or so we may expect to find such progress made as may induce a hope that we shall live to see it actually finished. Those who are old enough perhaps may recollect that the erection of the Column was entrusted to the Government in 1844, when the work was commenced in the most energetic manner; two men and a boy being at once employed upon it. This activity, however, proved so exhaustive of the funds which had been voted, that within a very few months there was a stoppage of the works; and the question being put to Government in 1857, it was stated that 'it was not thought desirable' just then to grant the needful. The matter then rested till the spring of 1889, when in consequence of their resuscitation of the Income-Tax it was discovered that the Government had in hand sufficient money to resume the works, and an order was thereupon given for the purpose: but as this had to pass through the formalities of several departments, we considered at the time that there was little chance that we should find it acted on within the current century. It will be owned that our prediction has been fully verified, and if the Column be completed within ten years' hence, the country will have every reason to be satisfied. . . .

Although a century has almost passed since NELSON died for us, our non-completion of his Column has at any rate served to keep him in our remembrance. It affords, we think, a striking proof of how much confidence is felt in the solvency of England, that in paying these her debts of honour, she is still allowed so long a credit.

A ROYAL NURSERY RHYME FOR 1860

'There was a Royal Lady that lived in a shoe,
She had so many children she didn't know what to do.'

Printed on the occasion of
the birth of Queen Victoria's
fourth child, Prince Alfred,
in August 1844.

Social Transformations

SERVANTGALISM VERSUS SCHOOLING

By no one shall we be accused of any wish to take our readers' breath away by advancing an extravagant and startling supposition, if we venture to assume that there are some of them who are not quite contented with their housemaids, and are sometimes to be heard even complaining of their cooks. Without going so far as to assert that servants are 'the greatest plagues in life' (which in the presence of street-organists and Income-Tax collectors it would scarcely be compatible with honest truth to do), we may yet presume to state that many a young house-keeper has found they are 'great worries,' and many an old one would declare, if she might speak her mind about them, that the minxes would exhaust the pocket of a CROESUS and the patience of a JOB. Smashed crockery, chipped furniture, spoilt cookery, and cheap finery, are enough to sour the feelings of the sweetest-tempered 'Missus,' and when to these failings is added a weakness for life-guardsmen and for reading penny novels, and a demand to be allowed to practise the piano, and to be excused from doing any needlework but crochet, we cannot wonder that complaints should now and then be heard that servants nowadays know neither their station nor their work.

With an ear to these complaints, and an eye to the instruction of girls in humble life, not merely in the knowledge of how to read and write but in the useful arts of sewing, cookery, and housekeeping, which are no more learnt by instinct than anatomy or algebra, geography or Greek, a lady four years since established a training-school at Norwich, where the object was, she tells us –

> 'To give the opportunity for gaining a good education, with the addition of plain sewing, mending, and cutting out; and also (what every mother was to understand on putting her girl to school) such practical acquaintance with cookery and housework, under my excellent housekeeper, that every girl might know how a house should be kept, and should acquire habits which would hereafter make all the difference between a tidy and happy home or the reverse.'

Surely children, one would think, would like a school like this, where as a relief from their arithmetic and spelling, some mornings would be spent in learning how to make a pudding, which, at the small charge of threepence each for dinner, the pupils were at liberty to eat when it was made. Surely, too, poor parents would like to see their daughters grow up handy, useful, clever girls, who would make good servants and good house-keepers when wives. But no, poverty and pride go often hand-in-hand, until they drag each other down into the dirt. After a trial of four years, the lady is compelled to own her scheme a failure, solely because she found the girls too proud to do the housework, and the parents so absurd as to encourage their refusal. In a letter to the *Norwich Mercury* she says: –

> 'I was not prepared to find the class of parents I had to do with would apparently accept the education, but make every excuse to evade the industrial work, or keep their daughters away when it was to be done, and threaten to remove them if the household duties were required of them. In corroboration of this latter may observe that twenty-three girls have been away from the school expressly because they do the housework. Whether in the present allowed to determine for themselves wha shall not do, or whether the parents recognise such industrial work as their children, it is not for me to on the result, and close my s willingly have continued th discouragement and oppos

Proper deference to part virtue of the rising genera his, perhaps, is more the fault o an of children, the case which we ha ed seems abundantly to prove. How far it may be true that poor people spoil their children because richer people do so, we think that it may possibly be worth while to inquire. It is fashionable nowadays to let one's children, as a rule, do exactly as they please, for mothers often are too lazy to pay much heed to their family, and so long as toys or lollipops will keep things quiet in the nursery, all attempts at proper training are parentally postponed. What wonder, then, that children are so often now such self-willed, pert, and stuck-up little creatures; and who can doubt that the example is, to some extent at any rate, followed by the poor? What great folks do, the less will prattle of and imitate; and while young ladies are allowed to think it ungenteel to make a shirt or mend a stocking, and to consider they lose caste by even entering the kitchen, we may depend that their inferiors will give themselves like airs, and prefer to starve as sempstresses than to grow fat in service.

Commenting upon the letter we have quoted, which should find its way to every cottage in the kingdom, a writer in the *Athenaeum* sensibly observes: –

> 'Is there not something out of joint in a society in which competent cooks, dairymaids, and laundrymaids are hardly to be got, while incompetent governesses and female artists are a drug? Is there not something alarming in a society where the superficial and false refinement of the girls of the lower classes unfits them for domestic life, and gives them tastes, habits, wants, which a large proportion of them can never satisfy in the safe but humble regions of virtuous labour? While this fatal misdirection is given to their training, we may confidently predict that the recruits to the ranks of vice will far more than fill the places made vacant by the efforts of reformers.'

Out of joints, as well as out of joint, will be society, if cooks, as we seem threatened, are no longer to be got. 'Every lady her own servant,' will become the general motto, and the sooner we prepare ourselves for this new state of things the better. If girls in humble life refuse to learn to cook and to keep house, schools for cookery and housekeeping must be opened for young ladies, and parents of the highest rank will have to send their daughters to them. Instead of bringing home rewards for drawing or deportment, our girls will charm our eyes by showing us their prizes for plumpuddings. ANGELINA will be 'honourably mentioned' for her pancakes, and AGNES be 'commended' for the genius she displayed in boiling a potato. If this plan be carried out, and 'Servants' Schools for Ladies' be generally established, we think, in order to ensure a home being made happy, every bride should be obliged, on the morning of her marriage, to produce before the clergyman her first-class cook's certificate, without which document, the ceremony should not be performed, and the engagement of the bridegroom should be legally annulled.

Caution to Young Ladies who ride in Crinoline on Donkeys

CRINOLINE'S RAGING FURY

OR, THE FASHIONABLE FEMALE'S SUFFERINGS

YOU rustic maids of England,
　Who dress yourselves with ease,
Ah, little do you think how hard
　It is French taste to please.
Give ear unto the milliners,
　And they will plainly show,
With what care, tight with air,
　They our Crinolines do blow.

The husband, and the lover,
　May simple gowns prefer,
That fit the form, and, in a storm,
　With safety let one stir;
Reproaches fierce, our hearts that pierce,
　Against our taste they throw,
Which we poor things endure,
　Whilst our Crinolines we blow.

We put on costly merchandise
　Of most enormous price,
So much we need of drapery,
　To follow this device;
We spend so much in drapery,
　Of such a size to show,
And with toil our shape spoil,
　When our Crinolines we blow.

THE MODERN GOVERNESS
A Young Lady's Idea of the Use of Crinoline!

211

THE FUTURE OF
THE FASHIONS

THERE was a time when girls wore hoops of steel,
  And with grey powder used to drug their hair,
Bedaubed their cheeks with rouge: white lead, or
    meal,
  Adding, to stimulate complexions fair:
Whereof by contrast to enhance the grace,
Specks of court-plaister decked the female face.

That fashion passed away, and then were worn
  Dresses whose skirts came scarce below the knee,
With waists girt round the shoulder-blades, and Scorn
  Now pointed at the prior finery,
When here and there some antiquated dame
Still wore it, to afford her juniors game.

Short waists departed; Taste awhile prevailed;
  Till ugly Folly's reign returned once more,
And ladies then again went draggle-tailed;
  And now they wear hoops also, as before.
Paint, powder, patches, nasty and absurd,
They'd wear as well, if France but spoke the word.

Young bucks and beauties, ye who now deride
  The reasonable dress of other days;
When Time your forms shall have puffed out or dried,
  Then on your present portraits youth will gaze,
And say what dowdies, frights, and guys you were,
With their more specious figures to compare.

Think, if you live till you are lean or fat,
  Your features blurred, your eyes bedimmed with age,
Your limbs have stiffened; feet grown broad and flat:
  You may see other garments all the rage,
Preposterous as even that attire
Which you in full-length mirrors now admire.

THE BLOOMER BALL

Not in vain the Bloomer movement. Forward! forward,
  let us range!
Set the world of fashion spinning – all improvement
  comes from change.
'Twixt the two extremes of folly common sense is
  always found,
'Twixt the skirt above the knees, and the skirt that
  sweeps the ground.

VIII · PLUS ÇA CHANGE

BOTTLED PUNCH

CAPITAL AND LABOUR

BIG BOY. 'How do you make out Threepence is Threeha'pence a-piece? There's a Penny for my Broom and a Penny for my Shovel – that's *capital*; and a Hapenny for you and a Hapenny for me – and that's *labour*.'

THE MARKETS

Done into verse by our own reporter

BARLEY is very dull,
  And wheat is rather shy;
Oats keep their prices full,
  But there's a fall in rye.

In oil, the chief transaction
  Has been confined to flasks;
Sugar gives satisfaction,
  Some has been sold in casks!

There have been strange devices
  Pepper to sell in bags;
But all the trade in spices
  Materially flags!

The cotton-trade lies fallow;
  Nothing is done in bales;
Th' attempt to get off tallow
  At present sadly fails.

Hyson is getting higher;
  Of rice they've sold one lot;
And there has been a buyer
  For – porter in the pot.

ACTIVITY IN THE DOCKYARDS

I STOOD in Portsmouth, on the Dockyard ground,
  And looked about for industry's display;
But when of work I did not hear the sound,
  I thought, of course, it was a holiday.

I was mistaken; things pursued their course
  According to the customary track:
I saw nine men uniting all their force
  To move what one might carry on his back.

I saw four stalwart fellows, tall and stout,
  Who with their arms compactly folded stood,
Looking at one, who as he stared about,
  Morticed – by fits and starts – a bit of wood.

I saw two brawny men with feeble blows
  An iron hoop upon some timber drive;
And when 'twas on – for practice, I suppose –
  To take it off again they did contrive.

I saw four others working at a mast;
  But their pursuit I scarce had time to con,
When I perceived with admiration vast
  Nine more at the proceeding looking on.

I saw two horses drag a single stone;
  At scarce two miles an hour their pace I fix,
Though by one horse the job could have been done –
  Not at two miles an hour, but five or six.

Yet Portsmouth boasts, they say, a model yard;
  We've heard that story many a time and oft:
But he who henceforth thinks they're working hard
  At Portsmouth Dockyard, will be precious soft.

Economic Grumbles

A COOL QUESTION AND A COURTEOUS ANSWER

MR PUNCH lately received the following polite communication from the indefatigable assessor of Income-Tax for the district in which *Mr Punch* carries on his labours for the benefit of his species: –

'2, Falcon Court, Fleet Street, February 3rd.
'You will please fill up the enclosed Form with the names and addresses of those Gentlemen who WRITE for *Punch*, in order that they may be duly assessed to the Income-Tax. Please return it to my office within Seven days.'

This letter took *Mr P.* by surprise. He had not been accustomed to consider that his distinguished, though anonymous, correspondents, were 'persons in his service or employ' – as specified in the heading of the Form enclosed by the assessor. Satisfied, however, that no assessor of Income-Tax could possibly have over-stepped the limits of law, still more, that such an official could have asked any question he had no right to ask, and thus have been guilty of an impertinence, *Mr Punch* loses no time in satisfying the curiosity of that official, and at the same time takes the opportunity of indulging the natural eagerness of the public for information as to the sources of the wit and wisdom that weekly irradiate his pages, by filling up the return as follows: –

No. 8 INCOME TAX

For the Year 1859, ending 5th April, 1860.

Christian and Surname of every Person in my Service or Employ (except Domestic Servants whose Total Incomes are respectively less than £100 a Year), whether resident in my Dwelling-house or not, and the Place of Residence of those not residing with the Master or Mistress.

Christian and Surname	Place of Residence of those not residing in my Dwelling-house.
BENJAMIN DISRAELI,	Grosvenor Gate, Park Lane and Hughenden Manor, Bucks.
THE RIGHT HON. VISCOUNT PALMERSTON,	Cambridge House, Piccadilly and Broadlands, Hants.
HIS ROYAL HIGHNESS THE PRINCE CONSORT,	Buckingham Palace, &c.
BARON NATHAN,	Rosherville, Gravesend.
JOHN JENKINS,	*Morning Post* Office, Wellington Street North
THE RIGHT HON. W. E. GLADSTONE,	Downing Street

(Signed) *Punch*.
Dated (by anticipation) the 1st day of April, 1860.

TOUCHING SIMPLICITY

LITTLE WIFE (*eagerly opening the door for dear Edwin*). 'Oh, see dear, what I have for you! – I'm sure Uncle has got you an appointment under Government at last – for here's a Letter marked immediate, and *"On Her Majesty's Service!"*'
(*Poor little soul! what does she know about Rates and Taxes?*)

THE UNCIVIL CIVIL SERVICE

IT is a subject of very general remark, that it is difficult to find a subordinate in the Civil Service who has got a civil tongue in his head. The Post-office authorities have hit upon a happy expedient at the Money Order Office in Charing Cross, where written directions are placed in front of the bars, behind which the bears are to be heard growling out their indistinct replies to any question that may be addressed to them. We recommend every one who applies for a money-order at Charing Cross to read the written directions, if he wishes to avoid the surliness and snappishness to which he will probably be exposed, if he ventures to ask one of the Civil servants a civil question. We strongly recommend the adoption of the same system at other Government offices; for there is undoubtedly much more politeness in printer's ink – notwithstanding its black looks – than is generally to be met with from the lips of official underlings. Perhaps their pay may be unreasonably low, but we are quite sure that the public would not object to the 'two-pence more,' which, according to the old anecdote, is the normal price at which instruction in manners may be acquired.

CODE OF INSTRUCTIONS

To be observed by the medical student preparing for examination at the Hall

1. Previously to going up, take some pills and get your hair cut. This not only clears your faculties, but improves your appearance. The Court of Examiners dislike long hair.

2. Do not drink too much stout before you go in, with the idea that it will give you pluck. It renders you very valiant for half an hour and then muddles your notions with indescribable confusion.

3. Having arrived at the Hall, put your rings and chains in your pocket, and, if practicable, publish a pair of spectacles. This will endow you with a grave look.

4. On taking your place at the table, if you wish to gain time, feign to be intensely frightened. One of the examiners will then rise to give you a tumbler of water, which you may, with good effect, rattle tremulously against your teeth when drinking. This may possibly lead them to excuse bad answers on the score of extreme nervous trepidation.

5. Should things appear to be going against you, get up a hectic cough, which is easily imitated, and look acutely miserable, which you will probably do without trying.

6. Endeavour to assume an off-hand manner of answering; and when you have stated any pathological fact – right or wrong – *stick to it;* if they want a case for example, invent one, 'that happened when you were an apprentice in the country.' This assumed confidence will sometimes bother them. We knew a student who once swore at the Hall, that he gave opium in a case of concussion of the brain, and that the patient never required anything else. It was true – he never did.

7. Should you be fortunate enough to pass, go to your hospital next day and report your examination, describing it as the most extraordinary ordeal of deep-searching questions ever undergone. This will make the professors think well of you, and the new men deem you little less than a mental Colossus. Say, also, 'you were complimented by the Court.' This advice is, however, scarcely necessary, as we have never known a student pass who was not thus honoured – according to his own account.

PROCTOR (*to Undergraduate*). 'Pray, Sir, will you be so good as to tell me whether you are a Member of the University, or a Scotch Terrier?'

Students

THE UNIVERSITY BOYS

SINCE the old abodes of letters
  Are inhabited by boys;
If they must be spendthrift debtors,
  Let them only deal in toys.

Stop them in their reckless courses,
  'Gainst their ruin quick provide;
Give them only rocking-horses;
  Such as schoolboys ought to ride.

Let not dealers, sharp and cunning,
  On their innocence impose;
With the horses made for running,
  Rapidly the money goes.

If they have a taste for glitter,
  Give not jewels rich and rare;
Sure Mosaic would be fitter
  For the silly boys to wear.

Out of debt and degradation
  Keep them by the aid of toys
Fitting to their mental station,
  Hapless, feeble-minded boys!

THE MODEL AGITATOR

Demagogues, and Drugs

He is born with the bump of Notoriety. This bump first expands at school. He heads all the rows. His special delight is in teasing the masters. As for punishments, they only whip him on to renewed rows. He is insensible to the cane, quite callous to the birch. At home the bump grows larger. He bullies the servants, and plays the democrat to his younger brothers. He is always in open rebellion with 'the governor,' and very seditious on the question of latch-keys. His love of talk bursts out on every little occasion. He will not ring the bell without an argument. He is very rich in contradictions, having always a No for everybody else's Yes. At last he revolts against parental tyranny, and is kicked out of doors. He is an injured man, and joins a debating club. The bump gets bigger. He attends a public meeting. The bump enlarges still more. He is called to the bar, and the bump has reached its culminating height. Henceforth he and Notoriety are two inseparables. He runs after it everywhere, and eventually, after numerous dodges through bye lanes, and heaps of mud, and narrow, dirty courses, and the most questionable paths, he catches the dear object of his pursuit. He is notorious! He has good lungs, and his reputation is made. He is a hearty hater of every Government. In fact he is always hating. He knows there is very little notoriety to be gained by praising.

The only thing he flatters is the mob. Nothing is too sweet for them; every word is a lump of sugar. He flatters their faults, feeds their prejudices with the coarsest stimulants, and paints, for their amusement, the blackest things white. He is madly cheered in consequence. In time he grows into an idol. But cheers do not pay, however loud. The most prolonged applause will not buy a mutton chop. The hat is carried round, the pennies rain into it, and the Agitator pours them into his patriotic pocket. It is suddenly discovered that he has made some tremendous sacrifice for the people. The public sympathy is first raised, then a testimonial, then a subscription. He is grateful, and promises the Millenium. The trade begins to answer, and he fairly opens shop as a Licensed Agitator. He hires several journeymen with good lungs, and sends agents – patriotic bagmen – round the country to sell his praises and insults, the former for himself, and the latter for everybody else. Every paper that speaks the truth of him is publicly hooted at; everybody who opposes him is pelted with the hardest words selected from the Slang Dictionary. A good grievance is started, and hunted everywhere. People join in the cry, the Agitator leading off and shouting the loudest. The grievance is run off its legs; but another and another soon follows, till there is a regular pack of them. The country is in a continual ferment, and at last rises. Riots ensue; but the Model Agitator is the last person to suffer from them. He excites the people to arm themselves for the worst; but begs they will use no weapons. His talk is incendiary, his advice nothing but gun-powder, and yet he hopes no explosion will take place. He is an Arsenal wishing to pass for a Chapel or a Baby-linen warehouse. He is all peace, all love, and yet his hearers grow furious as they listen to him, and rush out to burn ricks and shoot landlords. He is always putting his head on the block. Properly speaking, he is beheaded once a quarter.

A Monster Meeting is his great joy to be damped, only, by the rain or the police. He glories in a prosecution. He likes to be prosecuted. He asks for it: shrieks out to the Government – 'Why don't you prosecute me?' and cries, and gets quite mad if they will not do it. The favour at length is granted. He is thrown into prison, and grows fat upon it; for from that moment he is a martyr, and paid as one, accordingly.

The Model Agitator accumulates a handsome fortune, which he bequeaths to his sons, with the following advice, which is a rich legacy of itself: – 'If you wish to succeed as an Agitator, you must buy your patriotism in the cheapest market, and sell it in the dearest.'

FASHIONABLE LABORATORIES

Chemical evening parties now are all the rage. About a year ago nothing was heard of in fashionable circles but gun-cotton. Ether then was introduced after coffee, and flirtations carried on without either party being sensible – as is often the case in such matters – of what they were saying. Now Chloroform has invaded our parlours and our drawing-rooms. It is the inspiration of all our balls, and it is almost dangerous to talk at a *soirée* now; for at the very first breath you may forget yourself and behave in the most senseless manner. It will be the etiquette this season, we suppose, to ask a young lady, not to take an ice, but 'a glass of Chloroform;' and after-supper speeches will be conducted by the host inquiring of his guests, 'Now, gentlemen, are you all Chloroformed?' and then he will deliver his toast, to the very great relief, probably, of the company.

This chemical joviality, however, must be a very great saving. We don't know the exact price of Chloroform, but a whole hogshead of it cannot be so expensive, we imagine, as cold chickens and barley-sugar pagodas, to say nothing of *bonbon* mottoes and crackers, for a hundred people. We doubt if FARADAY would charge for a supper as much as GUNTER; though, in enjoying our midnight meal we must say that the economy of it is the very last thing that enters into our thoughts, or mouth, either. We would sooner have one tumbler of champagne than the very best bottle of Chloroform you could offer us. If we are to be insensible, we prefer choosing our own way of becoming so.

DOMESTIC BLISS

YOUNG MOTHER (*joyously*). 'The dear little Creature is getting on so nicely; it's beginning quite to take notice.'

FIRST MOTHER OF A FAMILY (*blandly*). 'Oh! my dear! that is not taking notice; it's only the wind.'

SECOND DITTO. 'You should give it a little Dill Water, dear. You would find,' &c., &c.

THIRD DITTO. 'Well, if it was my Child, I should,' &c., &c.

FOURTH DITTO. 'Now, when I was nursing my little Gregory, I used,' &c., &c.

FIFTH DITTO. 'Well now, I would not for the world that a baby of mine,' &c., &c.

SIXTH DITTO. 'Indeed I have known Children obliged to endure the most horrible agony,' &c., &c.

SEVENTH DITTO. 'Depend upon it, love; and you know I have had a large family – and if you will be advised by me,' &c., &c. [*Young Mother becomes quite bewildered, and gives herself up to despair.*

LIBERTY.

THE SHADOW OF ENGLISH
LIBERTY IN AMERICA

AMERICAN LIBERTY –
AMERICAN EGGS

THE American Eagle – the bird of Liberty – lays rotten eggs. This filthy fact is made evident by a letter written to the *New York National Anti-Slavery Standard,* by FREDERICK DOUGLASS. He and MR GARRISON lately proceeded as far as Harrisburg, to preach liberty to the benighted citizens of the freest nation of the earth. And their arguments were met with foul eggs, crackers, and brickbats – the arguments of the good and wise!

'I spoke only for a few moments, when through the windows was poured a volley of unmerchantable eggs, scattering the contents on the desk in which I stood, and upon the wall behind me, and filling the room with the most disgusting and stifling stench.'

Sweet odours – consecrated to the altar of Liberty – by free men! But the sacrifice was not completed – for pyrotechnic science bestowed 'a pack of crackers;' and other worshippers at the shrine of Freedom offered, not frankincense or myrrh, but 'cayenne pepper and Scotch snuff,' that 'produced their natural results among the audience!' And then arose a triumphant shout –

'Throw out the nigger! Throw out the nigger!' And thereupon the 'nigger,' leaving the room, and gaining the street, there followed a shower of 'stones and brickbats;' which are arguments so ready-made, and generally so easily obtained, that neither fool nor knave need be without them.

When FRANKLIN was consulted about the design for the American insignia, he gave his veto against the proposed eagle. It was a rascally, thievish, carrion bird, he said; and was unworthy of a free people. The Americans, however – as is proved in our time – knew better. They felt that the eagle would very admirably typify the spirit of American Liberty. The eagle steals its prey – America steals her blacks. The eagle will feed upon human flesh – so does America; that is, if the flesh have within it negro blood. The eagle – that is, the free American eagle – lays putrid eggs; nought wholesome, nought vital is produced from them. They are foul things; fit for no service. Oh, yes! They are arguments – strongest arguments against the liberty of the black – sweetest incense for the nostrils of the free white.

220

CUSTOMERS' PROTECTION CIRCULAR

LONDON tradesfolk have established an elaborate sort of spy system, for the purpose of protecting themselves against bad customers. There is regularly prepared, and circulated among tradesmen, a Black List, in which the names and histories of any persons who are supposed to be undesirable patrons of trade are duly printed, with any information that can be picked up about the parties; and the subscribers to this work, when a new customer presents himself, search the list, with a view to see whether he may be trusted. It has been felt that this is an excellent system, but should not be one-sided in its operation; and, inasmuch as for one dishonest buyer there are at least ten dishonest sellers, it has been thought that the purchasing public may well employ the same method of self-defence. *Mr Punch* has been requested to publish the following specimen page, and to edit the *Customer's Protection List*. He has acceded to the first request; but his numerous avocations, and the probability that, on the fall of LORD DERBY, he will be obliged to accept the Premiership, compel him to decline the latter. He will, however, be happy to lend his aid to a project which appears to him a fair one.

CUSTOMERS' PROTECTION LIST

Specimen page

A

ADDLEHEAD, Jehoshaphat (Chemist). Very ignorant, and has poisoned several persons by mistake in chemicals. Clever at sending in bills that have been paid, and rapid in County-courting you unless you have preserved receipts.

ADIPOSE, Samuel (Draper). Confirmed habit of giving servants and children bad money in change, and bullying when asked to make restitution. Either he or his father absconded with the rates of St Habbakuk, Norwood.

APPLEBITE, Cruncher (Linendraper). Professes to sell cheap and good articles, but mind that the goods put up for you are those you bought, if you take away the parcel yourself. You may be quite sure they will not be the same if you let him send the things home.

PROTECTION FOR HOUSEWIVES

'DEAR MR PUNCH,

'PACKING up some things in the newspaper one day last week, I happened to notice a speech made in Parliament, by MR DISRAELI; and in it a passage so interesting that I thought I *would* cut it out and send it to you. Here it is: –

' "The average price of meat in 1848 was 4s 5½d. That was the average of the temporary depression. Now, the average price of meat in 1850 (taking it from the official return from Smithfield) was 3s 8½d. (*Loud cheers from the Protectionists.*)"

'Most gentlemen talking politics, I have observed, ridicule the Protectionists, and say they know nothing about political *economy:* Well; now, *I* think there is *great* economy in paying 3s 8½d, instead of 4s 5½d for meat; and I must say, I think it was very *natural* and *sensible* of the Protectionists to cheer at the idea of such a saving, and I shall try all I can to persuade JOHN to vote for their side at the next election.

'Your sincere admirer,
'MARTHA NOTABLE.

'P.S. I suppose what Protectionists want is to protect us from being imposed upon, and to make everything as reasonable as they can. There *can* be no nonsense in that. M.N.'

ADVERTISEMENTS

TO THE FAIR AND THE FACULTY

MADAME PINCHIN, (from Paris,) Maker to the *Beau Monde*, respectfully invites the attention of Ladies and the Medical Faculty to her newly-invented Stays and Corsets, which will be found to act with peculiar efficiency in the alteration and compression of the figure. When it is considered how incompatible with Elegance and Beauty is a naturally-sized waist, and at the same time how necessary it is to the freedom of respiration and the digestive powers, it will be obvious that the Stays and Corsets of MADAME PINCHIN will equally suit the views of fashionable ladies and physicians. They secure for the wearer a Sylph-like form; and they guarantee to the Medical Man a constant patient.

BLENHEIM PALACE

THE DUKE OF MARLBOROUGH, feeling it necessary to march with the times, and to add to the attractions of Blenheim Palace, (a shilling a head being considered too much for the show in its present state,) is willing to treat with any Fire-eater, Slack-rope Dancer, or Spotted Boy – that he may be shown with the establishment, no additional charge being made to a patronising and discerning public. Keepers of menageries, wishing to dispose of second-hand monkeys, may hear of a purchaser. The best price given for ostriches with the pip. None but Principals dealt with. Apply at Woodstock.

Puff! Puff! Puff!

NOT content with the ordinary vans, the Advertisers have commenced plastering the omnibuses with their placards. It is too bad that the windows of these vehicles should be obstructed during the hot weather with announcements that put a stop to wholesome ventilation. Is there no other way of raising the wind than by preventing the free passage of air, and must a cheap tradesman's outrageous puff keep off anything in the shape of a pleasant blow from the riders in an omnibus?

Novelties

A STARTLING NOVELTY IN SHIRTS

OLD AND NEW TOYS

TOYS have been in a state of coma for hundreds of years. It is time that Science should pass her gentle hands over them, and unmesmerise them. When everything else is moving, toys should not remain at a stand-still. They must advance with the age. Children are too clever now to be amused with the simple kites that almost lifted us off our little legs in the happy days when we wore no straps. The infant mind has so expanded that it is content with nothing less than a Nassau Balloon. The old rocking-horse, too, with his red wafers and wooden tail, is now voted 'slow;' and depend upon it, long before the three years of the Income Tax have expired, that the NIMRODS of the nursery will ride nothing but a Megatherium, or at least a monster steam-engine, worked with real steam.

Fast boys will stipulate for a velocipede instead of a hoop, and the innocent amusement of blowing soap-bubbles will be quite exploded eventually, by the awful gasometer. Nurses will still be subjected to the playfulness of their young charges, only in a more powerful form!

Nurseries will be turned into miniature laboratories, and we shall have the satisfaction of knowing that our children, as they grow out of their clothes, are becoming men, or rather hobbedehoys of science, every inch of them. A lesson will be contained in every toy; our lamb's-wool dogs will be taught to bark chemistry; our speaking-dolls be made to talk ten languages, and the most abstruse sciences be made easy to the smallest understanding by the aid of a plaything.

The old

The new

The new kite

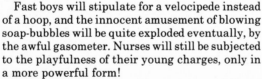

The old   The new

FINE LADIES AND THEIR TAILORS

THE boots with 'military heels' now commonly worn by ladies must have attracted the attention of many of our readers, because they are so conspicuously exhibited by the necessary practice of lifting up the excessively long clothes. The jackets also of a military character, resembling in design, if not in material, the tunics lately invented for some of the dragoons, must have been likewise remarked. These articles of attire apparently indicate that a certain change is coming over the female character – a tendency towards the masculine. To cap this, we may say, take further the wide-awake hats. The superior education which has of late years been given to woman may be the cause of these phenomena; the higher and harder cultivation of the understanding may express itself in the gentlemanlike boots, the tunics, and the wide-awakes. But the assimilation of ladies to gentlemen is not confined to outward habits.

The softer sex is beginning to emulate the sharper in habits of conduct. To one such habit in particular, attention has been drawn by 'An English Clergyman,' writing in the *Times*. He states that a celebrated and fashionable dressmaker's establishment in Pall Mall has lately failed by reason that duchesses and other ladies who dealt there would not pay their bills. This is a common trick with fine ladies, and it is a man's trick, a fast man's trick, equivalent to the common dandy's trick of not paying his tailor. Not to pay his tailor – or to pay his tailor – the dandy regards as a high joke. No doubt it is, in its way, capital fun, but it is not ladylike fun. It may be all very well for a duke, but it is unbecoming in a duchess. Moreover, it is the efficient cause of starving needlewomen. This system of tick is worse than *tic douloureux* to them. It is the tick of a death watch. It is easy to predict the consequences that must result from the adoption, by ladies, in regard to their milliners, of the behaviour of men towards their tailors. We shall have dashing young girls passing the Insolvent Court with fabulous milliner's accounts in their schedules, consisting partly of charges for bills discounted. They will take to billiard-playing and smoking cigars, and we shall see them seated on the counters of tobacconist's shops, kicking their military heels.

STEAM CHICKENS

WE believe it was the benevolent wish of Henri Quatre that his poorest subject should have a fowl in his pot. Mr Cantelo promises to realise the philanthropic desire of the royal mind to the benefit of all men. He proposes to prorogue the sittings of poultry sine die, and to supply the world with fowls, turkeys, guinea-fowl, and pheasants, by means of hot-water. 'Millions,' says Mr Cantelo, very boldly, 'have been spent in fruitless attempts' to relieve female poultry from the cares of a family – by hatching chicks in hot rooms or ovens. Now Mr Cantelo – the eggs granted – will produce any given number of chicks by the application of 'top contact heat,' conveyed by 'a current of warm water flowing over an impermeable water-proof cloth, beneath which eggs are placed.' Thus, chickens may be produced beneath a cloth, as multitudinous as mites in a cheese. Consequently, the price of poultry must drop to nothing. The guinea-fowl must change its name, and become at most, a bob-chick.

Our only fear of the success of the experiment – as explained by Mr Cantelo – arises from 'the artificial mother.' We have great fears that the filial affections of the poultry will ever be developed. For how can a chick feel its heart expand and heat towards a 'number of warm pipes, about an inch and a quarter in diameter, and about the same distance apart, resting on supports about five inches from the floor?' A step-mother is proverbially careless and indolent. What then may we hope from a steam-mother?

Nevertheless, according to Mr Cantelo, art is above nature. For instance, he charges it against the living mother that she 'often tramples on the chickens – this always injures and sometimes destroys them.' Again, she is apt to gad about; when, 'if the brood is following the hen, it is often over-fatigued, and fewer come home than she took with her!' When hens are made to acknowledge this, how very small they will feel themselves, contemplating the sobriety and maternal love of 'a number of warm pipes, about an inch-and-a-quarter in diameter!' With – filial yearnings – if they have any at all – towards steam, how curious it will be to watch a brood of chicks nestling about a tea-kettle.

Mr Cantelo has noble Spartan notions touching deformed chickens. We think his ideas on this head quite worthy of attention and practical imitation by Boards of Poor-Law Guardians. For Mr Cantelo with patriotic sternness observes –

'In all cases of deformity, it is most economical and humane to destroy the chicken. If a cross-bill, it always grows worse, and will finish by not being able to eat at all, and a stiff-leg is pulled about, and made miserable by the other chickens; and, inasmuch as a deformed chicken would not have left the nest of the mother, it is not worth while to attempt to do better artificially. I have hatched a duck with three legs, that is, an imperfect and extraordinary one, proceeding from

below the root of the tail. This lived and did well, as it had two good legs to stand upon; but the third one was often pulled at by the others.'

We confess to be greatly taken with Mr Cantelo's enthusiasm; nevertheless, the doubts we have must speak out. We fear, then, a great increase of cases of deformity. We fear that, in process of time, poultry thus artificially hatched, will, in their shape, assimilate to nothing but 'a number of pipes an inch-and-a-quarter in diameter.' Chickens, forlorn things, will be hatched without merrythoughts; and turkeys – like peace-loving 'friends' – think drum-sticks quite beneath them. . . .

CHICKEN FOR THE MILLION

MR CANTELO seems born for the refutation of the proverb which forbids us to count our chickens before they are hatched. He professes to be able, by his system of artificial incubation, to produce seventy-five chickens, on an average, out of a hundred eggs. In a letter to the *Morning Post*, he declares, 'I shall go on till I can produce poultry for the million.' He proceeds to give some startling statistics of the national deficiency in poultry, whereof he says, 'At present the supply is not half a fowl a year to every member of the community.' That is, a leg, a wing, a breast, and backbone, with the merry-thought, respectively to each. It would take,' according to MR CANTELO, 'from twenty-five to thirty millions of money embarked in the business, to give every one a chicken once a month.'

As the means are rather disproportionate to the end proposed, and thirty millions are hardly likely to be forthcoming just now, we have not much opinion of MR CANTELO's project, considered as a public undertaking. However, as a private speculation, we think highly of his scheme for producing cheap chickens. We really wish him every success; and if he can only provide us with poultry at a shilling the couple, we shall say that CANTELO has done more with his egg than COLUMBUS.

Spring   Summer   Autumn   Winter

PORTRAIT OF 1855

**The English
Climate**

'OH! THE MERRY MERRY MONTH OF MAY!!!'

THE DECIMAL COINAGE

THERE has been expressed, in some quarters, a desire for a decimal coinage; but most people are very well satisfied with the present coin of the realm; or would be if they only had enough of it. Englishmen object to change, except the change is such as may be now had for a bank-note or a sovereign, and though of all change preferring small change, would not like change so very minute as the integer which it is proposed to introduce under the name of Doit. The best use of that infinitesimal piece of money – should it ever be issued – would be to serve as a fee for homoeopathic physicians.

A FEW SIMPLE REASONS AGAINST SMOKING

By the mother of a large family and the widow of three husbands, who all smoked

1. BECAUSE it injures the curtains.
2. Because it is injurious to the furniture generally.
3. Because it is not agreeable to breakfast in the room when the gentlemen have been smoking overnight.
4. Because no man's temper is the better for it the next morning.
5. Because it keeps persons up to late hours, when every respectable person ought to be in bed.
6. Because the smell haunts a man's clothes, and his beard, and his hair, and his whiskers, and his whole body, for days afterwards – so much so that it is positively uncomfortable sometimes to go near him.
7. Because it is a selfish gratification that not only injures those who partake of it, but has the further effect of driving the ladies out of the room.
8. Because it is, also, an expensive habit which the ladies, not participating in its so-called enjoyments, cannot possibly have the smallest sympathy with or appreciation for.
9. Because it has the further effect of making gentlemen drink a great deal more than they otherwise would, and so weakens their purses besides ruining their constitutions, to say nothing of the many comforts and new dresses that their dear wives and children may have been unjustly deprived of, supposing the same amount of money had only been judiciously laid out at home.
10. Because it gives extra trouble to the servants who have to clean and to ventilate the room the next morning.
11. Because how are one's daughters to get married, if the gentlemen are always locked up in a separate room paying court to their filthy pipes and cigars?
12. Because it unfits a young man, who is wedded to it, for the refining influences of female society.
13. Because it puts a stop to music, singing, flirting, and all rational enjoyments.
14. Because it is a custom originally imported from the savages.
15. Because we see the nations that smoke the most are mostly the stupidest, heaviest, laziest, dreariest, dreamiest, most senseless, and worthless beings that encumber – like so many weeds, only capable of emitting so much smoke – the face of the earth.
16. Because when a man says he is going out to smoke a cigar, there's no knowing what mischief he is bent upon, or the harm the monster may be likely to get into.
17. Because it is not allowed in the Palace, or Windsor Castle, or in any respectable establishment.
18. Because the majority of husbands only do it because they know it is offensive to their wives. *And a thousand other good reasons, if one only had the patience to enumerate them all. Pray did* ADAM *smoke?*

SONGS OF THE HEARTH-RUG

The disgusted wife to her husband
YOU promised to leave off your smoking,
　The day I consented to wed.
How little I thought you were joking:
　How fondly-believed what you said!
Then, alas! how completely you sold me,
　With blandishments artful and vain;
When you emptied your snuff-box, and told me
　You never would fill it again!

Those fumes, so oppressive, from puffing,
　Say, what is the solace that flows?
And whence the enjoyment of stuffing
　A parcel of dust in your nose?
By the habits you thus are pursuing
　There *can* be no pleasure conferr'd;
How irrational, then, is so doing!
　Now *is* it not *very* absurd?

Cigars come to three-pence each, nearly,
　And sixpence an ounce is your snuff;
Consider how much, then, you yearly
　Must waste on that horrible stuff.
Why the sums in tobacco you spend, love,
　The wealth in your snuff-box you sink,
Would procure me of dresses no end, love,
　And keep me in gloves; only think!

What's worse, for your person I tremble,
　'Tis going as fast as it can;
Oh! how should you like to resemble
　A smoky and snuffy old man?
Then resign, at the call of Affection,
　The habits I cannot endure;
Or you'll spoil both your nose and complexion,
　And ruin your teeth, I am sure.

THE BATTLE OF THE STREETS

Smoke in the Streets

WHILE the battle of the gauges is dividing the railway world, the battle of the streets – the contest between the broad and the narrow – is revolutionising the metropolis. Unfortunately for the narrow, the broad carries, or rather knocks down, everything before it. We shall soon be utterly without a lane or an alley throughout the whole of London; while as to architecture, the old brick and tile order will be utterly superseded by the modern stuccoite. It is all very well to enlarge the streets if we can enlarge the means of the people sufficiently to enable them to live in them; but if the habitations of the poor are superseded by palaces, while pauperism still remains, we would simply ask what on earth is to become of it.

The old police principle of 'move on,' 'you can't stop here,' seems to be now generally applied to those of humble means, and the question is, 'where are they all to go to?' So as they are got rid of somehow, this is a question which gives little trouble to those who are bent on 'improving' a neighbourhood.

KING SMOKE

KING SMOKE was a vile old fellow,
    He suffered no sun to shine,
As he spread out his veil so yellow,
    The woof of the coal-black mine.
        Hurrah! hurrah! hurrah! for the coal-black mine,
        For the coal-black mine!

There railed on him many a maiden,
    With 'blacks' in her weeping eyne,
And her toilet with soot o'erladen
    From the reek of the coal-black mine.
        Hurrah! &c.

The chemist applied all his learning,
    And the poet bewailed these woes,
But their fuel men kept half-burning,
    Whence still the dark fumes arose.
        Hurrah! &c.

They railed on the vile old fellow,
    Who smirched all our buildings fine,
As he spread out his veil so yellow,
    The woof of the coal-black mine.
        Hurrah! &c.

OUR ANGLO-ITALIAN
CLIMATE

SOMEBODY has been saying that during the very hot weather we were favoured with an Italian sky, but we confess we never saw anything in London to remind us much of Italy, except Italian irons, Oil and Italian warehouses, Italian greyhounds, and those very unfortunate dogs, the Italian organ boys. As to the Italian climate, we will undertake to be whipped into an Italian cream, if any reasonable being could confound our confounded atmosphere of London smoke with the transparent air of Italy. Though MEUX and CO. may consume their own, and we may exclaim, '*Tant mieux*,' we cannot forget that BARCLAY and PERKINS, with a thousand others, published their daily volumes of smoke, in columns almost as thick and heavy as those of the morning papers, when the debates have been lengthy the preceding night in Parliament.

THE ANTI-STREET-
NOISE LEAGUE

MR PUNCH sees with satisfaction that an influential meeting has taken place in Marylebone, with a view to the Suppression of Street Noises. These abominable nuisances, which are daily growing more and more atrocious, must be put down by a determined effort, to which, in the interests of humanity (for no earthly sound can perturb His constant mind) he will lend all the assistance in his power. What are the parishes about? Let them all meet, and put the screw upon their representatives, and let a Bill be introduced declaring it a police-offence to raise clamour of any kind, vocal or instrumental, in the public streets.

He has recently appointed himself a Committee, and has been taking some evidence in the Disturbed Districts. A small portion of this he begs to submit, that the Legislature may know what the people suffer.

MRS MATERFAMILIAS. Resides in Pimlico. Has had illness in her family. When her youngest child was in a critical state, and quiet was necessary, it was nearly killed by the organs, which constantly roused it from sleep. When she had nervous fever,

the effect was the same. The organists would never go away at her entreaty, but her husband caught inflammation of the chest by going after a policeman one night, who refused to act, and the Italian not only persevered in playing next door, but sent a bag-piper and a hurdygurdy. It would be a real blessing to mothers and invalids if all the organs were driven away.

MR SWANQUILL. Is an author. Was deluded into taking a house in a quiet street in Brompton. Has never been able to write a page in his house for the incessant and irritating uproar in the streets. In one day there have bawled, shrieked, howled, or ground in his street, sweeps, orangemen, dustmen, knife-grinders, potboys, rabbit-sellers, periwinkle-vendors, fishmongers, match girls, watercress women, Jews, hareskin buyers, hearthstone boys, tinkers, cat's-meatmen, chair-menders, and musicians, to the number of sixty-three. His house is of no use to him, but he cannot get rid of it, and has to borrow a friend's chambers.

MR FIXTURE. Is a House-Agent. The value of the houses in his charge is daily diminishing by reason of the Street Cries, which render the place uninhabitable. When he mentions any of the 'quiet streets' to persons in want of a house, they almost abuse him for trying to entrap them.

MR BADGER. Is an M.P., but not a rich man, and lives in a quiet street. The House keeps late hours, and he is always roused from his first sleep by a miscreant whining and screaming after hareskins. Cannot see why he should be subjected to this nuisance – nobody but servant girls have any interest in this trade, and does not think a whole street should be disturbed at seven in the morning that a servant may get fourpence. Will vote for any Bill for suppressing the system.

SAMUEL SHIVERS. Is a little boy, son of a costermonger. Never goes to school, because his father makes him come out to scream turnips. Has generally a very sore throat, and is very miserable, but is always licked if he complains, and hopes the gentleman won't let his father know he has said anything.

MARY SHIVERS. Is sister of the above. Would like to go to school, but is always driven into the streets to sell onions, and is beaten if she brings them home again.

DR FEBRIFUGE. Is a medical man in a district infested by the peripatetic traders. Has no hesitation in ascribing the protracted sufferings of many of his patients to their inability to procure repose, in consequence of the incessant howling and noise which is carried on from an early hour of the morning to a late hour at night. He considers the suppression of these noises a sanatory movement of much importance.

MR BULL. Is an Englishman. Has heard that an Englishman's house is his Castle, but this is all rubbish, if a gang of roaring ruffians are to drive a man into his back rooms by their making it impossible to inhabit his front ones for the abominable riot the scoundrels kick up. Thinks it is a clear case for legislation.

HINTS HOW TO ENJOY AN OMNIBUS

1. On getting in, care neither for toes or knees of the passengers; but drive your way up to the top, steadying yourself by the shoulders, chests, or even faces of those seated.

2. Seat yourself with a jerk, pushing against one neighbour, and thrusting your elbow into the side of the other. You will thus get plenty of room.

3. If possible, enter with a stick or umbrella, pointed at full length; so that any sudden move of the 'bus' may thrust it into some one's stomach. It will make you feared.

4. When seated, occupy, if possible, the room of two, and revenge the treatment you have received on entering, by throwing every opposition in the way of a new-comer, especially if it be a woman with a child in her arms. It is a good plan to rest firmly on your umbrella, with your arms at right angles.

5. Open or shut windows as it suits you; men with colds, or women with toothaches, have no business in omnibuses. If they don't like it, they can get out; no one *forces* them to ride.

6. Young bucks may stare any decent woman out of countenance, put their legs up along the seats, and if going out to dinner, wipe the mud off their boots on the seats. They are only plush.

7. If middle-aged gentlemen are musical or political, they can dislocate a tune in something between a bark and a grumble, or endeavour to provoke an argument by declaring very loudly that Lord R— or the Duke 'is a thorough scoundrel,' according to their opinion of public affairs. If this don't take, they can keep up a perpetual squabble with the conductor, which will show they think themselves of some importance.

8. Ladies wishing to be agreeable can bring lap dogs, large paper parcels, and children, to whom an omnibus is a ship, though you wish you were out of their reach.

9. Conductors should particularly aim to take up laundresses returning with a large family washing, bakers and butchers in their working jackets, and, if a wet day, should be particular not to pull up to the pathway.

10. For want of space, the following brevities must suffice: – Never say where you wish to stop until after you have passed the place, and then pull them up with a sudden jerk. Keep your money in your waistcoat-pocket, and button your under and upper coat completely, and never attempt to get at it until the door is opened, and then let it be nothing under a five-shilling piece. Never ask any one to speak to the conductor for you, but hit or poke him with your umbrella or stick, or rap his hand as it rests on the door – he puts it there on purpose. Always stop the wrong omnibus, and ask if the Paddington goes to Walworth, and the Kennington to Whitechapel: you are not obliged to read all the rigmarole they paint on the outside. Finally, consider an omnibus as a carriage, a bed, a public-house, a place of amusement, or a boxing-ring, where you may ride, sleep, smoke, chaff, or quarrel, as it may suit you.

THE THREEPENNY FARE MYSTERY

PASSENGER. 'Sixpence! Why it's marked up Threepence!'
CONDUCTOR. 'Yes, Sir. Threppunse when you don't get in between Charing Cross and the Bank, or from Tuesdays to Mile End down to the Gate by Ungerfod, or Edger Road to Black Lion Lane or Rathbone Place and Blackwall Railway – or else you must get out at St Paul's Churchyard, or you can go to Pimlico all the way if you like – beyond that distance – it's Sixpunse!'

LONDON CABS

The dirty Cabs of London!
How lazily they stand
About the public thoroughfares,
Or crawl along the Strand;
The omnibuses pass them by
With a contempt supreme;
E'en the coal-cart overtakes them
With slow and heavy team.

The crazy Cabs of London!
How wretched is the sight
Of one of those old vehicles
That ply for hire by night!
There, cracked is every window-pane,
The door is weak and old;
The former lets in all the rain,
The latter all the cold.

The shakey Cabs of London!
How important the powers
Of one poor nervous female fare,
When fierce the driver lowers,
Swearing, with impudence sublime
And ruffianly frown,
He can't afford to lose his time;
'His fare will be a crown.'

The dear, bad Cabs of London!
In vain the public call
For a better class of vehicles
That can't be got at all.
Extortion must for ever thrive,
Cabs must be bad and dear,
Till Legislation looks alive,
And deigns to interfere.

Don't!

THE THAW AND THE STREETS!

Tomkins, who has just paid his Rate for Paving, Cleansing, &c., goes for a Walk in his immediate Neighbourhood. He is, of course, much gratified at the way in which the Cleansing part of the business is managed.

DREADFUL DESTITUTION IN BUCKINGHAM PALACE

IN the ignorance of our democracy, we envied the luxurious conveniences of Buckingham Palace. For hours and hours have we stood contemplating its body and two wings, and saying every five minutes, in confidence to ourselves – 'That's a Paradise of stone, that is! There's the Garden of Eden, *without* a snake.' And now – but our feelings are such that we must begin another paragraph to give vent to them.

The Royal Family criticised . . .

Now, we learn that the dwelling-place appointed for our Sovereign, her Prince, and babies, is a most comfortless abode; a place of nooks and corners; a place of racking noises and villanous odours. Her Majesty is absolutely lodged – but we take from MR BLORE's printed report: –

'The portion of the Palace occupied by HER MAJESTY and HIS ROYAL HIGHNESS PRINCE ALBERT as private apartments, is in the north wing; that they were not calculated originally for a married Sovereign, the head of a family; that the basement of this wing is also used by the Lord Chamberlain's department for store-rooms, workshops, &c., there being no accommodation in any other part of the Palace for these services; the conse-quence of this arrangement is, not only that *the noise and smell* from these workshops, in which cabinet-makers, upholsterers, smiths, &c., are constantly at work (independently of the obvious impropriety of such services being performed in a part of the building so contiguous to the Royal apartments), are at times positively offensive; but that the arrangement is not altogether free from the risk of fire, a quantity of oil being used, and large fires kept for boiling glue,' &c.

There! Who, now, will envy the QUEEN OF ENGLAND? Dear lady! whilst, in their ignorance, people think she is breathing airs of Araby, she is offended, stifled, by the fumes of a glue-pot!

The Wonder

ALTHOUGH HER MAJESTY and the PRINCE were not present at Covent Garden – although the Royal Box was the only box blank and empty – royal enthusiasm in the poetic cause was duly represented; the cheque sent by PRINCE ALBERT in aid of the funds being duly pinned upon the cushion.

A CASE OF REAL DISTRESS

'GOOD People, pray take compassion upon us. It is now nearly seven years since we have either of us known the blessing of a Comfortable Residence. If you do not believe us, good people, come and see where we live, at Buckingham Palace, and you will be satisfied that there is no deception in our story. Such is our Distress, that we should be truly grateful for the blessing of a comfortable two-pair back, with commonly decent Sleeping-rooms for our Children and Domestics. With our slender means, and an Increasing Family, we declare to you that we do not know what to do. The sum of One Hundred and Fifty Thousand Pounds will be all that will be required to make the needful alterations in our dwelling. Do, good people, bestow your Charity to this little amount, and may you never live to feel the want of so small a trifle.'

A PRINCE IN A YANKEE PRINT

AN American journal has cut out our *Court Circular*. The special reporter of the *New York Herald*, appointed to watch and record the progress of the PRINCE OF WALES, relates, with wonderful minuteness the performance, by his Royal Highness, of actions of which the importance is immense. For instance: –

'At the Newfoundland ball he danced eleven of the thirteen dances; but last night he was the hero of seven quadrilles, four waltzes, four gallops, and three polkas.'

Put that grand fact down, CLIO. Note this also, Muse of History: –

'This morning he was out in plain dress, walking with his suite.'

Book also the following memorable relations: –

'At eleven he appeared in uniform, and held a levee at the Government House, which was attended by 300 persons. At half-past twelve he stood, hat in hand, with his suite, and was photographed in the private grounds of Government House. At half-past two the Prince drove in an open carriage with LORD and LADY MULGRAVE, the DUKE OF NEWCASTLE, and LORD ST GERMANS, to the dockyard, and embarked amid the thunders of a Royal salute from the batteries and ships, and the cheers of a vast multitude, for the Nile, to lunch with the admiral, and witness the regatta.'

Of all the details in the foregoing narrative the most striking, perhaps, is the specification of the solemn circumstance, that the PRINCE OF WALES stood, hat in hand, with his suite, and was photographed in the private grounds of Government House at half-past twelve. It is much to be regretted that the republican chronicler of the princely movements was not, also, photographed at the same time. Standing, watch in hand for his part, to time every change and transition of occupation or attitude on the part of his Royal Highness, he must himself have presented a picture of considerable grandeur and dignity. Ah! if all historians had only paid equal regard to exactness in taking notes of the acts and deeds of illustrious personages, there would be much less controversy than there unhappily is about many vital points in history, sacred and profane. But now for an ascent to particulars, even exceeding in consequence the most tremendous things contained in the preceding narrative: –

'He afterwards went on board the *Hero*, and substituted for his uniform a pair of drab trousers, a dark-blue buttoned walking coat, with an outside breast pocket for the handkerchief, an ordinary black hat, and walking-stick.'

Here is a specimen of glorious word-painting indeed! For to what nobler purpose could words be applied than that of expressing the colours of the clothes of a Prince, and informing a breathlessly attentive world that his trousers were drab, that his walking-coat was blue, and his hat black?

Those who are not magnanimous enough to care about the boots or clothes in which the PRINCE OF WALES is astonishing the American mind, may yet rejoice to know that the wearer of those habiliments is comporting himself in such a manner as to increase the great popularity which he necessarily inherits.

A PRINCE AT HIGH PRESSURE

THOU dear little WALES – sure the saddest of tales,
   Is the tale of the studies with which they are
      cramming thee;
In thy tuckers and bibs, handed over to GIBBS,
   Who for eight years with solid instruction was
      ramming thee.

Then, to fill any nook GIBBS had chanced to o'erlook,
   In those poor little brains, sick of learned palaver,
When thou 'dst fain rolled in clover, they handed thee
      over,
   To the prim pedagogic protection of TARVER.

In Edinburgh next, thy poor noddle perplext,
   The gauntlet must run of each science and study;
Till the mixed streams of knowledge, turned on by the
      College,
   Through the field of thy boy-brains run shallow and
      muddy.

To the South from the North – from the shores of the
      Forth,
   Where at hands Presbyterian pure science is
      quaffed –
The Prince, in a trice, is whipped off to the Isis,
   Where Oxford keeps springs mediaeval on draught.

Dipped in grey Oxford mixture (lest *that* prove a
      fixture),
   The poor lad's to be plunged in less orthodox Cam:
Where dynamics and statics, and pure mathematics,
   Will be piled on his brain's awful cargo of 'cram.'

Where next the boy *may* go to swell the farrago,
   We haven't yet heard, but the Palace they're
      plotting in:
To Berlin, Jena, Bonn, he'll no doubt be passed on,
   And drop in, for a finishing touch, p'raps, at
      Gottingen.

'Gainst indulging the passion for this high-pressure
      fashion
   Of Prince-training, *Punch* would uplift loyal
      warning;
Locomotives we see, over-stoked soon may be,
   Till the supersteamed boiler blows up some fine
      morning.

The *Great Eastern's* disaster should teach us to master
   Our passion for pace, lest the mind's water-jacket
– Steam for exit fierce panting, and safety-valves
      wanting –
   Should explode round the brain, of a sudden, and
      crack it.

and (over-) chronicled. Punch issues a Warning

231

The Christmas Spirit

IT IS LUCKY THAT CHRISTMAS DOES COME BUT ONCE A YEAR

DEAR PUNCH, – I live in lodgings. I am one of those poor unfortunate helpless beings, called Bachelors, who are dependent for their wants and comforts upon the services of others. If I want the mustard, I have to ring half-a-dozen times for it; if I am waiting for my shaving water, I have to wander up and down the room for at least a quarter of an hour, with a soaped chin, before it makes its appearance.

'But this system of delay, this extreme backwardness in attending to one's simplest calls, is invariably shown a thousand times more backward about Christmas time.

'I am afraid to tell you what I have endured this Christmas. My persecutions have been such as to almost make me wish that Christmas were blotted out of the Calendar altogether.

'I have never been called in the morning at the proper time. My breakfast has always been served an hour later than usual – and as for dinner, it has been with difficulty that I have been able to procure any at all!

'This invasion of one's habits and comforts is most heart-rending; and the only excuse I have been able to receive to my repeated remonstrances has been, "Oh, Sir, you must really make some allowances; pray recollect it is Christmas time."

'Last week I invited some friends to spend the evening with me – but I could give them neither tea, nor hot grog, nor supper, nor anything – because, "Please, Sir, the servant has gone to the Pantomime – she's always allowed to go at Christmas time." . . .

'Now, Sir, it seems to me, that Christmas is, with a certain class of people, a privileged period of the year to commit all sorts of excesses, to evade their usual duties, and to jump altogether out of their customary avocations into others the very opposite of them. For myself, I am extremely glad that Christmas does come but once a-year. I know I shall go, next December, to Constantinople, or Jerusalem, or the Minories, or some place where the savage customs I have described do not exist; for I would not endure another Christmas in England for any amount of holly, plum-pudding, or Christmas-boxes in the world.

'I have the misfortune to remain, *Mr Punch*,
'Your much-persecuted Servant,
'AN OLD BACHELOR.'

THE CHRISTMAS-BOX NUISANCE

HOW much longer, we ask with indignant sorrow, is the humbug of Boxing-day to be kept up for the sake of draining the pockets of struggling tradesmen, and strewing the streets of the metropolis with fuzzy beadles, muzzy dustmen, and intoxicated – but constant – scavengers? We have received the usual intimation from our pertinacious friend who eases us of our dust, that he expects us to come down with our dust in another sense, at what the fellow sarcastically calls 'this festive season.' The gentleman who boasts of his 'constancy' in scavenging – as if he loved the mud and stuck to it – has apprised us, according to his annual custom, that we are to ascertain his genuineness by a dog with a black eye, a white nose, a red ear, an absent tail, a swelling on his left cheek, and other little symptoms of his having lived the life of a busy dog rather than of a particularly lucky one.

The Christmas Box system is, in fact, a piece of horribly internecine strife between cooks and butchers' boys, lamp-lighters, beadles, and all classes of society, tugging at each other's pockets for the sake of what can be got under the pretext of seasonable benevolence. Our cooks bully our butchers for the annual Box, and our butchers take it out of us in the course of the year by tacking false tails on to our saddles of mutton, adding false feet to our legs of lamb, and chousing us with large lumps of chump in our chops, for the purpose of adding to our bills by giving undue weight to our viands. *Punch* has resolved on the overthrow of the Boxing system, and down it will go before 1849 has expired.

A Christmas visitor

TRIPPING TIME

TRIP, tired Briton, gaily trip, man,
   To the forests and the moors;
Ship thyself on board a ship, man,
   Take a trip to foreign shores.
If our own coast will not suit thee,
   There to bask and have thy dip,
Let a foreign clime recruit thee;
   To another land trip, trip.

Trip to Athens or to Rome, JOHN,
   Trip to Cairo or Hong Kong;
Trip – to get away from home – JOHN,
   Anywhere – trip up Mont Blanc.
Down Vesuvius his crater,
   Lightly trip on tiptoe fleet,
And inside thereof a 'tatur
   All hot bake with lava's heat.

Thereabouts, among the various
   Things the natives have to show,
See the blood of Januarius,
   Find out how they make it flow.
There's another burning mountain,
   Burning in the midst of ice,
Boil your egg in Hecla's fountain;
   You will find it – oh, so nice!

Trip to Berlin and Vienna,
   Trip to Lisbon and Madrid;
Like a trip what rhubarb, senna,
   Salts, the frame of ails will rid?
If both trip and physic needing,
   Trip to Homburg; quaff its spring,
Where you may, if too unheeding,
   Be cleaned out of everything.

Trip, of course, you will to Paris,
   On your way abroad or back,
Every British tourist tarries
   There, in tripping on his track;
Tarries on his track in tripping,
   In his pockets puts his hands,
And amid a people skipping,
   Hopping, dancing round him, stands.

Home at length, before November,
   Trip again, my noble Peer,
And mine honourable Member,
   Back to British beef and beer;
With your spirits somewhat lighter,
   And your pockets lighter still;
Bit by many a foreign biter
   With proboscis – and with bill.

Holiday Mood

Why cannot your Wife travel for a Week
without taking with her Luggage for a Twelvemonth?

233